EARLY CHILDHOOD EDUCATION SERIES

Sharon Ryan, Editor

Twelve Best Practices for Early Childhood Education:
Integrating Reggio and Other Inspired Approaches
ANN LEWIN-BENHAM

Big Science for Growing Minds:
Constructivist Classrooms for Young Thinkers
JACQUELINE GRENNON BROOKS

What If All the Kids Are White? Anti-Bias Multicultural
Education with Young Children and Families, 2nd Ed.
LOUISE DERMAN-SPARKS & PATRICIA G. RAMSEY

Seen and Heard:
Children's Rights in Early Childhood Education
ELLEN LYNN HALL & JENNIFER KOFKIN RUDKIN

Young Investigators:
The Project Approach in the Early Years, 2nd Ed.
JUDY HARRIS HELM & LILIAN G. KATZ

Supporting Boys' Learning:
Strategies for Teacher Practice, PreK–Grade 3
BARBARA SPRUNG, MERLE FROSCHL, & NANCY GROPPER

Young English Language Learners: Current Research and
Emerging Directions for Practice and Policy
EUGENE E. GARCÍA & ELLEN C. FREDE, EDS.

Connecting Emergent Curriculum and Standards in the
Early Childhood Classroom: Strengthening Content and
Teacher Practice
SYDNEY L. SCHWARTZ & SHERRY M. COPELAND

Infants and Toddlers at Work:
Using Reggio-Inspired Materials to Support Brain Development
ANN LEWIN-BENHAM

The View from the Little Chair in the Corner:
Improving Teacher Practice and Early Childhood Learning
(Wisdom from an Experienced Classroom Observer)
CINDY RZASA BESS

Culture and Child Development in Early Childhood Programs:
Practices for Quality Education and Care
CAROLLEE HOWES

The Early Intervention Guidebook for Families and Professionals:
Partnering for Success
BONNIE KEILTY

The Story in the Picture:
Inquiry and Artmaking with Young Children
CHRISTINE MULCAHEY

Educating and Caring for Very Young Children:
The Infant/Toddler Curriculum, 2nd Ed.
DORIS BERGEN, REBECCA REID, & LOUIS TORELLI

Beginning School: U.S. Policies in International Perspective
RICHARD M. CLIFFORD & GISELE M. CRAWFORD, EDS.

Emergent Curriculum in the Primary Classroom:
Interpreting the Reggio Emilia Approach in Schools
CAROL ANNE WIEN, ED.

Enthusiastic and Engaged Learners:
Approaches to Learning in the Early Childhood Classroom
MARILOU HYSON

Powerful Children:
Understanding How to Teach and Learn Using the Reggio Approach
ANN LEWIN-BENHAM

The Early Care and Education Teaching Workforce at the
Fulcrum: An Agenda for Reform
SHARON LYNN KAGAN, KRISTIE KAUERZ, & KATE TARRANT

Windows on Learning:
Documenting Young Children's Work, 2nd Ed.
JUDY HARRIS HELM, SALLEE BENEKE, & KATHY STEINHEIMER

Ready or Not: Leadership Choices in Early Care and Education
STACIE G. GOFFIN & VALORA WASHINGTON

Supervision in Early Childhood Education:
A Developmental Perspective, 3rd Ed.
JOSEPH J. CARUSO WITH M. TEMPLE FAWCETT

Guiding Children's Behavior:
Developmental Discipline in the Classroom
EILEEN S. FLICKER & JANET ANDRON HOFFMAN

The War Play Dilemma:
What Every Parent and Teacher Needs to Know, 2nd Ed.
DIANE E. LEVIN & NANCY CARLSSON-PAIGE

Possible Schools: The Reggio Approach to Urban Education
ANN LEWIN-BENHAM

Everyday Goodbyes: Starting School and Early Care—
A Guide to the Separation Process
NANCY BALABAN

Playing to Get Smart
ELIZABETH JONES & RENATTA M. COOPER

How to Work with Standards in the Early Childhood Classroom
CAROL SEEFELDT

In the Spirit of the Studio:
Learning from the Atelier of Reggio Emilia
LELLA GANDINI, LYNN T. HILL, LOUISE BOYD CADWELL, &
CHARLES SCHWALL, EDS.

Understanding Assessment and Evaluation in
Early Childhood Education, 2nd Ed.
DOMINIC F. GULLO

Negotiating Standards in the Primary Classroom:
The Teacher's Dilemma
CAROL ANNE WIEN

Teaching and Learning in a Diverse World:
Multicultural Education for Young Children, 3rd Ed.
PATRICIA G. RAMSEY

The Emotional Development of Young Children:
Building an Emotion-Centered Curriculum, 2nd Ed.
MARILOU HYSON

Effective Partnering for School Change: Improving Early
Childhood Education in Urban Classrooms
JIE-QI CHEN & PATRICIA HORSCH WITH KAREN DEMOSS &
SUZANNE L. WAGNER

Let's Be Friends: Peer Competence and Social Inclusion in Early
Childhood Programs
KRISTEN MARY KEMPLE

Young Children Continue to Reinvent Arithmetic—
2nd Grade, 2nd Ed.
CONSTANCE KAMII

Major Trends and Issues in Early Childhood Education:
Challenges, Controversies, and Insights, 2nd Ed.
JOAN PACKER ISENBERG & MARY RENCK JALONGO, EDS.

(continued)

Early Childhood Education Series titles, continued

The Power of Projects: Meeting Contemporary Challenges in Early Childhood Classrooms—Strategies and Solutions
JUDY HARRIS HELM & SALLEE BENEKE, EDS.

Bringing Learning to Life: The Reggio Approach to Early Childhood Education
LOUISE BOYD CADWELL

The Colors of Learning:
ROSEMARY ALTHOUSE, MARGARET H. JOHNSON, & SHARON T. MITCHELL

A Matter of Trust
CAROLLEE HOWES & SHARON RITCHIE

Widening the Circle
SAMUEL L. ODOM, ED.

Children with Special Needs
MARJORIE J. KOSTELNIK, ESTHER ETSUKO ONAGA, BARBARA ROHDE, & ALICE PHIPPS WHIREN

Developing Constructivist Early Childhood Curriculum
RHETA DEVRIES, BETTY ZAN, CAROLYN HILDEBRANDT, REBECCA EDMIASTON, & CHRISTINA SALES

Outdoor Play
JANE PERRY

Embracing Identities in Early Childhood Education
SUSAN GRIESHABER & GAILE S. CANNELLA, EDS.

Bambini: The Italian Approach to Infant/Toddler Care
LELLA GANDINI & CAROLYN POPE EDWARDS, EDS.

Serious Players in the Primary Classroom, 2nd Ed.
SELMA WASSERMANN

Telling a Different Story
CATHERINE WILSON

Young Children Reinvent Arithmetic, 2nd Ed.
CONSTANCE KAMII

Managing Quality in Young Children's Programs
MARY L. CULKIN, ED.

The Early Childhood Curriculum, 3rd Ed.
CAROL SEEFELDT, ED.

Leadership in Early Childhood, 2nd Ed.
JILLIAN RODD

Inside a Head Start Center
DEBORAH CEGLOWSKI

Bringing Reggio Emilia Home
LOUISE BOYD CADWELL

Master Players
GRETCHEN REYNOLDS & ELIZABETH JONES

Understanding Young Children's Behavior
JILLIAN RODD

Understanding Quantitative and Qualitative Research in Early Childhood Education
WILLIAM L. GOODWIN & LAURA D. GOODWIN

Diversity in the Classroom, 2nd Ed.
FRANCES E. KENDALL

Developmentally Appropriate Practice in "Real Life"
CAROL ANNE WIEN

Experimenting with the World
HARRIET K. CUFFARO

Quality in Family Child Care and Relative Care
SUSAN KONTOS, CAROLLEE HOWES, MARYBETH SHINN, & ELLEN GALINSKY

Using the Supportive Play Model
MARGARET K. SHERIDAN, GILBERT M. FOLEY, & SARA H. RADLINSKI

The Full-Day Kindergarten, 2nd Ed.
DORIS PRONIN FROMBERG

Assessment Methods for Infants and Toddlers
DORIS BERGEN

Young Children Continue to Reinvent Arithmetic—3rd Grade: Implications of Piaget's Theory
CONSTANCE KAMII WITH SALLY JONES LIVINGSTON

Moral Classrooms, Moral Children
RHETA DEVRIES & BETTY ZAN

Diversity and Developmentally Appropriate Practices
BRUCE L. MALLORY & REBECCA S. NEW, EDS.

Changing Teaching, Changing Schools
FRANCES O'CONNELL RUST

Physical Knowledge in Preschool Education
CONSTANCE KAMII & RHETA DEVRIES

Ways of Assessing Children and Curriculum
CELIA GENISHI, ED.

The Play's the Thing
ELIZABETH JONES & GRETCHEN REYNOLDS

Scenes from Day Care
ELIZABETH BALLIETT PLATT

Making Friends in School
PATRICIA G. RAMSEY

The Whole Language Kindergarten
SHIRLEY RAINES & ROBERT CANADY

Multiple Worlds of Child Writers
ANNE HAAS DYSON

The Good Preschool Teacher
WILLIAM AYERS

The Piaget Handbook for Teachers and Parents
ROSEMARY PETERSON & VICTORIA FELTON-COLLINS

Visions of Childhood
JOHN CLEVERLEY & D. C. PHILLIPS

Ideas Influencing Early Childhood Education
EVELYN WEBER

The Joy of Movement in Early Childhood
SANDRA R. CURTIS

Twelve Best Practices for Early Childhood Education

INTEGRATING REGGIO AND OTHER INSPIRED APPROACHES

Ann Lewin-Benham

Foreword by Howard Gardner

Teachers College
Columbia University
New York and London

Published by Teachers College Press, 1234 Amsterdam Avenue, New York, NY 10027

Library of Congress Cataloging-in-Publication Data

Lewin-Benham, Ann.
  Twelve best practices for early childhood education : integrating Reggio and other inspired approaches / Ann Lewin-Benham ; foreword by Howard Gardner.
     p. cm. – (Early childhood education series)
  Includes bibliographical references and index.
  ISBN 978-0-8077-5232-6 (pbk. : alk. paper)
  ISBN 978-0-8077-5233-3 (hardcover : alk. paper)
     1. Early childhood education. 2. Inclusive education. 3. Educational tests and measurements. I. Title.
  LB1139.23.L48   2011
  372.21–dc22   2011005073

ISBN 978-0-8077-5232-6 (paper)
ISBN 978-0-8077-5233-3 (cloth)

Printed on acid-free paper
Manufactured in the United States of America

19   18   17   16   15   14   13   12   11   8   7   6   5   4   3   2   1

**For Daniel Shepard Lewin,
my best piece of work**

Contents

Foreword: Ann Lewin-Benham's *Vade Mecum*, by Howard Gardner   xi

Acknowledgments   xiii

Introduction   1

    Changing Practices   2

    The Book's Content   4

    Breaching the Reggio/U.S. Divide   6

1. When Belief Drives Practice   7

    Cultural Context of Reggio Emilia   8

    Reggio's Unique Beliefs and Features   9

    Correlations: Best Practices and the Reggio Approach   12

    The Structure Supporting Reggio Practices   16

    Conclusion: Using Reggio and Other Best Practices   17

2. Developing Self-Regulation   19

    Becoming Self-Regulated   19

    The Reggio Approach   21

    Montessori's "Normalizing" Method   28

    A Scripted Kindergarten   31

    Scheduled Early Education   32

    The Model Early Learning Center's Techniques   34

    Conclusion: Self-Regulation—The Basis for Learning   35

3. Using Documentation to Gain Parents' Trust   36

    What Is Documentation?   36

    Documentation as a Magnet for Parents   39

    A Project Emerges   41

    Robust Parent Involvement   47

Panels as Planning for Curriculum 49

Conclusion: Documentation—A System for Listening 51

4. An Open Flow Day **52**

Essential Features of an Open Flow Day 52

How Open Flow Looks 60

Moving Toward Open Flow 62

Conclusion: Differently Organized Days 65

5. The Environment *Is* the Curriculum **66**

When Design Fails to Support Children 67

Exemplary Features of Reggio Classrooms 70

Thinking About Design 71

Developing an Aesthetic Sense 74

Designing or Redesigning a Classroom 76

Conclusion: A New Take on Environment 79

6. The Art of Meaning-Full Conversation **80**

Defining Conversation 80

Holding Focused Conversations 82

Conversation Punctuates a Project 86

Techniques in the Conversation Tool Kit 90

The Impact of Focused Conversation 94

Conclusion: Conversing Toward Literacy 96

7. Intentional Teaching **97**

What Is Intention? 97

Intention in Reggio Teachers 99

Conclusion: The Teacher's Roles in Action 109

8. Materials and Human Development **111**

The "Languages" of Materials 111

Materials and Brain Development 116

"Framing" and the Brain's Attention Systems 118

Triggering Visualization and Imagination 120

Conclusion: The Romance of Materials 124

9. Materials and Relationships **125**

Why Materials Matter 125

Finding Good Materials 127

Asking Families to Help 134

Materials and Cognition 137

Conclusion: Finding Relationships 140

10. Documentation **141**

Walls as Curriculum 142

Documentation of an Experience 144

Walls That Encourage Mindful Activity 146

Documentation at Work 149

Using Documentation Reflectively 152

Conclusion: Walls That Intrigue Parents 153

11. Assessing Children's Progress **154**

Evaluation 155

Assessment 157

Authentic Assessment 157

Roadblocks to Authentic Assessment 163

Reconciling Authentic Assessment and Standardized Testing 164

Effectiveness of Authentic Assessment 165

Conclusion: "Proof" Is Not Attainable 167

12. Significant Project Work **169**

An MELC Story 169

A Reggio Story 173

The Contrast 179

Conclusion: Bucking Cultural Imperatives 181

13. EXCEL **183**

Understanding the Acronym EXCEL 183

Putting EXCEL to Work 187

Using EXCEL to Rate Yourself 195

Conclusion: Best Practices and Significant Work 196

Glossary **198**

References **201**

Index **204**

About the Author **210**

Foreword:
Ann Lewin-Benham's *Vade Mecum*

TRANSLATED FROM THE Latin as "go with me," my dictionary defines *vade mecum* as "a book for ready reference" and "something regularly carried about by a person." I can think of no better characterization of Ann Lewin-Benham's latest book. This book should be read by anyone interested in early childhood education—indeed, anyone interested in education, or in young children. That person is well-advised to keep this book nearby for ready reference, and perhaps even have it stored in a back pocket or displayed on the homepage of an electronic reading device.

In *Twelve Best Practices for Early Childhood Education*, Ann reflects on a lifetime in education: as a student, a parent, a teacher, the founder of important and influential educational institutions, including the Capital Children's Museum in Washington, D.C. But Ann is far more than an expert teacher and a founder of schools and museums. She is also a careful scholar of education, well-versed in the major theoretical schools, up-to-date on the relevant literature in the social and biological sciences. And she is an ingenious devisor of innovative practices in education—indeed, an educator and scholar for all seasons.

I've known Ann for many years. Over that period I have learned from her in a multitude of ways. I've benefited from her mastery of the approaches pioneered by Maria Montessori and by the brilliant educators in Reggio Emilia; her keen insight into the minds and the worlds of children, parents, and educators; and her brilliant intuition of what works, what does not work, what can be improved, how, and why. I've marveled at her combination of patience and steadfastness, so needed in education, particularly when one works with "at risk" populations, yet so rarely found in this era of "magical" solutions.

Yet, well-versed in Ann's thinking, writing, and practices, I was still not prepared for the power of this important book. As a constant learner and instinctive reflecter, Ann has always been intent on conveying to us what she has learned from the inspiring examples of others. She has done so powerfully, brilliantly. In this book, however, we encounter Ann's voice directly and authoritatively. To be sure, Ann still draws on those from whom she has learned—from Jean Piaget and Lev Vygotsky, from Reuven Feuerstein and Loris Malaguzzi, from the latest findings in brain science and school design. But the twelve practices on which she focuses are the ones that she herself has developed and worked through—and so we are treated to the unalloyed version of her own best thinking.

Let me mention a few examples. Nowhere else in the literature of early childhood education does one encounter such original and searching discussions of the nature of conversations in the classroom. Nowhere else does one encounter as skillful a delineation of the importance of self-regulation and how best to foster it. Nowhere else does one encounter so textured an account of a school day marked by open, regular, fulfilling experiences of "flow." Nowhere else does one gain an insider's view of intentional teaching. Nowhere else does one find as searching a comparison of the educational assumptions implicit in the Reggio approach, as compared to those dominant in the United States. There is so much more! Finally, Ann captures her conclusions succinctly in the powerful EXCEL concept: that vital synthesis of Environment, eXchanges, Conversation, Evidence, and Language which marks—indeed which makes—the most powerful educational experience, an experience, if you will, that bears the imprint of Ann Lewin-Benham.

It should be apparent that I am part of a large and enthusiastic group—admirers of the achievements and the writings of Ann Lewin-Benham. If you have not already done so, you are about to join its ranks. I predict that you'll place this book alongside those educational readings that you value most; and that, in the manner of a *vade mecum*, you will draw on it regularly for implementation, insight, and inspiration.

–Howard Gardner, January 2011

Acknowledgments

EVERY BOOK COMES FROM someplace in an author's mind. This book comes from impressions stored over decades of observing teachers, young children, and classrooms. Early childhood educators work harder than anyone realizes. The work requires special talents—the ability to listen, to see with eyes on all sides of one's head, to read children's behavior, to handle the tantrums and biting that can occur before children under age 3 transform "catastrophic global emotions into a pattern of regulated emotional signaling" (Greenspan & Shanker, 2004, p. 30). Without knowing if the cranky child had too little sleep, too much sugar, or no breakfast, or if there was a struggle at home over what to wear or getting out the door on time, the teacher will do everything she can to calm the child, to change his state from anger to joy, and to help him learn to calm himself. The teacher will never know if a child's violent behavior stems from watching too much beat-'em-up TV or from being hit—physically or verbally—by an overstressed parent. Whatever the cause, she will embrace the child, envelop her in her love, and shift the child's attention to something engaging and pleasurable.

Anyone who dares criticize a teacher should spend an hour responsible for a classroom of infants, toddlers, or 3- to 6-year-olds. Teachers are underpaid and underappreciated. Until recently, when the neurosciences began to provide research affirming the importance of the early years, programs for infants, toddlers, and young children have been off the budget and their teachers and environments have been under the radar screen.

My first words of appreciation are for teachers of young children. Elana Nougouchi has boundless love. Mary Ann Banta has contagious humor. Frances Hawkins (deceased 2006) had priceless wisdom. Tanya Clark has dignity and passion. Named and nameless, you are my heroes.

This book is for teachers. I have tried in these pages to show you the best examples I can assemble of exemplary early education. I thank the many teachers who welcomed me in their classes where I collected the stories you will read here.

I thank the neuroscientists who, brain cell by brain cell, are unraveling the complexities of how the mind works. Your work has opened a new horizon that, in time, can help my profession—educators—better understand the meaning of children's behavior and the implications for how children act in the classroom. Michael Posner, John Ratey, Frank Wilson, Eric Kandel, and many others—your writings are powerfully illuminating the shadows in the classroom.

I thank the psychologists who bring understanding of how we learn to the practice of how we teach. Mihalyi Csikszentmihaly, Reuven Feuerstein, Howard Gardner, Rochel Gelman, David Perkins, Steven Pinker, and many more—may the time not be distant when we walk easily on the path you are laying, plank by plank, between the research lab and the classroom.

Educators in the Infant/Toddler Centers and Preschools of Reggio Emilia, Italy, have forged a new vision of what early education can be. I draw on their classrooms, exhibits, lectures, and writings for inspiration. They have made their remote town a world center to showcase teachers' new roles, communities' influence, and children's competence.

Colleagues who read the manuscript, Marcia Ruth and Holly Blum, are mature teachers and experienced educators. Thank you for your diligence to large ideas and small words. Your efforts clarified many sticky places. Younger colleagues, Jennifer Azzariti and Alex Cruickshank, brought their energy fresh from the classroom to contribute, criticize, and hone numerous passages. Your minds and your work are precious to me. Thank you. Other teachers' laughter and love of children echo in my mind, especially Sonya Shoptaugh and Wendy Baldwin.

In another category, Alex Cruickshank, a computer whiz, assisted on the figures, sharpening lines, corners, and text.

My husband is all enduring as I spend hours at the computer. I love you, Robert.

My editor at Teachers College Press, Marie Ellen Larcada, was a steadfast advocate for this book. She is the kind of editor every author hopes to have: insightful, clear, ever-available, full of wisdom and warm words–and humor. Susan Liddicoat, another Press stalwart, taught me how to write a book when she edited my first book, *Possible Schools*. I continue to learn from everything she touches on a manuscript and thank her for thoughtful, detailed review. Karl Nyberg knows everything there is to know about turning a manuscript into a book; I am fortunate that he is my production editor and appreciate his technical prowess. I am also fortunate to have had the good eyes of copyeditor Tara Tomcyzk, whose extreme care caught every misplaced comma, even the fly specks!

Introduction

B EST PRACTICES IN early childhood education draw on old and new traditions. Some go back to John Dewey's ideas about learning through experience; others reflect Friedrich Froebel's understanding of the importance of play. Two sources of best practices come from Northern Italy–the work of Maria Montessori and the work of Loris Malaguzzi and the many educators who worked with him to develop what is known today as "the Reggio Approach."

Drawing on these strong traditions, I have organized this book to describe 12 practices that, in my opinion, are essential, or in the word of the title, "best." These practices include:

1. how we put what we believe about young children into practice;
2. how we help children become self-regulated;
3. ways to integrate the life of school and home by involving families;
4. how to structure time so that there is Open Flow, long uninterrupted periods in which children can concentrate on what interests them;
5. how to design a classroom environment that is interesting enough to provoke long, concentrated work;
6. how to hold Meaning-full Conversation, supported by a group of techniques I call a Conversation Tool Kit;
7. what it means to be an Intentional Teacher and what it looks like to teach with Intention;
8. what it means to use a multitude of materials and to introduce children to their attributes, functions, and histories;
9. how to introduce children to a plethora of things to do with materials from the natural and man-made environments;
10. how to develop evidence of children's growth through observing what they do and listening to what they say;
11. how to assess children by using the evidence of what they do and say as the way to see their growth;
12. how to engage children in projects that tap their interest, competence, and creativity and result in the production of Significant Work that is creative, complex, competent, language-full, and joyful.

These 12 practices are demonstrated, one per chapter in this book, with scenarios from classrooms, dialogues of children and teachers, and work samples showing the outcome of using each practice. Used together, the 12 best practices constitute a new structure for early education.

When I began to teach, I was 26 years old and the mother of a 4-year-old. I had just earned a Montessori certificate in a 9-month/7-hour-a-day training course. Memories of my experiences from the ensuing 4 years with a class of 35 children in a Montessori school are vivid. Some are the foundation for beliefs I hold today about learning.

Rigorously schooled in Montessori practical life activities, I structured exercises to enable 3-year-olds to manage complex routines. So, I kept only six juice glasses, ensuring that glass washing would take place several times each morning. The activity was constrained: You could only have juice if there was a clean glass. Likewise, the fishbowl could only be changed once a day. One morning, an urgent chorus of voices interrupted the lesson I was giving: "Mrs. Lewin! Quick! Come!" There on the table, the goldfish was flapping and gasping. The child changing the water had missed his target. Water was everywhere, a matter of no concern, but the fish seemed about to perish. I grasped it and put it in the little water remaining in the fishbowl. The fish revived. A child brought a bucket, another a mop, a third a sponge, and all helped the child who had spilled the water to clean up.

The episode showed that children have empathy for living creatures and for one another, that they can follow complex procedures—even ones fraught with peril, take "failure" in stride and recover, and spontaneously help one another. Daily, I saw how critical the years before 6 are for language learning (confirmed by today's research in neuroscience), how aware young children are of one another's emotions and competence, and how important structure is.

I was subsequently hired to introduce Montessori methods in what was then called a "play school." Neither the director nor teachers had any desire to learn about Montessori, but with a grant from a wealthy parent to "introduce" the Montessori method, they had to do something. The staff held a then-common belief that the Montessori method was somehow wrong, that showing a child how to do something would destroy creativity.

My memories from that school are of a free-for-all—painting with shaving cream, which the children gleefully squirted all over one another; "creative snacks," which meant grabbing spaghetti from the large bowl and using your hands to smush it into the table; leaving toys in disarray; no morning meeting or other structure. The teachers called everything "creative." The only evidence that the teachers felt anything was amiss was their exhaustion at morning's end.

As years passed, the split between structure and creativity in early education widened. This book is grounded on my belief that structure is essential and my concern that it is difficult but possible in early childhood classrooms to establish a structure in which children simultaneously build self-regulation and skills, *and* express creativity. I have spent my life striving to create foundations for educational practices that are worthy of children's competence and joyful nature.

CHANGING PRACTICES

In 1984, I first heard about the Reggio Approach, the short name that refers to early education in the Municipal Infant-Toddler Centers and Preschools of Reggio Emilia, Italy. Only after founding the Model Early Learning Center (MELC) in 1988, and flailing and all but failing to make it a model, did I conclude, in 1992, that we should adapt the Reggio philosophy and practices.

The Reggio Approach evolved under the leadership of Loris Malaguzzi (1920–1994), founder of the schools and a driving impresario. With strong parent involvement and a cadre of educators who agreed with his vision, they created schools in which children's rights were deeply respected and children's responsibility was built along with the rights. If you know anything about the Reggio Approach, you understand its attraction: Classrooms are aesthetic, children's work is sophisticated, parent involvement is high. The Reggio Approach is truly a new and visionary picture of school before grade school.

A few American educators became interested in the Reggio schools in the 1980s, but I place the serious start of American interest in 1990, the first year that the National Association for the Education of Young Children (NAEYC) scheduled a presentation on Reggio at its annual conference. The room held 30 people; 100 showed up.

Today, most early educators have heard the word *Reggio*, about half know it refers to Reggio Emilia, a city in Northern Italy, and about 1,200 American schools use the word in their name or mission statement to show that they are inspired to try to emulate Reggio practices. U.S. interest was boosted by a 1991 article in *Newsweek* that stated Reggio Emilia had the "world's best preschools" (Kantrowitz & Wingert, pp. 50–52).

What makes a "best" school is a cluster of "best practices"–those things that teachers do to prepare interest-laden environments, to help children become self-regulated, and to foster the drive to learn that is a human's birthright. The practices that are the foundation for Reggio work are the same that underlie any best early education practices. Thus, whether you desire to use the Reggio Approach or to align your teaching with best practices, this book will give you the foundation.

There are strong similarities and significant differences between the Reggio Approach and the Montessori method, another example of a "best practice": Briefly, both respect young children's enormous competence and rely on intentional teaching, on a well-prepared environment that children learn to manage responsibly, and on children being self-regulated, choosing activities based on their interests, and concentrating for long periods. They differ in the role of the teacher–Montessori teachers are lone practitioners, the aide usually not acting in a teaching role. Typically, Montessori teachers introduce materials and then, for the most part, step aside and let the children use the materials as they have been presented. In Reggio classrooms, there is no aide and the adults are co-equals. Reggio teachers collaborate with children and intervene regularly as they make suggestions and work alongside children.

Montessori and Reggio use different materials: Montessori uses beautifully designed and comprehensive sets of diverse apparatus to teach sensory, language, math concepts, and much more. The objective for each material is carefully spelled out. Reggio uses a wealth of natural and man-made materials to encourage children to collaborate on complex tasks with outcomes that emerge as the tasks progress.

The differences stem from the underlying theories of the two systems: Jean Piaget's (1950) idea, that intelligence unfolds naturally in stages with no adult intervention, supports the Montessori method. Lev Vygotsky's (1934/1986) idea, that adult intervention is essential in learning, is the cornerstone of Reggio practices.

As a teacher, I lived the daily rhythm of classroom life. Then, as founder/director of schools and of one of the first hands-on children's museums, I experienced the devilish process of change. When children's museums began, they threatened many museum professionals who insisted that these "hands-on" places were not museums.

When I founded two junior high schools, public school educators perceived them as a threat.

Because of these experiences, I recognize the hopes, fears, frustrations, and successes of educators whose vision lies on the fringe of our culture, as Reggio practices do. In this book, I try to allay those fears and frustrations through stories, key points, and questions about the foundations for Reggio or any other best early education practices.

After hearing an inspiring lecture on the Reggio Approach, seeing an exciting PowerPoint presentation, or visiting a dynamic classroom, teachers' spirits are high. But they falter when facing "What to Do on Monday." There is no one entry to the process of change. Changing teaching practices is not like first removing, then protecting the furniture before painting the living room. Classroom life is complex, and teachers begin in different ways to question what they are doing, to harness their individual strengths, and to make changes. Change can happen in a sudden fit of ripping everything commercial off the walls, but usually begins gradually–the toe-dipping I know so well as a non-swimmer who is afraid of the water.

In this book, I try to speak to both "rippers" and "dippers." I use real classroom stories to show teachers' doubts, confusion, eventual attempts, and successes so that you see the thoughts behind their actions. Thus, the book is like a mental rehearsal of what you might want to try in your own classroom. The practices I have included address the "sticky" places–those aspects of teaching that are new, unclear, or contradictory to mainstream early education in the United States.

As I reflect on many classroom observations and workshop audiences' questions, I am struck by how far American interest in Reggio has spread, by the similarities in where teachers get stuck, and by a common misinterpretation that the Reggio emphasis on children's choice denotes a laissez-faire approach. This is as strong a misconception as is the notion that there is no creativity in the Montessori method.

Each of the powerful practices I present is a plank in the structure that supports any best early education system. All the practices are essential before children can do the kinds of stellar work we see in Reggio schools or the concentrated effort at hard work we see in Montessori schools.

THE BOOK'S CONTENT

This book is not formulaic and has no preconceived scripts. Rather, scenarios highlight children's and teachers' competence. For example, in Chapter 2 on self-regulation, you see teachers who turn children's unsettled or chaotic behavior into focused activity. In Chapter 4 on an Open Flow day, you see how teachers establish a structure in which children can choose from a mass of provocative materials and use them for an extended time. In Chapter 6 on conversation, you sit in on teacher/child exchanges and learn why some are and others are not conversations.

This book expands my earlier writing so that teachers can see (1) the foundations for practicing the Reggio Approach and (2) how to put them in place in a classroom. For example, buried in a paragraph in my book *Possible Schools* (2006) are 24 words describing a project called Our Families and Us that provided the impetus for the MELC's parent program. Here, that project is presented in a full chapter (Chapter 3) about involving families in a school.

I have built the book in response to educators' questions. The Director of a large cluster of early childhood centers said, "Educators from our community went to Reggio, we have explained its wonder to our colleagues, we have held discussion groups among ourselves. It's time to stop saying, 'This is complex.' It is time for us to *get down to business and do something!*"

I avoid calling the Reggio Approach "complex," "subtle," and "difficult," but in this book I show teachers' minute-by-minute decisions–selecting children and considering topics for projects, determining how long projects should last, or how to segue from project to project. You cannot see the structure in a Reggio day as you can in a scheduled day; thus, Reggio classrooms are often mistaken as laissez-faire, on one end of a continuum with "readiness" at the opposite end, where skills are drilled for kindergarten or 1st grade. There is nothing laissez-faire about Reggio teaching! Expectations are clear and enormous emphasis is placed on skill development.

I believe that the structure and practices that form the foundation of the Reggio Approach can be learned. This book is a tool to

- examine beliefs about children and teaching–Chapter 1;
- build self-regulation in children–Chapter 2;
- engage children in the process of drawing their families into a school's daily life–Chapter 3;
- structure and manage Open Flow, a long daily period during which children can focus without interruption–Chapter 4;
- design classrooms so children's interests replace lessons from Teacher's Guides as the driving force–Chapter 5;
- hold "meaning-full" conversations with children–Chapter 6;
- learn to be an intentional teacher–Chapter 7;
- understand the multiple roles of materials–Chapters 8 and 9;
- document children's activities–Chapter 10;
- use authentic assessment to show children's progress–Chapter 11;
- undertake projects–Chapter 12.

Throughout, I identify key points, and at the end of chapters, I pose questions to help you think more deeply about the content. To conclude the book, Chapter 13 provides a self-assessment tool. Structured around the acronym EXCEL, questions are grouped in five areas–Environment, eXchanges, Conversation, Evidence, and Language–to assist you in examining your practices and those of your school. Answers indicate your facility with or readiness to engage in best practices. If you use EXCEL to assess your practices before reading the book, then adopt some of the practices and again use EXCEL, you will see your own growth. The potential of this book lies in its use as a catalyst for changing teaching practices.

Best practices are compatible with findings from the new science of teaching/learning and recent research on the brain, and I show where theory and practice intersect. The research with the most impact on this book is Michael Posner's work on attention (Posner, Rothbart, Sheese, & Kieras, 2008). Posner's work established the neurological basis for children's self-regulation, a theme that runs throughout this book.

The fact is, certain practices must be in place in order to do Reggio-inspired or any other work that is "best." The beliefs and techniques that I explain provide a foundation for any early education that exemplifies best practices. Hallmarks of such practices, which form the backbone of this book, include

- silencing the impulse to "teach" in favor of listening and observing;
- intervening in children's activities with intention;
- working one-on-one or with a small group while most of the other children work independently;
- encouraging collaboration among children, between teachers and children, teacher to teacher as peers, and school and family;
- admitting frustration or failure and asking colleagues for help;
- looking reflectively at every aspect of the classroom.

Most essential is what you believe about children. Reggio educators believe in children's competence, their right to an aesthetic and thoughtfully prepared classroom, and to teachers who are enthusiastic, joyful, avid learners and astute listeners.

BREACHING THE REGGIO/U.S. DIVIDE

The Italian and American cultures are dramatically different, as is each country's history of early education. In Reggio Emilia, high value is placed on aesthetics, philosophy, and intellectuality. American culture values the newest "thing," commercial production, quick solutions, and sound-bite analysis (an oxymoron!).

Reggio practices have been evolving for 65 years. Current U.S. early education is evolving in an era when the need for out-of-home care in children's earliest years has exploded. New standards that have been developed over the short period of the past decade pay more attention to judging children against predetermined measures of "readiness" than to fulfilling each child's potential. A difference with great consequences for American classrooms is that English is only 40 to 60% phonetic but the Italian language is over 95% phonetic. Therefore, unlike American teachers, Reggio teachers are not pressured to teach phonics before 1st grade.

Those Americans trying to use Reggio practices are to be saluted for an effort that requires them to go against the grain of our culture. This is perhaps most evident when we look at the watchword of Reggio education: "Joy!" I hope that children's joy is evident in this book, that it is contagious, and that it surrounds the practices I advocate.

CHAPTER 1

When Belief
Drives Practice

Alice: "Would you tell me, please, which way I ought to walk from here?"

"That depends a good deal on where you want to get to," said the cat.

"I don't much care where," said Alice.

"Then it doesn't matter which way you walk," said the cat.

—Lewis Carroll, *Alice's Adventures in Wonderland*

Scenario 1. Johnny and Tom are fighting again. The teacher walks purposefully toward them to intervene. She catches sight of Jenny, the class' peacemaker, going toward the boys. The teacher stops mid-step, confident that Jenny can arbitrate the fight and can do it better than she, the teacher, because Jenny was closer to the dispute and could better see and hear what went on.

Scenario 2. Johnny and Tom are fighting again. The teacher walks purposefully toward them to intervene. She separates the boys, and talks to them about their behavior.

THE TEACHERS IN SCENARIOS 1 and 2 hold different beliefs. Teacher 1 believes that some children are capable of spotting their classmates' interpersonal problems and resolving them. Because of this belief, she encourages children to play the role of arbitrator by allowing them to do so. If she has seen a child successfully arbitrate, the teacher trusts that child's ability to the same extent she would trust her own. Teacher 2 does not believe that children can arbitrate among themselves. Therefore she does not give them an opportunity to practice that skill and because they do not have the opportunity to use it, the skill does not develop.

Where we go and what we do reflect our beliefs. I believe that Reggio educators' practices are effective. I believe American children can thrive if teachers adapt these practices. And because I hold that our beliefs determine all we do, I start this book by explaining Reggio beliefs and contrasting them with American beliefs about early education.

First, in this chapter, I give a brief overview of the culture in which the Reggio schools exist. Then I describe the Reggio beliefs and explain why the differing American and Italian beliefs make it difficult for American educators to adapt Reggio practices. I end by examining the structure underlying the Reggio Approach.

CULTURAL CONTEXT OF REGGIO EMILIA

A unique mix of circumstances gave birth to the Reggio Approach. One was a rare leader. Others were the spirit of the era and characteristics of the people and place.

Loris Malaguzzi (1920–1994) was the founder of the Reggio Approach. As a young educator, he learned that a group of parents in Reggio Emilia, a city near his native town of Modena, had built a school with bricks from a bombed-out building and a bit of money from the sale of tanks and guns littering their environs at the close of World War II. Devastated by the destruction of large swaths of their city and countryside, parents determined that something good must follow the war and started a school initially called Villa Cella. Malaguzzi rode his bike to Reggio, liked what he saw, and stayed the rest of his life.

> The war was still hot and palpable. . . . Only a few days had passed since the Liberation and everything was still violently topsy-turvy. . . . There was no telephone. . . . That is why I got on my bicycle and rode out to Villa Cella. . . . [W]ithout a penny to their names . . . the people, women, farm laborers, factory workers . . . [were] build[ing] a school with their own strength, brick by brick. . . . [The school] remained an uninterrupted lesson given by men and women whose ideals were still intact, who had understood long before I had that history can be changed, and is changed by taking possession of it, starting with the destiny of the children. (Malaguzzi, 1985, pp. 13–15)

Over time, Malaguzzi cultivated a band of dedicated teachers and parents who, with him, forged the practices, fought for the funds, rallied political support, and gradually grew the schools we know today. Since Malaguzzi's death, a corps of passionate educators has stepped into the many roles he played or responded in new ways to the increasing deluge of requests from all over the world for information and support as educators try to adapt what has become known as the "Reggio Approach."

The city of Reggio Emilia is about a 2-hour train ride southeast of Milan and an hour northwest of Bologna. It is located in the verdant, prosperous northern region that yields bountiful agricultural products. Just as its schools are famous among educators, Reggio's collaborative manufacturing is renowned in industrial circles. Industry includes production of Reggiano Parmesan cheese, vintage years of balsamic vinegar, and luxurious Max Mara clothing. Reggio Emilia is known in financial circles as a model of citizen participation in the government budgeting process. Given the emphasis in the schools on collaboration, it is no wonder that now, two generations after the schools' inception, collaborative endeavor in the region is seen from farm to finance.

Reggio Emilia lies on the Via Flaminia, the ancient road from Rome to the Adriatic Sea. Although not on most tourists' agendas, the city could be. Remains of Roman structures attest to its ancient heritage. Outlines of the medieval walled town stand out clearly in aerial photos. Subtle, muted facades of centuries-old buildings maintain their character and coloring. Town squares regularly host lively traveling markets that sell everything from corsets and crockery to culinary treats. Its government building and central opera house are in the grand tradition of Europe's finest. In the opera house, children's whimsical, colorful drawings were enlarged to dazzling size to decorate the theater curtain. Pageants that reenact historical events include many

Key Point:
Reggio practices are embedded in their city's and country's long history and culture.

roles for youngsters. Reggio calls itself "the city of children," so deeply do its citizens value children's presence and joyous spirit.

REGGIO'S UNIQUE BELIEFS AND FEATURES

The Reggio schools are unique because the philosophy that underlies all their practices is consistent. Beliefs and practices are seamlessly integrated. You cannot discuss beliefs without referring to practices, nor describe any one belief without referring to the others. Belief and practice are fully interwoven in Reggio classrooms. Like the three-legged stool that topples if a leg is missing, the Reggio philosophy stands the test of practice because its structure has integrity.

A Cohesive System

The cohesive features that comprise the Reggio Approach have evolved over many decades. Practices continue to evolve because Reggio educators study and reflect as naturally as they eat pasta. Because their practices are evolving, any description is a work-in-progress. Here is my current interpretation of the key features:

- *Belief in children's competence.* Reggio educators say that from birth children are "rich, strong, and powerful," that they have *rights*, not needs, and that schooling must ensure that those rights flourish. Teachers base everything they do on the competencies they observe in each individual child.
- *Work in small groups.* Small-group work, which constitutes most of the hours in a school day, enables teachers to closely observe individual children's strengths and to tailor daily activities to develop those and other strengths.
- *Organization of space and time.* Space is designed in minute detail because the environment is considered a "third teacher." Floor plan, furniture placement, and materials result from teachers' conscious choices. Teachers analyze the aesthetic quality and potentialities of every item, from type of glue to variety of plants. Within their thoughtfully designed spaces, they see time as a valuable commodity that must be protected from trivial pursuits, boring lessons, and, above all, interruptions. There are no breaks for music or gym, no interfering loudspeakers. As a result, long blocks of time are available for challenging activities, some chosen by children, some suggested by teachers, most resulting from teacher/child collaboration.
- *Studio/Studio teacher.* The Studio is the "heart" of the school because it contains a repository of materials and tools that, along with the expertise of its Studio teacher, are resources children use to make meaning of experiences. In the process, children hone complex skills. By using materials and tools, children heighten their sensory awareness, their gross and fine motor skills, and their expressive capacities.
- *"100 languages."* With these poetic words, Reggio educators refer to the human capacity to receive information and to express ideas–through written word, symbol, speech, music, movement, drawing, facial expression, clay, wire, paper, looms, shadow, light, gesture, and more. They consider that each capacity is a "language." The idea of "100 languages" corresponds to

psychologist Howard Gardner's (1983) theory of Multiple Intelligences and to Israeli psychologist Reuven Feuerstein's (Feuerstein, Feuerstein, Falik, & Rand, 2006) understanding that humans can receive information and express ideas in limitless ways.

- *Teachers as researchers.* Reggio teachers think of themselves as researchers. Research involves the intention to
  - suppose what might occur in the classroom;
  - observe what actually occurs;
  - listen thoughtfully to what children say;
  - analyze reflectively what children's words and actions mean;
  - use their reflections to deliberate with the children on what to do next (see Chapter 7).
- *Documentation.* The use of documentation as a means of reflection was, initially, unique to Reggio. The process involves:
  - recording children's words and photographing their actions as the means of listening and observing;
  - selecting those comments or actions that express pivotal moments in an experience;
  - using what is selected as the basis to reflect with children;
  - encouraging children to relive an experience by explaining what they thought and did and what they might do next.
- This active reflection builds children's memory and focus. They learn to articulate the story of their activities in a logically related sequence. Lively exchanges among children and teacher ensue as they debate past experiences. The process extends projects in unexpected directions. As they interact with children, teachers encourage the children to undertake challenges.
- *Family involvement.* Amelia Gambetti, retired Reggio teacher and Liaison for Reggio Children to schools worldwide, said, "A school without families is like a body without arms." Family participation has incalculable value. Teachers involve families as intentionally as they interact with children. Teachers engage families in numerous ways to
  - make furniture and playground equipment;
  - harvest unusual recyclable items;
  - host dignitaries;
  - prepare regional specialties for guests;
  - serve on a council that lobbies at all governmental levels for support;
  - advocate strongly for their schools.
- Evening meetings about what goes on at school may last until midnight, with parents intellectually stimulated by discussions of what their children's activities mean.
- *Teacher growth.* The Reggio system offers:
  - continuing professional development;
  - collaboration with specialists;
  - reasonable hours;
  - thoughtful adult/child ratios;
  - ample staff support;
  - budgets for well-designed furnishings and well-made equipment;

– plentiful materials;
– decent pay.
- Leading psychologists, philosophers, educators, and others interested in excellent early education visit frequently. Their questions stimulate Reggio educators to reflect and redefine their work.

> **Key Point:**
> What children in Reggio schools produce far exceeds expectations of what young children can achieve.

Foundation: Socio-Cultural Theory

Socio-cultural theory, initially developed by the groundbreaking Russian psychologist Lev Vygotsky (1934/1986), provides a theoretical basis for the Reggio Approach. Vygotsky's fundamental insight was that human development results from the relationships that people form with their environment, but especially with the persons around them.

Small Groups. As mentioned earlier, the structure of a Reggio classroom is small groups of children collaborating with a teacher. This reflects the basis of socio-cultural theory that close contact with others–peers and adults–is essential for development. Small-group work fosters imitation that, beginning in infancy and continuing throughout life, is a primary way that humans learn.

Vygotsky's theory and Reggio practice are both supported by the recent discovery of "mirror neurons," the cellular basis for imitation. *Science Daily* reports on current research by Itzhak Fried, UCLA Professor of Neurosurgery, Psychiatry and Bio-behavioral Sciences:

> Mirror neurons fire both when an individual performs an action and when one watches another individual perform that same action; it's thought this "mirroring" is the neural mechanism by which the actions, intentions and emotions of other people can be automatically understood. (First direct recording made of mirror neurons in human brain, 2010)

Conversation. A cornerstone of Reggio practice is Meaning-full Conversation that is long, intense, and focused on a topic (see Chapter 6). I use the word *Meaning-full* with the unconventional spelling and capitalize it along with the word *Conversation* to refer to a particular technique that recognizes the importance of conversation in children's learning to speak and use language. The two words together reflect another basis of socio-cultural theory that language is (1) the main tool the brain uses to think (Greenspan & Shanker, 2004; Wilson, 1998; Wolf, 2007), and is (2) essentially social– necessary to communicate with, influence, and relate to others. Vygotsky says: "The child's intellectual growth is contingent on his mastering the social means of thought, that is, language" (Vygotsky, 1934/1986, p. 94). I intend the word *Meaning-full* to convey the necessity for conversation to have significant and robust content *and* to convey the role conversation plays in the brain's constant quest to make meaning of experiences. (For a fuller discussion, see Vygotsky's *Thought and Language,* 1934/1986; Chapter 2 in Berk & Winsler, 1995.)

Conversation is a living thing. It cannot be scripted in advance. Everyone involved in the conversation must be a good listener. The teacher is the orchestrator who establishes the behaviors that make conversation possible.

A Reggio Day

A Reggio day is driven by children's interests, organized through *conversation*, based on *collaboration*, and assessed through *reflection.* These practices are the mortar in the structure. They integrate life in the classroom and connect everything that goes on.

So, a morning begins with conversation among the full class, and throughout the day conversations occur between teacher and an individual child, teacher and a small group, and among children themselves. Through conversations, teachers hear what excites children, what they know, and where their confusions lie. Using and extending what children know is the goal of work on which they—a small group of children with a teacher—collaborate. Teachers thoughtfully distill what they hear and, using the children's own words, read back to the children what they have said, converse with the children about it, then reflect together on what they might do next.

Key Points:
- Belief in children's competence is the driving factor in all Reggio practices.
- The environment is a "third teacher."
- Teachers are researchers who listen and reflect on what they hear with one another and the children.
- Meaning-full Conversation is all important.
- Listening and reflecting play a central role in learning.

CORRELATIONS: BEST PRACTICES AND THE REGGIO APPROACH

Four aspects of the Reggio Approach put it at the top of my list of "best practices":

1. The underlying belief is that from birth children are competent. Belief is the core of any approach. Practices either reflect or belie espoused beliefs.
2. Activities are bottom-up; that is, they are not pre-formulated but grow out of what has gone before in children's experiences at school or at home (see Chapter 4).
3. The aesthetics of a classroom relate to what the children do there; that is, the environment must appeal to the senses that, along with movement, are the avenues through which young children learn (see Chapters 5, 8, and 9).
4. Assessment and documentation are integral parts of all activities (see Chapters 10 and 11).

Here, I briefly contrast these four aspects of the Reggio Approach with beliefs in other early childhood programs.

Underlying Beliefs

The mission statements of many early childhood programs read as if they are in sync with Reggio practices. The differences become apparent when you watch how

Figure 1.1. Making use of a conversation may require reading it again at a later time and further conversation to clarify the meaning.

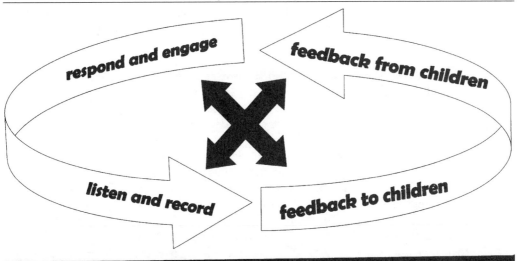

beliefs translate into teachers' actions. The head of the early childhood program at a large state teachers college and I attended a lecture by a leading Reggio educator. As we walked back to campus, she ticked off several ways in which the classes she supervised were no different from what she had just seen: "We have good materials in our classrooms, our teachers do projects with the children, we work hard to cultivate parent involvement," and, she concluded, "we do everything the lecturer talked about." She continued, "I tell my teachers, 'You'd better have something for those high-functioning children who go through everything you set out in 3 minutes and for the low-functioning children as well who cannot do anything you set out. If you don't, they'll come up with something on their own and I guarantee you won't like it one bit.'"

The professor's checklist may seem accurate, but it is diametrically different from the Reggio Approach. In particular, her last comment belies a belief in children's competence and suggests that she would not use children's ideas and actions as the basis for structuring experiences. Thus, the professor directly contradicts Reggio beliefs. If you truly believe in children's competence, you will prepare an environment and structure experiences based on children's interests. You will also ensure that experiences challenge children in areas where they are skilled and build skills in areas where they are challenged. This shift in perspective has immense implications for changing teaching practices. (See Chapters 4, 7, and 12.)

In the typically brief time that most visitors spend in Reggio classrooms, it is not possible to see the processes that gradually build self-regulation and other skills. Moreover, most of the Reggio educators' books and conference presentations do not show how their processes work. The Reggio book *Shoe and Meter* (Malaguzzi, 1997) is a notable exception (see Chapter 12).

> **Key Point:**
> Our beliefs are dictators that determine what we do.

Top-Down or Bottom-Up: The Space/Time Paradigm

Top-down practices use predetermined objectives and children learn bits of this and that. Bottom-up practices have evolving objectives and children learn skills to solve problems.

Top-Down Practices. These time-driven practices are based on predetermined schedules for specific subject matter that teachers must cover and children must know to repeat back on tests. Teacher talk dominates, as does direct teaching, often to the entire class at once. The schedule drives the day: "Put *this* away now and do *that.*"

A school where I once taught was pressured by competition from other private schools to have specialist teachers in music, gym, art, foreign language, and religious instruction. Additionally, in response to parents' expectations, the teachers followed a calendar of religious observances that dictated what they did with the children: "Sing these songs, make that art, cook this food, hear those stories." As a consequence, the children spent a lot of time coming and going to classes or, in their own room, making formulaic "products" that assured parents that their children were "learning" about their religion.

Bottom-Up Practices. In a bottom-up curriculum, time is open-ended within a general plan. Bottom-up work is successful because the environment is prepared in such detail that it captures children's interests. Their interests stimulate what they do, and conversation is the entry point to explore their interests. Conversation extends interests and sparks projects that continue until interests wane naturally. This relationship—environment, interests, conversation, projects—is the basis for children's using time and space well and reveals whether teachers do, in fact, believe in children's competence.

> **Key Point:**
> A bottom-up curriculum stimulates interest that motivates children to focus on (neuroscientists say "attend to") an activity for an extended period of time.

Michael Posner, respected researcher on the brain's attention systems, says, "Any training that truly engages the interest of the child and motivates the child can serve to help train attention" (Posner et al., 2008, p. 2). Attention means the abilities to select a stimulus, focus on it, and stay focused. Children who lack these skills have difficulty learning.

Aesthetics' Influence on Behavior

Aesthetics narrowly defined refers to beauty; broadly defined it refers to the characteristics of the material world. The Reggio Approach emphasizes aesthetics because the material aspects of an environment impact children's behavior. Typical American early childhood classrooms have bright, intensely saturated colors, commercially produced graphics, cramped "centers," and bulky furniture. With so much clutter, everything takes on equal importance. As a result, children see nothing as special.

In Reggio schools, each item, down to the smallest bead or individual label, is attractive and suggests an activity that is meaningful or leads to something related. There are no commercial hangings. Much of the furniture is made to fit classroom spaces, so shelf units, for example, are not too high, too deep, or too bulky. The color palette is distinct, original, and varied, with a great range of what Reggio educators call "lightweight colors (pale hues)" (Reggio Children, 1998, p. 61). They say

Key Point:
When an environment appeals to children's sensory and movement imperatives, and when it is quiet, varied, and challenging, children respond thoughtfully.

that because soft colors and natural materials are muted, they are calming. In this quiet surround, visual stimulation comes from thoughtful use of light and mirrors, careful placement of materials, artful display of children's work, and the colors added to the environment by materials and people's attire. Further, they say: "The richness of the chromascape [range of colors] in a school enables children to develop certain sensitivities and understandings which, if not set in motion at a young age, are difficult to recover as an adult" (p. 68).

Assessment

The recent proliferation of standards has spawned a big business to develop and sell assessment tools, both paper and electronic. Some assessments are too long–hundreds of measures to evaluate the students and the program. Others are elaborate electronic programs to align curriculum and reporting tools, and tie lessons, activities, and outcomes to state objectives or Head Start performance standards.

Standards-based evaluation leaves little, if any, room for teacher innovation. Some administrators, school systems, states, or federal programs require all children to achieve certain results by a specific time, based on the No Child Left Behind (NCLB) Act of 2002. This means that the standardized curriculum in each classroom must be identical. It turns teachers into clock watchers and page turners, pushing an entire predetermined curriculum forward regardless of whether children are interested in the material or understand it. Ensuring that children can answer test questions becomes the teacher's business and virtually eliminates activities that engage teachers' and children's creativity. Young children vary greatly in when they develop different skills. Being held accountable to predetermined standards–everyone on the same page at the same time–imposes a norm at an age when the optimum conditions for growth are directly opposite. In the early years especially, it is important to nurture individuality (see Chapter 11).

Assessment in Reggio schools is an integral part of the curriculum. That is, rather than test children, teachers base what they teach on what they observe children doing or hear them saying. If they observe that a child is weak in, for example, drawing, they include that child with a group of other children in an experience that will help drawing skills develop. All work product is saved and accumulates over 3 years so that what a child does now can be compared with what she did a month or a year ago. These comparisons provide evidence of children's growing skill.

Key Point:
The Reggio Approach to assessment is dramatically different from the evaluation-driven practices being imposed with increasing frequency in the United States.

Summary

Based on underlying beliefs, top-down versus bottom-up programs and the use of time/space, the value placed on aesthetics, and the approach to assessment, typical American early childhood curricula and the Reggio Approach are far apart. Understanding the structure in which Reggio practices flourish is the first step to using the Reggio Approach as a best practice.

THE STRUCTURE SUPPORTING REGGIO PRACTICES

Today, more than 2 decades after I founded the MELC based on Reggio practices, I realize that the success of the Reggio Approach results from the structure I describe here.

Self-Regulated Children

Between 1992 and 1995, when I traveled frequently to Reggio Emilia to visit their schools and spent hours in many classrooms, I never saw the behavior problems common in America. Children's engagement had a quality that psychologist Mihaly Csikszentmihalyi (1990) calls flow–deep concentration for extended periods. Because extended concentration was the norm, it generated what is called "social pressure"–the many influence the few, who consequently adopt the dominant behavior. Equally important, in establishing self-regulation, teachers converse frequently with small groups of children about rights and responsibilities and encourage the children to formulate the classroom rules. Thus, children learn why rules make sense and the connection of rules to behavior. Moreover, each classroom has climbing and other physical equipment that children use whenever and for however long they want. These factors help children achieve the self-regulation (see Chapter 2) that is essential before beginning the work typical of Reggio children.

> **Key Point:**
> Children must be self-regulated for Reggio practices to flourish.

Uninterrupted Time

Children cannot learn to concentrate if their activity is interrupted before they have a chance to settle into something that strongly compels their attention. Compelling activity is challenging in the way that Csikszentmihalyi (1990) defines challenge–not so easy that it bores nor so hard that it frustrates. In Chapter 4, I explain how to establish an Open Flow day that gives children long, uninterrupted periods of time. Here, it is enough to say that how time is used determines whether children will learn to persist in challenging tasks. Many do so naturally. Others need to be "trained" to concentrate. Throughout the book, I use the word *trained* as neuroscientists use it when they speak of "training the brain" (Posner et al., 2008).

> **Key Point:**
> Children must be able to persist at tasks for Reggio practices to flourish.

Aesthetic Space

Materials must be appealing, plentiful, and not cluttered or broken. As essayist Charles Lamb (1823/1913) said, "Man is not a creature of pure reason; he must have his senses delightfully appealed to" (p. 40). Some materials, like blocks, must be open-ended and must easily incorporate other objects. Some, like a housekeeping area or grocery, must entice children to enact daily life routines–an important means of developing procedural (long-term) memory. In Chapter 5, I discuss aesthetics, and in Chapters 8 and 9, I discuss materials.

> **Key Point:**
> Children must have access to an aesthetic environment for Reggio practices to flourish.

Teacher-Shared Perspectives

Co-teachers—or teacher/aide—must share the same beliefs of what children can do, how to help them become self-regulated, and how time and space are used. It is counterproductive for one teacher to refrain from assisting children if the other teacher overrides children's initiative by helping them.

Beyond this, teachers must clearly understand that the act of teaching has two distinct aspects: One involves interacting with an individual or small group of children with the intention of conveying meaning, building skill, or encouraging development of the cognitive capacities that enable children to form relationships. The other aspect involves managing, by which I mean constant attention to care of the environment, to children's behavior, and especially to those children who are not self-regulated. These aspects are both essential teaching behaviors. If there are two teachers, they can agree that each will assume one of the roles. But both teachers should understand and be able to function in either role. (See Chapters 2, 4, and 7.)

> **Key Point:**
> How teachers understand their role is a main reason Reggio practices work.

Family Involvement

The desire to involve families is often more words than reality. Just as it is important to define the two aspects of teaching, parent roles require definition. "One size" does not fit all schools. In the diverse American culture, families may be immigrant, affluent, economically disadvantaged, blended, gay or lesbian, single-parent, or a combination. Each family's different culture requires a meeting of minds between teachers and parents on the role that families play.

In Chapter 3, I show how the MELC teachers reached out to draw economically disadvantaged families into the school's life. In an affluent school where I worked, the question was how to reduce parents' pressure for 3- and 4-year-old children to be high achievers in literacy skills. All families are bombarded by messages about what children "should" do, how they "should" dress, and what "should" occupy their time. Schools may require an outside expert to get parental expectations on track. Lacking an expert, school leaders—a wise teacher, parent, or administrator—must step into the role.

> **Key Point:**
> Expectations for parent/teacher relationships must be well defined for Reggio practices to flourish.

CONCLUSION: USING REGGIO AND OTHER BEST PRACTICES

The first steps in adapting best practices are different for every school and teacher. It is less important which step to take than it is to understand what is to be accomplished. This, in turn, requires confronting basic beliefs. It can be overwhelming to compare initial efforts to the accomplishments of Reggio schools but comforting to remember that they are 65 years away from their beginnings.

In 1994, when I accepted Reggio's Certificate of Accreditation for the Model Early Learning Center —the only American school so accredited—I said it was humbling, that for our school it meant a "huge responsibility of continuing along a complex and challenging path, [and] helping others learn from our experience" (Reggio Children,

1995, p. 6). I said we were obligated to demonstrate how early education functions when it is based on the belief in every child's power, strength, and richness.

In the years since I wrote that, extensive research on the first years of life has shown beyond doubt that children's readiness to learn begins before birth. And the field of American early education has burgeoned, serving greatly increased numbers of children at younger ages and for extended hours.

Today, some educators venture bravely into the world of Reggio practices and against the grain of American culture. And many other educators seek best practices wherever they can be found. These educators are torchbearers for how to harness the power of young children. They are in a privileged and demanding position. They have an opportunity to use the hours of school–which today can be very long–to foster the growth of children's minds and to hone the functions of the brain on which success in future learning depends.

Questions to Consider

1. Describe the cultural context of your school. Then compare the context of your school with the cultural context in the United States in general.
2. Describe your beliefs about young children.
3. How do your practices reflect your beliefs?
4. List specific competencies that you observe in your children; then, organize your list by category.

CHAPTER 2

Developing Self-Regulation

Tom, Tom, the piper's son,
Stole a pig and away did run;
The pig was eat, and Tom was beat,
Till he run crying down the street.

—Mother Goose

OM'S PUNISHMENT SEEMS too severe when we realize that the "pig" was a meat pie. The rhyme reminds us how thorny questions of discipline are. What *does* discipline mean in an age when opinions vary from favoring old-fashioned punishment to eliminating the very word *discipline*? There are no simple answers. Think about these children:

The 3-year-old raced around the classroom, painting smock flying from his shoulders, shouting, "Baaaat Maaaan!" The 4-year-olds next door sat on the floor facing the teacher. One youngster snuck behind a classmate, poked his ribs, then as the child turned, quickly and craftily looked away. Next he crawled off under tables, oblivious to the lesson, causing some classmates to titter. In the kindergarten nearby, an angelic-looking girl was screaming, "I don't have to do this stupid work. If you make me, I'll tell my mother." These children were isolated instances in classes that were otherwise settled—Batman was a general disturbance; the poker/crawler, a nuisance; the screamer, a model of disrespect. These classrooms were fortunate to have only one disruptive child. Some classes have many.

In this chapter, I discuss children's self-regulation and explore how the following systems, schools, or teachers approach discipline and self-regulation:

- the Reggio Approach;
- Montessori's method;
- a curriculum-based school;
- a school run by a large day-care chain;
- the Model Early Learning Center.

BECOMING SELF-REGULATED

The words for behavior have changed—disciplined, then self-disciplined. Montessori used "normalized." Psychologist Mihaly Csikszentmihalyi (1990) uses "in flow." Some use "creative guidance." Teachers understand self-regulated behavior differently.

Children's behavior during a full-class conversation shows whether they are self-regulated. In an economically advantaged private school, I was demonstrating conversation techniques with a classroom of 4-year-olds I had never met. The school's full staff was observing. Generally, I start by asking what "conversation" is. I have heard 4-year-olds give dictionary-perfect definitions. In this class, one child answered: "It's a door." Another launched a rambling description of a TV cartoon, another gave a detailed account of a trip to her grandparents' house. Meanwhile, another was having a whale-sized tantrum, another half dozen were paying no attention but were chattering busily among themselves, and a few crawled away.

I had assumed that the children would be self-regulated and attentive. I was wrong on both counts. The exchange was not what I consider "conversation." I felt like a failure. At a meeting with the full staff observing, I asked for comments. No one mentioned the children's lack of conversation or discipline. They saw nothing unusual in what they had observed, and the teachers of the demo class took umbrage when I stated that, in my opinion, these children did not know how to have a conversation and were not self-regulated—a remark I regretted even as I said it.

What does self-regulation mean? Ultimately, every child is different. There is no one-size-fits-all way to help children learn self-control. No other aspect of teaching requires as much flexibility or such different responses to different children.

Yet in the United States when it comes to addressing children's behavior, similarities within early education are more apparent than differences. Many highly regarded preschools—both private and public—espouse a carefully articulated philosophy, are well equipped, and are run by staff with advanced degrees in early education. Most of these staff members say that they respect children's individuality and consider their overall well-being as having primary importance. They say they aim to foster children's social, emotional, physical, and intellectual growth. Nonetheless, discipline typically

- is addressed by a high ratio of adults to children;
- uses "time out" as a disciplinary technique;
- engages children in frequent one-on-one discussion with teachers about how others' behavior affects our feelings, how we treat others, and how we want others to treat us;
- involves considerable teacher time to discuss children's emotional reactions with them.

In schools that are rigorously scheduled with visits to music or art teachers, field trips, or special programs, short timeframes mask acting-out behavior. Schedules make misbehavior less noticeable than it would be if the child spent all morning in one room.

From the amalgam of approaches, from parents' desires and concerns, schools' ethics, and communities' expectations, teachers forge their own discipline techniques. Many new teachers feel unprepared for what to expect in children's behavior and say they lack strategies to address discipline and instill self-regulation.

Key Points:
- Discipline should come from within, from children's own understanding of how to behave and their growing ability to behave well in whatever circumstances they find themselves.
- Threats, rewards, punishments, or teacher interventions should not be the motives for children's behaving well.
- The marks of self-regulated children are sustained focus and understanding and respecting the rights of others.

THE REGGIO APPROACH

The city of Reggio Emilia was homogeneous and had been for centuries—a stable population with the same culture. In the mid-1990s, an influx of Eastern Europeans and North Africans began. The population shifts posed new challenges for teachers: children who did not speak Italian, families whose child-rearing practices differed from one another and from those of long-time Reggio residents, varied parental expectations, behavioral challenges from the children. Reggio educators' response was not to look at the problems but to look at the strengths the new families brought, to find what would enable families to participate, and to observe what worked in drawing children into the school culture.

A new position, called a "cultural mediator," was established to legitimize foreign languages and to be a link between immigrant families and the schools. The first level of mediation was to help families with transitions to a new place, culture, and school system. Educators recognized families' different attitudes toward mediation and school. Some families wanted to keep children home to learn their mother tongue first and send them to school at age 5 to learn Italian. Others questioned the use of financial resources for children under age 5. Others were concerned about outward signs of religion. For others the presence of the cultural mediator legitimized school excursions.

The educators found the families' questions helpful in establishing these issues as a focus for the school's role in acculturation:

- Language barriers suggest that school/family communication is not deep enough.
- Families who have been in school for a while are good resources at welcoming meetings where the goal is to begin to understand differences within differences.
- Listening must be a continuing process because experiences evolve and we change as we listen.
- The cultural mediator should not be involved automatically but only as needed.
- Cultural mediators help the teachers see other cultures more dynamically.
- Cultural mediators can be very helpful in supporting communication in morning meetings where their presence legitimizes the use of different languages.

- Factors designed to encourage parents to participate include meeting in smaller groups, at different times, and in the classrooms, and ensuring that the school is flexible.
- More "fun" encounters, such as parties, should be held. The educators found that storytelling is important because when people relate a narrative it ensures that they have a voice. As people tell their stories, the listeners enter into the folklore of a country. This gives value to different cultures.

From the perspective of children, the educators saw that work in small groups and especially work with materials enabled children who did not speak Italian to communicate, to use gesture and movement, to share their skills or make other contributions, and thereby to become important to the other children. Sharing artifacts or other objects enabled children to reveal themselves in ways that generally remain private. When teachers saw children using the message center, they added symbols from other cultures and encouraged children to make their own symbols for words or phrases in common use in the classroom. When cultural mediators expressed uncertainty about how to talk about issues such as life, death, or religion, the Reggio teachers explained that they (the teachers) were always honest and clear, but made sure to tell children or parents that they were speaking only from their own perspective.

What the educators ultimately learned was the importance of

- making each person a mediator;
- using direct experience with another culture as the means to reevaluate themselves and their practices;
- amplifying the facets of other cultures, and as different immigrant families continue to arrive, rethinking Reggio Emilia, a city they thought they knew.

Above all, the educators recognized that children could give new meanings to things that the adults did not experience growing up. For example, the children made maps showing places that their new friends found significant—the Mosque and the Ghanaian Church, stores, and other places of cultural exchange. The teachers discovered a city they did not know, a city oscillating between past and future. They reconceived the school's role; now it became forming a bridge—between the real and the imagined, the static and the dynamic, and the new ways of understanding their city.

The significance of Reggio educators' emphasis on strength, not on problem, is that it reflects their entire approach: They recognize problems. They analyze problems with persons who have different perspectives, in the above case teachers, the cultural mediator, and the *pedagogista,* a specialist who works with several schools and collaborates with teachers to address matters involving families, children's behavior, or classroom practices. There is no comparable position in American school. After defining an issue, the educators determine what to change in the classroom or between family and school to address the issue. Their clues for what to do come from what they have heard as families' concerns, attitudes, and desires.

Key Point:
What might have been defined as a problem—children's different responses to school—was seen as an opportunity to reevaluate beliefs and teaching practices.

Watching Self-Regulated Children

Visitors to Reggio schools comment on how well behaved the children are. They go about their work purposefully, concentrate for long times—sometimes days on end—cooperate readily when teachers suggest an activity, collaborate well with teachers and other children, and choose what to do largely on their own initiative. I observed this in all the classes I visited—about two dozen in all—and colleagues reported the same.

On several occasions, I saw what I feared would disrupt a class:

- Five children became engaged in loud, strenuous physical activity—tumbling, climbing, jumping. But the rest of the class worked quietly, took no notice of the tumblers, continued as if their own work were the only thing going on, which, for them, it was.
- In another class, four boys, unsettled and wandering, went off on their own, out of the teachers' sight, into a small room adjacent to the classroom—with the door closed! It turned out that they spent the morning building an incredibly complex structure.
- I watched a child have a tantrum, smashing china plates she was supposed to be setting out for lunch. She was calmed by several other children who were also readying tables for lunch; the teacher seemed not to have seen, although she must have because the episode was videotaped.
- I watched a child almost stab another with a trowel, frustrated that "his" space had been *invaded.* As with the plate-smasher, the would-be stabber was detained by friends who took the trowel away and reprimanded the child. Again, no teacher needed to intervene.
- I observed a class of toddlers engaged in shadow play: Nearly 20 were supposed to be small fish, represented by their holding small paper fish mounted on sticks. They were urged by their teacher to *swim* (run) from another child who, wearing a shark's head, was urged by the teacher to chase them. Later, the teacher explained that the toddlers were dramatizing a book that had been their favorite for many months. Not for an instant did the activity show signs of deteriorating into a general melee nor did the teacher interrupt the play acting to caution children about their behavior.

> **Key Point:**
> Teachers who believe in children's competence trust that they can respect one another and behave well.

In each instance, I was amazed that boisterous or potentially dangerous activity remained contained and caused no harm. There was no hint of chaos among the children and no need for a teacher's intervention.

Structures That Build Self-Regulation

Reggio children are self-regulated for several reasons: First, the equipment and materials in the classroom are complex and thoughtfully chosen to arouse interest and incorporate movement. Second, teachers intervene in markedly different ways from American teachers. Third, when children are selected for groups, the purpose is often to encourage relationships that will build children's responsibilities along with their rights. Here, I examine these three practices.

Stimulating Movement. Classrooms are carefully detailed and encourage children to do what they naturally want to do. For example, gym equipment–tumbling mats, wall-mounted climbing rungs, ropes to swing on–is in every class. Young children need to be physical. Some cannot sit for the amount of time certain activities require. Others need to move vigorously, and not on schedule! Teachers recognize these differences and prepare the classroom to offer the same opportunity for strenuous physicality as for fine motor control.

Classrooms are also well equipped to support small-scale movement. So, a sand table is used as a construction site; the sand stabilized the construction made by the unsettled boys who by age 4½ had long since outgrown the funnel/pail/shovel/sifter activities that typify sand tables. The sand provided the means to make a complex construction.

Figure 2.1. Two-level climbing structure in the MELC with ladder, rope ladder, slide, tumbling mat, and ropes.

Figure 2.2. Complex construction in sand at the MELC using an oversized sink as the sand table and a large assortment of unusual props.

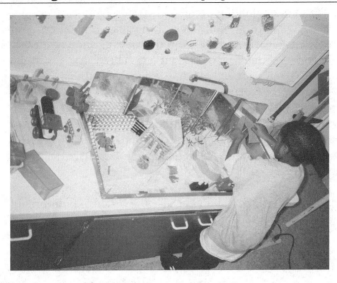

The toddlers involved in the dramatic play were strenuously engaged, running and dodging every which way to avoid the shark's jaws. For toddlers, movement *is* development. Their movements were not random, but followed a story line. The human brain is wired to follow a story, and toddlers do so long before they have the vocabulary, grammar, or vocal musculature to recite stories. The props emphasized the relationship between story and movement.

Movement centers in the brain are activated in every thinking act. Clinical psychologist John Ratey (2002) at Harvard Medical School says that movements "directly influence our ability to learn, think, and remember" (p. 178). Divorcing movement from classrooms in children's early years keeps the brain from functioning well. Even at age 8 and beyond, children solve problems most effectively when they can move objects that represent the parts of the problem. *Example for 3-year-olds:* How many spoons do we need at this table? (Children are most likely to solve the problem if they can go to the table and touch the chairs or placements.) *Example for 8-year-olds:* Regroup the number 324 into units, tens, and hundreds. (Children are more likely to solve the problem if they can use Deines Blocks, Montessori beads, or other manipulative materials designed to make place value tangible.) Reggio teachers understand the importance of movement and design the classroom to foster it.

When children are restrained from moving, cognitive areas of the brain shut down, and children squirm, wiggle, crawl away, or do whatever they must to engage the brain's movement centers. Materials stimulate attention when they are thoughtfully chosen for their potential to elicit varied and increasingly complex or precise movement.

Teacher Intervention. With situations like the "plate-smasher" and the trowel "almost-stabber" where the children's behavior was potentially dangerous, Reggio teachers believe that other children who are on the scene can better resolve a dispute than teachers who may be out of sight and earshot. Reggio teachers trust children's judgment, and children live up to expectations that they will be competent and fair arbitrators.

This does not happen by accident. It results from conversations in which teachers discuss with children what friendship means and their rights and responsibilities in treating others. Teachers do this through conversations with the full class, in small groups of two to six children, or one-on-one. These are conversations—reciprocal exchanges of ideas among members of a group. They are not lectures by adult to child. As Malaguzzi (1991) explains,

> Children are naturally endowed with the art of making friends or acting as teachers among their peers . . . They steal and interpret patterns from adult teachers; and the more these teachers know how to work, discuss, think, and research together, the more children get. (p. 17)

Children develop self-regulation because the teachers both provide active guidance and frequently converse with children about topics such as empathy, collaboration, friendship, and children's rights.

Rights and Responsibilities. Children are self-regulated because Reggio teachers believe they must accord rights to children—the right to a beautiful environment, plentiful materials, nourishing and tasty food, choice of activity, big challenges, and more—*and* rights must be matched by responsibility.

So teachers tour the classroom and discuss each area with small groups of children. The teachers do this whenever new children arrive, or early in the school year, when new things are added to the classroom, or if children's care of the environment falters and they need to review rights and responsibilities. Teachers spur the children to think about each area: How many children can play here at once? Why? How should the materials be used? Why? What should the area look like when you finish using it? Why? How can you ensure that it will? As they tour the classroom, the groups proceed from area to area, with teachers taking notes on children's comments.

Weeks later, after small groups of children have studied the whole school, teachers emerge with documents that are, literally, statements of rights and responsibilities *generated* by children. Then, together, teacher and children study the document, discuss it, refine their understanding, and revise their statements. Later, the children illustrate their thoughts and the work becomes a booklet. Later still, they use the booklet to explain the rules to other children. In time, every child takes part in small-group activity in which they analyze their rights and responsibilities to use the environment, to make choices, to be friends with others.

Typically in the United States, teachers in early education talk to children about their behavior when a "situation" occurs—some child has taken another's toy, hit, or otherwise behaved antisocially. Teachers supply children's words: "Tell John, 'I'm sorry I hit you, John.'" Teachers coach: "What do you tell Alice about hitting her? Can you say, 'I didn't mean to hit you, Alice?'" The teacher's tone of voice carries lots of "shoulds." Some teachers lecture about how it feels to be hit (have a toy taken, be bitten) and ask, "Would you want John to bite you?" The child being coached or lectured may feel humiliated. Some learn shame.

In contrast, Reggio teachers converse about the meaning of friendship or about children's rights, but *not* in the middle of a fray! They converse at neutral times, not

Figure 2.3. As Sonya and a small group tour the Big Room at the MELC, they consider where the Unifix Cubes are stored, how to carry and return them to their place, where to use them, and what might be done with them.

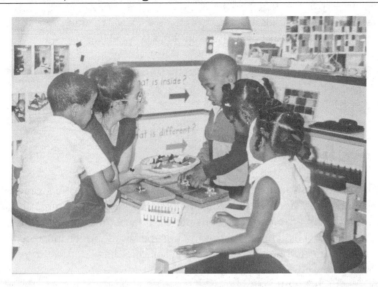

during "situations." Such conversations might start by a teacher's asking, "What if one child pushes another?" The teacher would not recall a particular situation or name a child. The tone is conversational, not preachy. Teachers do not tell children what to say; they ask more than they tell and they listen to children's answers. Such conversations are ongoing.

The Reggio-published book *A Journey into the Rights of Children: As Seen by Children Themselves* begins with the words, "The unheard voice of children" (Malaguzzi, Castagnetti, Rubizzi, & Vecchi, 1995, p. 1). The words mean that, outside Reggio schools, children are rarely called on to exercise judgment in regard to discipline. The authors, who are Reggio teachers, describe how the book came to be. Subjects were

> Identified by children themselves during a series of meetings. The first session involved full-class conversations (25 children) on the concept of rights and the definition of various rights. Then children divided into groups of three boys and three girls, and conversations were tape-recorded. In subsequent meetings, previously recorded material was re-proposed to two large groups—girls and boys—to further exchange ideas in more depth.
>
> The rights included in the Charter were chosen from a vast amount of material gathered, and the texts have been faithfully transcribed from recorded conversations. (p. 61)

The authors summed up the teachers' reactions to the whole process:

> What made the greatest impression on us was the children's sense of justice and equality, the social maturity of their judgment, a real feeling of responsibility and solidarity, the beginnings of which we see germinating in [their] thoughts and concepts. (p. 12)

These features, when used intentionally, consistently, and systematically, enable children to develop self-regulation.

Key Points: Self-regulation is the norm because Reggio schools provide:
- an environment prepared so that it is interest-laden;
- apparatus selected because it fosters children's innate tendency to move;
- novel and complex activities that keep the brain stimulated and engaged;
- trust in children's desire to be arbiters and their ability to be fair in judging others;
- strategies, such as serious and frequent conversation, that engage children in thinking about rights, responsibilities, friendship, and empathy;
- involvement of families in critical issues.

MONTESSORI'S "NORMALIZING" METHOD

Maria Montessori's first school opened in 1906 in the slums of Rome where she was asked, as medical doctor and anthropologist, to keep prostitutes' children from destroying new government-built housing. Early accounts provide few details, but we can imagine the challenge of gathering unsupervised, undernourished slum children from undereducated homes and instilling self-discipline.

"Normalized" Children

Montessori's concept of self-regulated children–in her word, *normalized*–refers to children who become deeply engrossed in work of their own choosing and who

- respect others' rights;
- treat classroom furnishings and materials with care;
- maintain the environment sensitively.

Each Montessori class has children of mixed ages from 3 to 6. Generally, children are accepted only at age 3 and 4; therefore, older "normalized" children influence the behavior of new, un-"normalized" children. The mixed age group is essential for this process.

We had a 3-year age spread in the MELC. At the start of each year, we brought returning children in before new children, discussed rights and responsibilities, and considered how new friends might act. This process prepared older children to help settle new children. The question is, how to "normalize" a class when all the children are new?

New Children

Montessori had specific techniques for classes of new children. Some techniques relate to the environment because the environment critically affects how children behave:

- Few items are on the shelves except those that can be used with little, if any, introduction by a teacher–blocks, objects-into-holes, puzzles, other tabletop items–anything where the use is obvious.

- The extensive Montessori apparatus is introduced gradually, with the teacher showing each piece in an individual lesson, one-on-one, to each child.
- Introductions include precise movement: how the object "works," and how to carry, lay out, and return the object to its place. The child first watches as the teacher models, which gives the brain a sequence of movement to follow. The demonstration makes use of the brain's natural inclination to imitate and young children's fascination with movement.
- An introduction includes *where* to use the object—tabletop or floor; and, if floor, how to lay out a mat so that a work place will not be walked on by other children.

Each morning begins and ends with group lessons to the full class. In between is a period for children to choose what they want to do from among the items in the classroom. Many of the lessons to the full class are designed to teach skills children need to become independent. Teachers intentionally and systematically determine what lessons to present to the full group and how children are dismissed from the full group. With a new class many lessons focus on movement.

As children are being dismissed from a full-class meeting to begin work, teachers encourage them to think about what they want to do that morning. Each individual child says what he or she has decided, and the teacher dismisses the child to do what he or she has stated. The aide ensures that children do, in fact, follow through, or if children change their minds, guides them to choose something else.

If free-choice time becomes a melee, the teacher stops the class and has the children put away the materials. She does not allow the class to continue working independently when a significant number of children cannot maintain their focus or are disturbing others. The teacher then gathers the class for more group lessons. She does not talk about behavior but engages the children in singing, reading, movement, the playground, conversation, or group games. She did not stop work time to punish the children, but because they have not yet developed sufficient concentration to sustain a long work period. The issue is not punishment, but change of pace to something that children find engaging.

Group Lessons. With both new and returning children, group lessons are short, varied, punchy, well paced. In other words, teachers are showmen with many preplanned "tricks up their sleeve"—the more skilled, the better. Group lessons place strong emphasis on learning how to move. The teacher demonstrates, then children practice many challenging movements, for example:

- carrying classroom furniture such as tables and chairs;
- unrolling and re-rolling mats (for work on the floor);
- walking around furniture so as not to bump it;
- walking around mats so as not to step on them;
- carrying a great variety of fragile, brimful, or other items that present a challenge.

As more Montessori materials are introduced, there are increasingly difficult things to carry, such as full baskets, pitchers full of liquid, pails or basins of water, a large box with hundreds of letters of the alphabet, a large puzzle map of each continent with each country a separate piece—maps so large that two children often carry them.

"Grace and Courtesy." Children love the exercises in this category, which are done with the full class:

- practice bumping into something, dislodging it, and rectifying the situation;
- practice bumping into some*one* and learning to say "excuse me";
- inquiring if they may join someone;
- asking if they may use what another child is using so they do not barge in without another's acquiescence;
- opening a door quietly so that the knob makes no noise, the keeper does not rattle, and the door does not bang (the keeper is the small triangular prism that retracts when a doorknob is turned and extends when the doorknob is closed).

Making these kinds of movements and having these kinds of experiences are high-level cognitive challenges between the ages of 2 and 4 when movement centers in the brain are developing, ideas about social engagement are forming, and the ability to self-regulate is increasing.

"Walking on the Line." The "line" is a large ellipse made from colored plastic tape. It is an organizing device for many full-class activities. For example, a single child may demonstrate a skill, such as walking on the line while carrying a bell without ringing the clapper. Or the full class may move along the line, then "freeze" at a pre-agreed-upon signal. Montessori suggests dozens of movement activities "on the line." All build precision in the control of gross and/or fine movement and develop the neuronal networks in the brain that enable it to coordinate eye, hand, and body. Games include music—march, run, tiptoe, swing, crawl, according to tempo. Montessori specified varied piano music (for teachers who play). She also advocated using as many variations on these activities as teachers can imagine.

As a Montessori teacher, my showman skills improved as I overcame shyness and learned to be a "ham." The more I acted, the more rapt was children's attention, encouraging me to become a better actor! By "acting," I mean being precise in isolating and exaggerating each bit that makes up a complex movement. The more I exaggerated, the more attention children paid to my demonstration, and the more carefully they performed the movements themselves. The children loved group time. I always planned far more than I had time to do, varying the pace of the children's engagement from exuberant to silent, active to still, noisy to silent, intense participation to equally intense observation.

Young children's innate fascination with movement impels them to move precisely. Most have probably been scolded for spilling the milk, bumping into things, or breaking something precious. So they welcome the opportunity to practice moving carefully and learning how to apologize acceptably.

A great joy in working with very young children is that most are compliant, eager to please, excited by new things, desirous of mastering the ways and whys of their environment, eager to do what adults do. The same activities that fascinate 2- to 4-year-olds would be unlikely to hold the attention of 5- or 6-year-olds unless they themselves do the teaching, which older Montessori children are frequently asked to do. Teaching reinforces an older child's skill, builds competence, and develops confidence.

The procedures and activities described here merely hint at the huge repertoire of ways Montessori teachers develop self-regulation. Because most activities demand concentration and high-level skill, children take pride in mastering them, realizing that they are being trusted to do challenging things that adults value. When children are infantilized, even the youngest know their competence is being demeaned. Children live "down" to expectations as much as they live up to them.

> **Key Point:**
> The natural state of children is not aimless running around and flitting from thing to thing, but—with a prepared environment and well-trained teacher—deep, extended attention.

A SCRIPTED KINDERGARTEN

In response to a request from a principal, I spent a day in a kindergarten that was scheduled according to a Teacher's Guide with scripted lessons by the teacher to the entire class. The prescribed curriculum covered beginning literacy, numeracy, and isolated facts unconnected to anything else being taught. For example, the teacher spent several minutes drilling the class on how to make the sound of the letter "e" (as in *bed*). There was no conversation, just drill.

The class of 25 children sat clustered on the floor in a wedge-shaped group, with the teacher at the point and the children fanned out. Four of the 25 children paid some attention for a while; the others wiggled, squirmed, poked, or hit each other. And they chattered, making a constant hum. Lessons were punctuated with the teacher's frequent cries of "Shhhhh!" or "Quiet!", which added to the din. Sometimes the teacher called a particular child's name, arresting that child's attention for a second or two.

The Behavior Chart

On the wall was a large chart with each child's name down the left side and rows of rectangles stretching horizontally. When a child continued talking or poking, despite the "shhhses" and name-calling, the teacher put an orange or red "smiley face" on the chart–except that the mouth was frowning. Children who paid attention, neither moving nor talking, received dark green or light green smiley faces. Children who were bordering on disruptive received yellow faces, with the mouth in a straight line.

The Day's Activities

The morning proceeded with lesson after lesson that, by the end of 2 hours, left all the children squirming, gyrating, or talking. (I dare anyone reading this to sit perfectly still for 2 hours without taking their attention off someone who talks about unfamiliar things and switches the subject every few minutes.)

Finally, there was free-choice time when, calling the names of three to five children, the teacher told them which center to go to–blocks, housekeeping, grocery store, books, and so on. Centers were poorly equipped. Materials were jumbled, with many broken, mainly scratched and dented plastic, parts missing. Three children who had too many red or orange faces were not allowed free time, but had to sit at a table, hands folded, head down, still and silent. After 15 minutes of free choice, full-class lessons from the Teacher's Guide resumed until lunch. There was no playground recess.

After lunch, the children went to the library to see a film. The librarian, in stentorian tones, announced that they would continue watching *Shrek*. She used a remote control to fast-forward through parts she considered unsuitable for young children, leaving gaps in the story's logic. Frequently, her voice boomed across the room, singling out a particular child: "D'Antonio," she said sarcastically, "you *don't* want to sit next to Ms. _____, do you?" That temporarily silenced the child, who, on the next reprimand, was removed to Ms. _____'s side. As the period began, there was no recap of the video and at the end there was no discussion of what the children had seen or what might happen next. Silently, the children filed back to their class to finish the day with more full-class lessons. As they left, the teacher gave them an amount of candy that reflected what kind of smiley faces they had received. Children with mainly orange and red faces received none.

> **Key Point:** This kindergarten fostered neither self-regulation nor cognitive growth, and for many children, failed to build pre-reading skills. It was, in effect, a year wasted at an age when the brain is primed to strengthen, expand, and build new networks.

After school, I asked the teacher how she liked the curriculum. "I hate it," she replied. She used it, she told me, because she would be fired if she did not. The class exemplified discipline by punishment, threat, and reward.

SCHEDULED EARLY EDUCATION

At a commercial early education center, the schedule was prominently posted on the wall outside the 3-year-olds' classroom along with the names of the two teachers and 20 children. The classroom had a block area, dress-up clothes, and housekeeping furnishings; an easel alongside a shelf with thick markers, crayons, construction, and used copy paper; dolls, a huge dinosaur, and some other stuffed toys; puzzles and a basket of mixed plastic figures—people, dinosaurs, insects, farm and zoo animals; and wooden stringing beads, sewing cards, and some plastic pull toys. There were also some toddler toys, donated by families. They were worn, with missing pieces, or broken. Someone on staff who had read about Reggio schools had built a light table. It was well intentioned, but the wrong Plexiglas caused the fluorescent tubes to glare so you could not see anything on the table—if there had been anything! No transparent items were in evidence. However, the chain used the word *Reggio* in its literature.

This is how the children's day proceeded:

> 7:30–9:30. The children drifted in and meandered around the room. A few settled down with the blocks, dressed up, or played in the housekeeping area. At about 9:30, when all the children were there, the teacher blinked the lights a few times, then asked them to gather. Five ignored the group and continued to play with the toys. For about 10 minutes, the teacher struggled to focus the children's attention on the calendar. But whether she counted numbers with one child or said the days of the week with another, the rest squirmed.

9:45. The teacher abruptly stood and told the children to line up, that they were going to music. (The teacher went to the teacher's lounge.) The music teacher played a CD to which the children were to sing along for the full half hour.

10:20. The children returned and dispersed to play. The aide took a few to the toilet, and at 10:40 set a long table for snack. The teacher asked the children to form a line at the sink, wash their hands, and go to the table. They were not allowed to eat until all were there. The teacher said a prayer, and the children had apple juice and saltines.

11:00. The children were lined up again, this time for Spanish class. Again, the teacher went to the lounge. The class was a sit-still, face-front, repeat-after-me experience. Most of the children talked and wiggled their way through the half hour.

11:30. The children returned. Teacher and aide helped them use the bathroom, wash their hands, and put on their coats to go outdoors. They returned at noon. While the aide took children's coats off and hung them up, the teacher read a book, sang some songs, then told the children that whoever was sitting still and quietly could wash their hands and go to lunch. Reading, singing, dismissal to lunch, and hand washing took almost an hour.

12:30. Teacher and aide circulated, helping children open lunchboxes, unscrew thermoses, open plastic containers, snip tops off small packages of yogurt or other foods. Most of the children ate what was sweet or salty and left the rest. The teachers neither sat with the children nor encouraged them to eat. While the teacher supervised those still at lunch and sent them to nap as they finished, the aide spread cots, darkened the room, and put on some music.

1:00. All napped, some for 30 minutes, some until they were picked up. The children who woke were taken to the bathroom then to the playground or classroom, depending on playground availability. The morning aide left at 1:30.

3:30. The teacher went home, and the afternoon aide, who came at 3 with her own child, supervised the children's play and organized them for snack. She stayed until 6:30 when all the children left.

The day ran by schedule. The children were not rowdy in the morning but by afternoon, as the group dwindled, those who were left were restless and cranky. Little in the schedule demanded that the children regulate their behavior, except waiting to eat and story time, which not everyone was required to attend. The 4-year-olds' class next door had essentially the same schedule and toys.

Nothing in the schedule amused, engaged, challenged, or offered complexity. The program was sterile:

- the clock determined when to do what;
- the environment had little stimulation;
- the teachers did little more than caretaking.

Key Point:
Developing self-regulation requires point blank attention from the teacher using the kinds of techniques described in this chapter to help children build internal control. A year or two of the dull routine will make active children wild and calm children comatose.

THE MODEL EARLY LEARNING CENTER'S TECHNIQUES

At the MELC, we began with an out-of-control class with a tantrum-thrower, a screecher/crawler, and two hitting/punching/kickers. These four raised the other 32 children's tone to chaotic. The four took enough teacher time to eclipse other responsibilities. Four directors were helpless (two resigned, and the other two were asked to resign). As the founder, I was considering closing the school. My last hope was hiring as director a clinical child psychologist, a woman with decades of experience as a Montessori teacher/school director. Her clinical skills, teaching experience, and directorial skill turned the school around. She instructed the staff in how to handle problems and, more important, how to manage a class. With the problem children, she

- found special placement for the screecher/crawler whom, she suspected, was born with some form of addiction;
- counseled the tantrum-thrower's mother, who refused to acknowledge a problem and withdrew the child when confronted with the facts;
- physically constrained the hitter/kickers by holding them on her lap lovingly and firmly and restraining their arms and legs to prevent them from pummeling others. They settled down very quickly.

We had estimated that it would take 6 months for the children to become calm and self-regulated. In fact, it took 6 weeks. While dealing with "the four," the director also turned her attention to the teachers:

- One person was to be Classroom Manager, paying sole attention to behavior, focusing on unsettled children, guiding them to select and stay with an activity, keeping track of who used which materials, and making sure children put away what they used before choosing something else.
- Teachers were to teach, giving full attention to one-on-one or small-group lessons. Note: These were *not* lessons from Teacher's Guides. They consisted of conversation, how to use items requiring explanation, experience with new materials (such as glue or wire) or new skills (such as scissors), literacy activities, and such.
- Teachers themselves were to speak quietly; when a teacher is loud, the tone of the entire class becomes loud. If they needed to intervene, teachers were to walk determinedly, not run. When teachers rigorously adhere

---

Key Points: The MELC children became self-regulated because
- The teachers rigorously followed a plan to help the children learn to focus and to take responsibility for the environment.
- The environment was prepared to stimulate children's diverse interests.
- In conversations with small groups, the teachers focused on how to use the environment and the rights and responsibilities involved. (In Chapter 6, self-regulation is seen from another perspective—its role as the basis for focusing during Meaning-full Conversation.)

to behaviors they want children to emulate, children copy. That is what psychologists mean when they say humans are "adaptive."
- Teachers were to guide children to follow four rules:
    - Use your quiet voice.
    - Use your walking feet.
    - Put things away.
    - Keep your hands to yourself.

CONCLUSION: SELF-REGULATION—THE BASIS FOR LEARNING

Call it guidance, discipline, or self-regulation, the significant, intentional problem solving that Reggio schools exemplify, the kind of concentration that Montessori activities stimulate, and the success achieved in the MELC will not occur if children cannot regulate their own behavior. Until children are self-regulated, they cannot engage meaningfully in challenging activities, persist in conversations, or, in a word, concentrate. Helping children become self-regulated is the first essential step in undertaking Reggio practices.

Questions to Consider

1. How would you describe the different approaches to discipline and self-regulation shown in this chapter?
2. Which techniques do you use? Which are most effective in helping your students become self-regulated?
3. Which techniques that you do *not* presently use might you try?
4. Choose two techniques. Think about how and why you selected them. What is your plan for using them?

CHAPTER 3

Using Documentation
to Gain Parents' Trust

Birds of a feather flock together.

—Mother Goose

THE GOAL OF A PARENT PROGRAM is to make teachers and parents part of the same flock regardless of whether their feathers match. In this chapter, I show how documentation was used to draw the families of the MELC children into the school. In doing so, I briefly describe what documentation is *not* and what it *is*.

WHAT IS DOCUMENTATION?

As pioneered by the educators in the Reggio Infant/Toddler and Preschools, documentation is the ongoing recording of children's learning by taking notes on what they say and photographing key activities. The practice has a visible end-product: large panels that hang on the walls in a school and show in words and photos (and sometimes objects or children's work) the intention and meaning of what different small groups of children have been doing.

The purpose of documentation is reflective, to help teachers and children think about what they have done in order to build relationships to something they might do. Its purpose is not to decorate walls or fill wall space with displays.

Documentation Is Not . . .

Examples of what I consider decoration but not documentation are:

- bulletin boards or wall hangings with colorful backgrounds, patterned edges, and other commercially produced content;
- high-quality pictures of natural forms—birds, shells, trees, rocks, mountains, beaches;
- reproductions of famous works of art;
- all work by every child in the class mounted in a group.

These examples might be part of documentation *if* they were used to engage children in conversation about what the display means or if they stimulated reflection about something the children did or might do. Wall hangings are not documentation unless they are associated with an experience that has meaning for children.

Children's art becomes documentation when, along with the art, there are

- an explanation of why the art was done;
- the comment or question of a child that stimulated the art;
- children's comments as they made the art, and
- information about the context in which the art was done or how it reflects a larger experience.

Documentation is not photographs of children at work and play, even when they are wonderful photos or have captions or longer descriptions.

In the central office of a Reggio-inspired school system I saw three large, dry-mounted, professional photographs of beautiful children: One showed a child smiling, another a serious child, a third showed two children holding hands. But, beautiful though they were, the images showed isolated moments that were divorced from the children's daily life at school. Even though the photographs may have been taken at school, they were not documentation.

I have seen photos of children on field trips, children eating snacks, carving pumpkins, painting, making things from found objects, listening to stories. Some have captions: "This Halloween we all decided to carve the pumpkin's face so that it had cat eyes and we put whiskers on it." Some have entire paragraphs:

> We took a field trip to the zoo. It was the first time Sam and Gayle had ever been there. The animals some of us liked best were the lions. They reminded us of the book *The Friendly Lion.* Others liked the monkeys best. They reminded us of the book *Curious George.* We ate our lunch on picnic tables and our teacher brought everyone animal crackers because they have zoo animals. We got to go to the zoo store so we could buy something to remember the trip. We will tell our family that we went to the zoo and want to go back again.

Experiences that occur once, are isolated from something that came before, and will not continue are unlikely candidates for documentation.

Documentation Is . . .

Documentation is the records in words, photos, work product, or objects of what children have done. Work that exemplifies particularly potent moments in an experience may be selected to be made into panels. Panels are studied for their past and future meaning. For example:

- Children in Reggio Emilia visited the fountains in some of the city parks because they intended to build a fountain at their school.
- MELC children saw the IMAX film *The Blue Planet* because they were searching for the causes of pollution and wanted to see images of planet Earth from space.

Documentation captures children engaged in something that has *continuity* from photo to photo and from panel to panel.

Documentation of ongoing experiences at the MELC occupied many panels. The school's cat, Coco, developed a relationship with a turtle; the stories covered nine panels. Children's lengthy involvement with the Statue of Freedom, called the Capitol Project, covered numerous panels that were hung on both the side and end walls in a long hall. When Reggio children investigated the stone lion in a city square, they transformed the experiences into clay, paint, marker, pen, sculpture, shadow play, and other media. The panels documenting their initial experiences with the statue and subsequent interpretations covered the walls from floor to ceiling in the vestibule to their studio.

Documentation of the MELC children's visit to a pumpkin patch revealed how the school was building a relationship with families and the many ways the excursion involved families in the planning, the trip itself, and the arrangements for the Octoberfest celebration that followed. Documentation panels make clear to a viewer *why* the activity took place:

- whether some conversation sparked it;
- if reading a book motivated it;
- if it answered children's questions;
- if it were antecedent to a Big experience.

Documentation contains the "presence of children"–their words, a piece of their work, some special object. In other words, it reveals more about the children than just their physical images. Documentation makes evident what the children's minds pondered, wondered, imagined, questioned, found puzzling or exciting, or considered in any other ways.

The Function of Documentation

Documentation tells stories. What is going on here? Why did it occur? What meaning do the children in the photos see in what they are doing? What is that structure doing there? Did the children visit it? Make it? Use it? How? Why? And what happened as a result? Documentation tells the stories of what has occurred in children's lives in the classroom, on an excursion, at home, during a celebration. Not: We dressed up for Halloween, but: We dressed up for Halloween because. . . .

Documentation is hung on the walls as a reminder of an experience. It is prominently displayed and on view (rather than in a scrapbook or photo album) where it draws the children's attention, is a constant reminder of some Big experience, and is readily available for discussion. Documentation enables the small group of children who had the experience to revisit and reflect on what they did by studying the documentation with teachers who orchestrate a conversation about it. When they reflect, children recollect the feelings the experience evoked. They become animated as they remember themselves in the moment, carry the experience forward into new experiences, and share the story of what happened with others–friends, teachers, parents, or visitors to their school. By looking at documentation, a viewer can understand:

- the motive for what took place;
- how it evolved;

- why it concluded as it did;
- what else happened because this event took place, this action occurred, this object was made;
- who was involved;
- what materials were used;
- what challenges the activity presented;
- what the antecedents and outcomes were;
- who are
  - the protagonists;
  - the antagonists;
  - the problem solvers.

> **Key Point:**
> Documentation is defined by *how it is used* more than by what it consists of.

Some documentation shows children at the very moment when they realize they need to solve a problem, how they do so, the solution, and their new ideas. (See Chapters 10 and 12 for examples of other effective documentation.)

DOCUMENTATION AS A MAGNET FOR PARENTS

Without living through it, I am not sure I would have believed that documentation would be the impetus to involve parents in the daily life of the MELC. In my description of our experience, some of the conversations quoted are children's or parents' verbatim remarks. Other dialogue is based on notes or photos of children's reactions.

Barriers to Family Involvement

It is not easy to involve parents in a school's daily life. Many parents do not have time. Some believe that they have no place in the school. Others are intimidated by what they perceive as teachers' superior education and knowledge. Some immigrants fear the school as an institution that would turn them in, so they avoid contact. There are as many barriers to families becoming involved as there are families.

In addition to barriers specific to families, schools face challenges to parent involvement. What is the best way to reach family members? Face-to-face? Memo carried home by the child? Phone? Email? Which is most likely to get a parent's attention? Do teachers have the time and energy to invest in building school/home bridges? Do they really want the parents to have intimate knowledge of what happens at school? Some teachers fear that parents are better educated and will challenge what they know. Some teachers disagree with their own school's policies and worry that, if challenged, they could not defend a position. Some teachers fear they will be unable to manage a group meeting if things get out of hand. Others assume there will be a we/they mentality between home and school. Most teachers resent parents' insistence that their children do more academic work.

These feelings put up invisible barriers so that invitations from school are perfunctory. When teachers feel that parent meetings are one more burden in an already too-full load, their effort to reach out is, at best, half-hearted. The barriers and fears on both sides are reasonable. After all, it is human to fear what you do not know, and most parents and teachers do not know one another.

At the MELC, we stumbled by accident onto something that worked, turning out to be a powerful beginning to a parent program that ultimately flourished. In my book *Possible Schools* (Lewin-Benham, 2006), I describe the stumbling. Here, I describe activities that gradually accumulated and eventually led to a successful parent program as we turned what we learned into an ongoing technique to involve families.

> **Key Point:**
> Documentation can become a tool to break down barriers, erase fears, and establish a relationship between school and home.

Gathering Records, Asking Questions

We knew how important it was to have an active parent program but didn't know how to begin. The idea that became the initial hook to grab parents' interest was that most children like to see photos of themselves and their family displayed. This realization began in a conversation with the full class of children. With the intention of eliciting the children's ideas about what might bring their parents to school and of motivating children to answer thoughtfully, we considered what questions to ask. We settled on the question: What would make your parents want to visit our school? We knew we had hit on a good question because the children's ideas flowed freely, their comments tumbling one after another:

GERALD: They likes to see where I go in the day.
AKEESHA: They likes to know what I do.
DERRICK: My momma always be saying, "Derrick! What you do in school today?"
WENDY BALDWIN, *MELC teacher:* What do you answer?
CHORUS OF VOICES: [indistinguishable]
COURTNEY: I tell 'em, our teacher say you can visit.

Two days later, the teachers returned to the topic with the full class at the end-of-morning meeting. Wendy used her notes from the previous conversation to remind the children: "The other day you said your parents wanted to know what you did at school. How do you think we can get them to visit so they can see what you do?" Again, ideas poured out: They could send a school bus to bring them. They could have a big party with McDonald's hamburgers and promise every parent a hamburger. "No! Five," Rashida chimed in. "No! 100!" added Gerald. Clearly, the children were excited about the idea of getting their parents to school!

The teachers knew several things about conversation:

- Good ideas do not always come fast.
- Sometimes it takes 2 or 3 weeks for an idea to evolve.
- Time must elapse before the solution to a problem becomes apparent.
- Sometimes solutions that seem good don't work.
- Children's different ideas spark even more ideas. Children have no lack of ideas that are vast and complex!

The teachers had learned to trust that in time a good idea would emerge. They had also learned to trust the process of

- conversing and note taking;
- reflecting together as a group of teachers about their notes;
- agreeing on what children meant by their remarks;
- deciding which children's words to read back to the full group, which words would
  - remind children of the conversation;
  - spark children to continue the conversation;
  - generate ideas that would lead toward solutions to the problem at hand.

> **Key Point:**
> The process of documentation has its own structure.

A PROJECT EMERGES

The next week, Sonya Shoptaugh, an MELC teacher, brought up the topic again by reminding the children that last week they had talked about how to get their parents to visit our school. She reminded them that Derrick had said his mom always asked what he did in school. Then Sonya asked a provocative question that introduced a new idea: "Can you think of anything we could *send* to our parents to make them come?"

A Galvanizing Question

Another good question! Ideas poured out. The children named dozens of items in the school that parents would like to receive: the trains, spaghetti from their lunches, the beautiful shells from the Lab, and a whole bunch of markers "'cause we ain't got none at home and I think my mama, I think she like drawing with them." The teachers wrote down every suggestion.

During the past year, it had become a regular practice at the MELC to document the children's activities in photos and to hang large panels showing the evolution of an activity. So, it was not surprising when Venyce said, "*We could send them a photo* 'cause my momma she like photos and she always be saying, 'Now Venyce you be still and smile 'cause I want a picture with Venyce smiling.'" Other children chimed in about photo taking at their homes. The teachers did not know it yet, but they were on to something. That afternoon, they met together to reread their notes of what children said they could send to entice parents. Mixed in with ideas of trains and spaghetti the teachers found a gem—photographs.

Three days later, at their regular weekly staff meeting, the teachers again discussed the issue of parent involvement. The topic had been on their minds for a full year, but as yet there was no answer to the question of how to get parents involved and no plan. They reviewed their notes on the class discussions, aware that the idea of sending a photo was a possible hook, but unsure how to develop the idea!

None of the MELC teachers were of the low socio-economic status of the school's families. All harbored fears of the unfamiliar, the hesitation to ask anything of parents whom they knew lived financially unstable lives. They did not want to burden families they knew were stressed in many ways. Long ago, they had ruled out skating parties and other off-school events that would be fun for the children but that required admission fees. Above all, they did not want to ask parents for anything that involved spending money.

An Apparent Thread

As they reread their notes on the children's comments, the teachers realized that "photos" were a thread. The children had segued from talking about sending photos to their parents to talking about photos. It seemed their families took photos! Like all families, they treasured these photos, and the children understood their importance. Photos were part of their life experience. Things with the most meaning for young children are those they themselves have experienced.

The teachers decided to have another conversation with the children. It took a little puzzling to phrase the key question, and they finally decided to turn Venyce's comment around. The question would not focus on sending a photo from school to home, but on sending a photo *from home to school.* The realization led to their forming this question: "What would you do if your family sent a photo to school?" The children were very serious in offering their thoughts:

> "I'd show it to all my friends."
> "I'd show it to *everyone.*"
> "I'd carry it to Ms. Sodartha's office." (school administrator)
> "I'd carry it to Ms. Ann." (school director)
> "I'd hide it in my locker. I don't want it . . . That my momma's photo. I don't want them to tear it or nothing."
> "I'd hide it in my folder in the Studio."
> "I dunno if my momma wanna let that photo go. She say, 'That your best picture ever.'"

When the teachers met to survey the harvest from the latest crop of remarks, they came up with this list as the critical factors in asking families to send a photo to school:

- The idea of photos appealed to all the children.
- No one objected that they had no photos at home.
- Protecting the photos from harm would be essential.
- They would need to be precise about what kind of photo they wanted.
- They would need a concrete plan for what to do if photos arrived at school.

Carefully, they selected those particular statements by the children that revealed the appeal of the idea, the range of different thoughts, and the children's concerns. A plan had not yet emerged, but the teachers felt the excitement that comes when you know you're on the right track. As the song from *West Side Story* goes: "The air is humming! And something great is coming!"

Looking back, it appears that there was a straight line from the introduction of the idea of photos to the project that emerged. But, when the teachers were in mid-process, trying to see where the idea might lead and what questions to ask, the way ahead was not obvious.

Honing In on Home

At the full class meeting a few days later, the question the teachers used to return to the matter of parent involvement was, "How can we get a photo from home?" The children had many ideas:

"Ms. Wendy! She can ask my momma when my momma bring me."

"I can ask, right now later, when I get home, I'm gonna say to my momma, Momma, I wanna. . . . Can I have a photo? And we're gonna get photos at my school."

"I know what. I'm gonna say, 'We be real careful so no one scratch or hurt that photo.'"

The children's answers continued to show their enthusiasm mixed with concern for the photos' safety.

More than 2 weeks had passed since the idea of photos emerged. The teachers realized they were still a long way from a plan. They could have worked one out themselves, but they knew that if the children worked it out, their enthusiasm would remain high and the project was more likely to be successful. The teachers were beginning to understand the value of the process that was under way in that it

- engaged children in thinking about the future;
- developed children's ability to plan;
- gave children practice in formulating steps that follow logically from one another;
- increased children's ability to put thoughts into words;
- extended the children's memory;
- welded the children's bonds as a group because everyone was focused on the same idea;
- gave every child a chance to contribute;
- gave the children experience in collaborating to devise a solution to a problem;
- sparked children's imagination.

The next question was: "What do you want to be in the photos?" The children mentioned everything from photos of their Christmas presents–still fresh in their mind from the holiday–to a goldfish and a dog. The meeting to discuss photo content lasted almost 30 minutes. It took three meetings to hone in on this list of what should be in the photos: moms, dads, grandparents, sisters, aunts, uncles, brothers, cousins, and friends. But they still were far from finished. Questions remained of how to communicate their ideas to their families and what to do with the photos once they arrived. The process in which they were engaged involved many meetings, teachers' active listening and note taking, teachers' reflection among themselves, then more conversations with the children about next steps.

A Parable

In James Thurber's tale *Many Moons* (1943), the Princess Lenore, who is ill, wants the moon. Her father, the King, is very disturbed–the moon is large and far away. The Court Financier, Mathematician, and Astronomer prepare long treatises telling the King just *how* large and far, which give the King an enormous headache. Seeing the King's distress and before the King can stop him, the Court Jester slips off to ask the Princess how big and how far away the moon is. "It is just a little smaller than my thumbnail," she said, "for when I hold up my thumbnail at the moon, it just covers it [and it] is not as high as the big tree outside my window," said the Princess, "for sometimes it gets caught in the top branches."

Again, the advisors tell the King it is impossible to get the moon and inform him of the many rare substances the moon is made of. Again, the King is in distress, and again the Court Jester goes straight to the princess to ask. Again the princess knows: The moon is made of gold. But the King's agony is greater because his advisors remind him that a new moon rises every month. Again, the Jester takes the problem to the princess and she explains: When the unicorn loses its horn, a new one grows; when you pick a rose, a new one grows; when she loses a tooth, a new one grows, so a new moon will grow.

> **Key Point:**
> Adults who listen carefully over a period of time will learn how young children mix imagination with every fact at their disposal to solve problems.

Children under age 6 still have much to learn about how the world works and they are eager to solve problems that are important to them. They use every experience they have had, many things they have heard, and invent their own logic in ways that are highly imaginative. So they arrive at solutions no one has previously envisioned.

Slowing Down

The MELC teachers did not rush but allowed time for ideas to formulate. Days when they did not discuss the topic gave the children time for ideas to generate, time for the brain to turn over the last experience and consolidate ideas that would become the basis for the next conversation. That conversation would be richer because of the time lapse—long enough to cogitate but not long enough to forget. The teachers allowed this to happen. Reggio educators call it "slowing down." The MELC teachers were learning to slow down.

In the middle of week 3, the teachers returned to the topic. They now knew photos were the hook to engage parents and that they would have to take special care of any photos the parents sent to school. But they did not yet know how they would acquire the photos. That was this day's business—to see what the children would suggest as ways to get the photos.

> **Key Point:**
> The process of documentation is more like the irregular zig-zagging of a bee's flight than the straight line of an arrow's.

A Letter Home

The children decided that they should put all the photos on the wall for everyone—especially their parents—to see. They also decided that the best way to get the photos would be to write to their parents and ask. The idea of writing to parents to ask for photos had come in a full-group meeting, but the actual letter writing was a collaborative endeavor by three children and Sonya. When the teachers considered which children were most excited about the idea, they concluded that Yesheie, Rashida, and Venyce had had the most to say. Sonya worked with them to draft the letter, and Venyce drew the picture.

At the next full-class meeting, Sonya read the letter to all the children. They were very excited. Together teachers and children formulated this plan:

- The full class would discuss the letter so the children would be familiar with its contents; hopefully, this would overcome literacy issues because the

Figure 3.1. Request to families for photos in a letter drafted and edited by children and teachers.

MARCH 19, 1993

DEAR PARENTS,

We WOULD LIKE TO COLLECT PHOTOGRAPHS OF YOUR CHILD WITH HIS/HER FAMILY - MOMS, dads, grandparents, sisters, aunts, uncles, brothers, cousins, friends, guardians - to display at school along with drawings the children make and words they say about the photographs. This will be a wonderful opportunity to form ties between school and home, and also to encourage dialogue among parents, teachers and children. There will be a folder in the studio for the photographs. Venyce asks you "To bring from home one of the pictures you have to school so I can decorate the walls." Yesheie wants "a picture of your family so I can hang it on the school walls." Rashida also wants "you to bring one of your pictures to school." Thank you for your cooperation. We will be extremely careful with the photographs.

— MELC

Venyce Larry "This is me, my grandmother and my mommy."

---

children could "tell" their parents what the letter said.
- Each child would take home a copy of the letter.
- As each child was picked up, the teacher would tell the family member that a letter was coming home.
- The children would tell their parents what the letter said.

As they were leaving school that afternoon, Wendy reminded each child to "read" the letter with their parents.

The Families' Responses

The next morning, Galeesa brought a photo. Immediately after the morning meeting, Sonya met with her one-on-one and asked her to talk about her photo. Reams poured out, and Sonya recorded every word. They also discussed a safe place for the photo and together put it there.

That afternoon, there was an impromptu meeting of the teachers. No one had expected such a fast response. It showed them that many questions still needed answers:

1. What would they do with the photos?
2. What should they do with children's descriptions?
3. Were there other logical extensions of this project?

Answers and action came quickly. That afternoon, Jennifer Azzariti, Studio teacher at the MELC, would mount a panel containing the first photo. Sonya would edit the text, read it back to Galeesa, incorporate any changes, and she and Galeesa would print and mount it on the panel under the photo. Wendy suggested asking the children to draw their interpretation of the photo. Bingo! A project took shape. Wendy and Sonya would collect the stories one-on-one as soon as possible, preferably the day the photo was received. Jennifer would begin a project in the Studio for children to interpret the photo in their own drawing. She would archive everything and mount it as soon as possible.

Early the next morning, two children discovered the new panel, recognized Galeesa in the photo, and dragged her over. Galeesa brought Wendy to read the text. Word spread quickly; photo fever—the desire to examine and discuss the family photo—touched every child. They talked of little else: Galeesa at lunch: "Hey y'all. Y'all gonna come see my family?" Within a short time, all 36 children had seen the photo and heard the story, which Galeesa now knew by heart.

A group of photos arrived from home shortly thereafter and were mounted immediately. Soon after, a parade began—parents wanting to see the photos. Sonya or Wendy—whoever had recorded the story—read it with the children. As with Galeesa, it did not take long before children could tell their own story. The stories revealed children's impressions of their life at home—who lived with them, some typical activities, a few sad stories, like Tamika's (name changed): "Black eyes, Tamika, black eyes. This Tamika. She in jail. I want to see her. Now I can see her eyes. I went home, was Tamika there? No. In jail! Sad."

The Panel

The panel, which was titled Our Families and Us—a title devised with the children—made a strong connection with the families. It became an ongoing project that continued for a month and a half. A few parents told a teacher privately that they had no camera, so the school sent one home. The first photo was mounted on a large, nearly empty panel. The blank space said, "There's room for everyone here," providing additional motivation for the families to send photos. By the time all 36 photos, stories, and drawings were mounted, the work spread across two huge panels and covered an entire long wall. In time, parents brought extended family members to see their photo on the panel. It was a sign that the school had become an important part of their life.

Figure 3.2. Family members study the panels with their photos and the children's words and drawings.

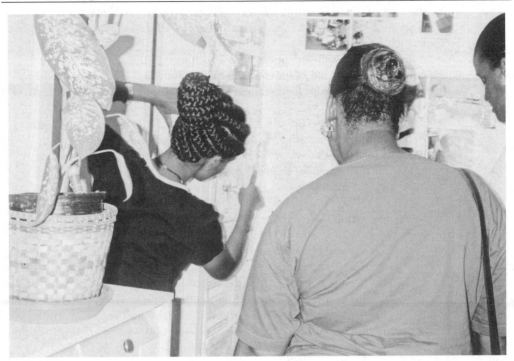

Malaguzzi explained why the family was an integral part of life in the Reggio schools: "Families have a great hunger for information, even when you hardly ever see them. It is impossible in a society where information has such huge value for the *school* not to give information as well" (quoted in Lewin-Benham, 2006, p. 131).

> **Key Point:**
> The continual exchange of information between school and family is an exchange of values as much as ideas.

ROBUST PARENT INVOLVEMENT

The Families panel began a different life in the MELC's parent program. Two aspects stand out—the traffic in information between school and home, and the amount of face-to-face contact in meetings, outings, and celebrations in which families took an active part.

Traffic in Messages

We were fortunate at the MELC to have Amelia Gambetti, just retired from 20 years teaching in Reggio, in residence for a full school year. We learned from Amelia how to keep families informed. Her gesture is indelibly impressed on my mind: bringing her two hands together as she rapidly slid one past the other, urging: Send it immediately! Now!

We wrote memos about

- information on the school, short statements of its mission, facts about hours, family contact information, teacher contact information;
- the flow of the day, a copy of each week's "doings," written at the end of the week after we knew what had actually happened, not what we had supposed *might* happen;
- notices relating to health and welfare, such as immunization shots, eye clinics, or breakfast and lunch menus;
- a monthly calendar of forthcoming events including Parent-Teacher Committee meetings;
- details about outings—the trip to the pumpkin patch, trips to the National Arboretum (many families' favorite), picnics, excursions to museums;
- requests for families to provide many things the school needed, such as letters cut from newspaper headlines, items for the dining room, and materials (see Chapter 9).

During only one school year, the teachers sent families more than 66 pieces of correspondence.

> **Key Point:**
> Messages were a vehicle to drive home/school contact.

A process evolved: Teachers would talk about each memo with the full class; often, teachers would handwrite the memo in front of the children, or children themselves would write some of the words. Children always decorated the memos; the teachers always read the finished memo and talked about it with the children. The process was reciprocal: Children saw teachers write and watched parents read the memos or told them what the letter said.

Face-to-Face Contact

Parent meetings were lively. The teachers gave tours of the school, presented slide shows about an experience, or read transcripts of what children had said. Meetings revolved around what children were doing. The school offered child care for students and siblings, and there was always food. Celebrations were huge—elaborate feasts prepared by parents, teachers, and children. Together, we celebrated the opening of school in the fall; an Octoberfest, Thanksgiving, and several holidays reflecting diverse families' traditions and culture; and at year's end graduation of children leaving for 1st grade.

Outings were joyous—hay riding at the pumpkin patch, crunching through mounds of leaves at the Arboretum, shuffling through drifts of cherry blossoms on the Mall, picnics on the school's playground or in a favorite park, excursions to take part in citywide happenings. Each child's birthday celebration followed rituals established by the Parent-Teacher Committee and detailed by a small group of children (the birthday child's best friends) and a teacher.

During 1993–94, we hosted 17 family meetings, as well as working with the Parent-Teacher Committee to arrange field trips, celebrations for birthdays, and other special occasions. Russell's mother said, "Parent meetings were most helpful for me. All of them . . . They let me know what is going on" (Lewin-Benham, 1998, p. 356).

> **Key Point:**
> Families respond positively when requests for involvement are genuine and families have been involved in shaping the plans.

PANELS AS PLANNING FOR CURRICULUM

Panels are not only a means to reflect and a way to attract parents, but are also a vehicle for planning children's activities. Panels shape curriculum when teachers study what is on a panel as the basis for what to do next.

Panels as Planning

When Reggio educators use panels to plan, they use the Italian word *projettare*, meaning "to predict," more like making a hypothesis. An architect would call it the conceptual stage of a project; the head of an organization would call it envisioning. Reggio educators consider it research: What if . . . ? The process of documentation is like a spiral: You come at the same question again and again, but each time you answer it differently because you have learned from your earlier trials.

The process of panel making can be frustrating because what to do next is not always apparent. Sometimes an idea goes nowhere. Preplanned lessons are safe because you know the outcome in advance; thus, no risk is involved. But "safe" is unlikely to generate complexity or new thinking. It is more difficult to reread dialogue, organize questions, realize your questions were not good, and so go through the process again! In the United States, when we see panels made by Reggio teachers, we do not see the questions they asked that went nowhere. We only see the questions that worked! Teaching with risk-taking requires expending effort, organizing thoughtfully, and generating many hypotheses of what *might* happen. It requires flexibility–you think you are going somewhere, but end up somewhere else.

The MELC teachers stumbled onto the trial-and-error approach they used in the families/photos project. They were not going through an exercise to arrive at a solution they had predetermined. They were genuinely stymied about how to involve parents.

Key Point:
Panels show children that their ideas are genuinely wanted, are heard, and are valued.

A teacher who does not have an answer in mind works with children differently from a teacher who has already thought of a solution. Children's responses are genuine when they see that their opinions are sought honestly and taken seriously. They intuitively know that teachers' probing for one right answer is different from teachers' probing for solutions to real problems. Teachers who know what answer they want hear their own voice, not children's. By age 6 or 7, if children learn that teachers don't really want their ideas, children stop generating them.

What Makes Panels Effective

Teachers in the United States who are inspired to try to document and make panels for the first time are often confused about how detailed they should be. Teachers may resent the huge amount of time it takes to make panels. Teachers who persevere get the hang of it; once they do, panels require less time. The more experienced teachers ease newer teachers' difficulties by assuring them that they also had problems at the beginning. It takes about a year to learn.

At one recently "Reggio-inspired" school, a teacher commented on the outcome of attempts at documentation:

I think our school used to look like an art gallery of children's work. Now it looks like a newspaper written by the teachers. I like the art gallery and I think the children like looking at their creative work much more than the typed words the teachers have put on the panels.

The other teachers present broke into applause.

The teacher's comments were on the mark. Her school was still struggling with how to make panels; no one had yet made a breakthrough with the techniques. Panels should not be detailed or crowded; they should contain only the information essential to the story they are telling. Stories should be told in as few words as possible. If teachers' attempts at documentation look like newspapers, no one, least of all children, will read them. If "documentation" looks like a newspaper, it is not documentation.

Reggio schools look like art galleries, although different from the way the teacher quoted above describes. In Reggio, small groups, not the full class, make the art, and if it is displayed, an individual piece may be selected or just a few pieces used. Reggio teachers select art that will help to tell a past story or stimulate a new one.

Time Spent on Documentation

Making documentation is especially time consuming when teachers are learning to document. As with any new skill, there is a learning curve. Early attempts may take a lot of time because teachers overwrite; that is, they say much more than necessary. Editing text on documentation panels to just those words that are essential is a skill teachers learn gradually. At the MELC we used children's words for as much text as possible and we selected words that would recapture the moment, explain the story, or drive it forward.

Making documentation is also time consuming if teachers are unsure how to lay out a panel. At the MELC, we evolved a typical layout that provided a consistent place for title, subtitle (used occasionally), short statement of context (used occasionally), and the photos and captions that drove the story. We also evolved documentation guidelines that included

- standard-size panel, the size determined by the board we bought–3 foot by 4 foot Bristol board. If wall size was irregular or content demanded a long linear or some other shape presentation, we cut the board;
- white background, the color of the board we purchased;
- standard type face;
- standard-size fonts so if we needed to change something we could remember what we used and keep the look consistent;
- no borders or colored backgrounds to distract from the message;
- standard-size photos–8 x 10, 5 x 7, 4 x 6, or rarely, 2.5 x 3.

These guidelines helped us to reduce clutter and shorten production time.

Distinction: Panels Versus Labels

Labels are isolated words that teachers post on or beside a part of the room or an object in the room. The rationale for using labels is that they are a way to promote early literacy. Labeling is entirely different from documentation. It is not a practice I support because

- Most children cannot read the labels.
- Few teachers engage children with the labels beyond attempting to read them, and many do not even do that.
- Words on labels have no context; therefore, they have little meaning unless a teacher engages a child in making the label relate to something.
- A room looks cluttered when it is plastered with labels.
- Labels are top-down and teacher generated. They do not result from children's interests unless used as described below.

Better, I believe, to play a game in which teacher or child writes a word about an object in the room, and the child affixes it where it belongs for the duration of the game. Labels can also cause action—short messages: "Give me a kiss," "Get the pen," "Put the glass on the table." Commands convey the fact that writing is speech without talking. When children are beginning to read, a teacher can add baskets with labels and commands to the literacy area for children to put around the room—and return the labels to the basket when the game is over.

CONCLUSION: DOCUMENTATION—A SYSTEM FOR LISTENING

The amount of time the MELC teachers spent on documentation lessened as they systematized a process for making panels. They learned to "steal" time; that is, they used nap time or lunch time for making panels. They learned to make the panel as a project developed, not to wait until the project was over.

The impetus for documentation at the MELC was twofold: The panels were powerful magnets to draw families to the school, and teachers' realization that panels spurred reflection, and reflection, in turn, spurred new bursts of activity, keeping the children interested in what they had done and motivating them to continue. This was sufficient reward for the effort. In later years, as the teachers saw how panels drove the curriculum, they developed a fuller understanding of their importance and a greater commitment to making them. They learned that documentation was a powerful way to listen to children, to entice children to listen to themselves, and to enable parents to hear what their children said.

Questions to Consider

1. Can you concisely explain what documentation is?
2. What is the difference between "documentation" and "panels"?
3. Why are documentation panels different from labels?
4. Think of a recent experience, and imagine you are making a panel:
   - What would you title it?
   - What would you put on it?
   - What would photos show?
   - What would text say?
   - How would you engage the children in reflecting on the panel?
   - How would you use the panel to involve families?

CHAPTER 4

An Open Flow Day

Time by minutes slips away
First the hours then the day.

—Mother Goose

T IME IN A SCHOOL DAY is as much a commodity as pencils and paper. Time is used differently in different systems. Here, I describe the Open Flow day of Reggio schools, Montessori classes, and the MELC. Open Flow provides a long period of time in the morning and afternoon in which children work or play with materials for as long as an activity holds their attention. The goals for children are long engagement, independence, and responsibility. The goals for teachers are many; the one I emphasize in this chapter is having the time to work in small groups or provide individualized instruction so children can learn to focus and become independent and so teachers can observe children closely.

It is not difficult to schedule Open Flow time. But it is devilishly difficult to make Open Flow happen in real classrooms. There are several reasons. In this chapter, I first describe features of an Open Flow day, then show how to overcome barriers and move toward adopting Open Flow.

ESSENTIAL FEATURES OF AN OPEN FLOW DAY

Replacing a schedule with Open Flow time is frightening, like facing an ocean with no life raft. The ocean is the sea of children, and the life raft is the schedule–the means to get from early morning to the end of the day. In typical early education centers, the schedule provides the structure. In an Open Flow day, structure depends on space-oriented, not time-oriented factors. Space-oriented factors include

- what items are available;
- items' organization;
- how teachers change the structure of time and space over time.

Each feature is described below.

The Items in a Classroom

In an Open Flow day, children's activities are based on what draws their interest; therefore, the environment must contain items that interest children and appeal to their diverse tastes. Items must be well organized and children must be "trained" to use things responsibly. The word *trained* is offensive to some; I use it as neuroscientists currently use it when they speak of "training the brain" (Posner et al., 2008, pp. 1–10; see Chapter 1).

In the era when most moms were home, few young children went to school before kindergarten. In 1964, acquaintances looked askance when I put my son Danny, age 3, in school from 9:00 until noon. Today, schools must accommodate parents who require child care from 7:00 A.M. to 6:00 P.M., sometimes longer.

In the 1960s, kindergarten was an exciting experience for 5-year-olds who had not had access to classroom staples such as sand and water tables, make-believe areas, or unit blocks. Everything was new and therefore fascinating because novelty hooks the brain's attention. Moreover, the day was 3 hours long, maybe less, so children left eager to play with things the next day. Today, by age 5, many children have already been in school for 2 or more years and are familiar with classroom staples. Some have been in school since infancy. Former experiences rob items of novelty.

The issue in equipping a class is choosing items that will fascinate children day in and out during the vital years of zero to 6 or 8 when the brain craves stimulation because it is literally building itself. By fascinating, I mean items that engage long periods of concentrated activity. The old stand-bys may not be sufficient.

Blocks. Some children are passionate about playing with blocks. For those who are not, it requires additional items to make blocks interesting–small-scale sets of people, houses, vehicles, animals; small-scale trees, mountains, roadways, train tracks; miniature and other blocks that differ in shape or scale from unit blocks; ropes, streamers, paper, or fabric to make roads, highways, land, and water; architectural elements or found objects that children can invest with their own stories (see Chapters 8 and 9). A block area will be interesting if it is augmented with as many items as you can collect so children can simulate a built environment and the traces of nature that crop up in it, or so they can make whatever fantasy structures they imagine. The more varied the collection, the more fascinating the play is to children.

Water Table. Consider the water table. If children have used plastic sifters, funnels, and water wheels as toddlers, at age 3 more is required to grab their attention.

The Discovery Center in Murfreesboro, Tennessee, has an exhibit called Water Works (http://www.discoverycenteronline.org/exhibits.html#Water) where children can "crank, funnel, pour, squirt, measure, float [and] discover the wonders of . . . [water] through interactive systems of pulleys, pumps, wheels, and pipes that demonstrate how we manipulate the multi-functional power of water." The exhibit contains enough water challenges to interest children from toddlers on. Adults could study physics at this complex exhibit.

Although it is beyond most schools' resources to create a Water Works, were a school so inclined, parents could adopt ideas for playground or bathroom and teachers could adopt ideas for the water table.

Complexity. Whether blocks, water, or any other item, the issue is complexity. The brain is continually active, but when stimuli are commonplace, dull, or overused, the brain's attention systems shut down. Classroom items that lack complexity fail to alert the brain's attention systems.

Eric, age 3, in my Montessori class, had–please pardon me–mosquito-like traits. He was in constant motion, buzzed about, lighting for a few seconds, then taking off again. The cylinders, pink tower, and other items that attract most 3-year-olds did not interest Eric. Nor did pouring, washing, or polishing activities. One day, urgently wanting to see if Eric could settle down, I reached for the Trinomial Cube. This three-dimensional set of 27 cubes and rectangular prisms only fit in their box when built precisely. (It can be found on line for about $60.) A child must pay attention to the pattern of shapes and colors on the box cover. Rarely did I offer the Trinomial Cube to children under 4, choosing for younger children the Binomial Cube, a similar set with only 8 pieces. Eric beamed as I reached the coveted Trinomial Cube off a high shelf, immediately sat at the table where I placed it, and settled down for the first time since starting school. He spent nearly an hour building and rebuilding the complex puzzle, thereafter often asked for it, and never failed to concentrate on it.

Challenging items stimulate the brain and keep it focused. When children meet a challenge that interests them and that is within their grasp (but not beneath their capacity), they settle down and concentrate. Today, because we know that young children's experiences build the brain circuits that will serve them (or not!) throughout life, it is imperative that we pay attention to whether classroom items are challenging enough.

> **Key Point:**
> If there are not enough complex items, if children have met everything before, if there is little that is novel, children will not settle into the long, unscheduled, concentrated work time of an Open Flow day.

Organization

I am not talking here about a classroom's "footprint," layout of shelves, or placement of furniture, but about the *items* that children use. If you count every peg, puzzle piece, and sheet of paper in a well-equipped classroom, there are thousands. Teachers are overwhelmed at the thought of organizing so much. Visitors to MELC most frequently asked: "Do the children *really* take care of the materials?" The answer was yes, they really do. The reasons were the classroom organization, children's self-regulation, and teachers' engendering respect for the environment.

> **Key Point:**
> Classroom organization must set children up for success.

Items must be organized to be accessible, available, and manageable, and must have utility and aesthetic quality. Further, the organization must make sense to children so they can follow the logic and thus care for the items. Age is a factor. Toddlers may not be able to sort crayons into a dozen or more shades, but might sort them into warm and cool. Or, toddlers might be unable to return blocks to a stack, but could return them to a basket.

Accessibility. Accessibility means that items are within reach of children's eyes and hands. Seeing something is one of the greatest spurs to interest. Many factors make items visually *in*accessible:

> **Key Point:**
> Teachers must examine every item in the classroom for its visual accessibility.

- height—they are too high to be in children's line of sight;
- depth—they are too far toward the back of a deep shelf unit to be seen;
- stacks—items are piled on top of one another;
- containers—items in opaque or translucent containers cannot be seen;
- cupboards and drawers—keep items out of sight.

Availability. Availability means having whatever a child might need to accomplish something when the child needs it. Consider these comments as Sonya and a group of children drew portraits. The project involved adding portraits to an existing panel so that the portraits would fit in a tight space alongside a photo of each child. Because the teachers were new at projects, they did not realize that the paper would have to be cut to exact size in advance so the children's work would fit. Sonya's notes provide the basis for the following conversation:

> Courtney, enjoying the process of drawing, wanting to make more pictures, and intrigued by the small-sized paper she had not used before: "Sonya, could you keep giving me this size paper . . . ?"
> Sonya, suddenly aware that, although small, the papers were not small enough to fit on the panel: "We can't use your pictures if you're going to use that size."
> Courtney, finishing her sentence and explaining why she wants to make another drawing: ". . . 'cause I want to take it home and let my mommy see it."
> Sonya, realizing she is going to have to re-launch the project with paper that will fit on the panel: "Rashida, I would like you to draw me another one, this time I'm going to give you the right size paper."
> As a note in her documentation, Sonya writes: "Sonya learns a lesson—have paper cut *before* kids get there. *Obviously!*"

Availability requires planning. If the environment is to lead the children to many different possibilities, it is necessary to think ahead of what will be required to realize those possibilities and of items children might request, such as certain color paints, pencils, markers, favorite books, or particular sized paper. A 1st-grader I tutored loved a particular version of the book *Aladdin and the Magic Lamp.* At every session, he brought the book from the librarian's desk and we read a few pages. After spring break, the library was being reorganized, the book was not in its place, the librarian could not find it, and we could not continue the story.

The child took the loss of the book in stride. Children in economically depressed neighborhoods rarely can count on continuity or stability. The missing book became a missed opportunity. As Langston Hughes (1951/1994) said, "A dream deferred is a dream denied" (p. 314).

> **Key Point:**
> When specific items are available, children can carry out what they have in mind, continue a train of thought, or accomplish the objectives of a project.

Note: Availability does not mean catering to pampered children who want things at their beck and call. The child who demands a "neon orange" glaze, throws a tantrum if there is none, and will settle for nothing else, has different lessons to learn!

Manageability. Manageability means children can control things independently. Consider manageability in terms of children's having a snack when they want and fixing it themselves. If the pitcher is too big, children won't be able to lift or tilt it. If the spout dribbles or sloshes, children won't be able to pour without spilling. Items must be chosen to fit the size and strength of children's hands. Consider children's caring for the environment. If brooms, brushes, dust pan, pails, sponges, and other items are not child-sized or if they do not really work, it is futile to expect children to use them effectively. *Note:* Real items with handles cut to size are often more manageable than items "made-for-children" because real items function.

Containers that are manageable hold items without spilling, are the right size, and are sturdy without being too heavy. If you rearrange the furniture for movement games and want children to help disassemble and reassemble the room, chairs and tables must be light enough for children to lift. If you expect children to hang up their coats, hooks must readily accommodate coat loops or children will not use them. If you expect children to find clean clothes independently if they soil their pants, spill juice, splatter paint, or splash through puddles, the clothes must be in a container a child can reach, lift down (if on an upper shelf), open, and return, and there must be a place for soiled clothes. A sure way to infantilize children is to have unmanageable items that thwart their desire for independence.

> **Key Point:**
> The preparation a teacher puts into the manageability of items determines how independently children can function.

Utility. Utility is the degree to which something is suited for its intended purpose. A teacher of 3-year-olds structured painting so that children could use the easel when they wanted. But the paint frequently spilled. On close examination, the teacher noticed a brush wiper in the paint pots that hindered children's taking the brush out without tipping the pot. Switching to glass baby food jars stopped the problem. Another teacher noticed that children were tearing long sheets of paper towel from the roll. She switched to a single sheet dispenser and stopped the problem. The swinging lid on the garbage prevented children from putting things inside. The teacher switched to a can with a foot pedal and a user-friendly lid.

> **Key Point:**
> How well-suited something is for its purpose determines how children can use it.

Aesthetics. Information enters the brain through the senses. Children are attracted to items because of their visual, tactile, auditory, or olfactory character. "The way information enters our brain affects its final state as much as any other step in cognition [thinking]" (Ratey, 2002, p. 54).

Items' aesthetic qualities determine how they affect us. Are we drawn or repulsed by them? Some young children react strongly to tactile experience, unable to sleep without their soft object or unable to tolerate a garment that feels scratchy. Glue's stickiness bothers some children; clay's smell bothers others. We all know that children have strong food preferences that result from the taste, smell, appearance, or feeling of food in their mouth. The reason for caring how items look, sound, feel, and smell is because the senses are so strongly affected by these qualities.

We speak of refined senses. This means that some people naturally (and others by training) can make fine sensory discriminations. For example, persons born with perfect pitch can name the notes they hear; in others, relative pitch can be trained. This is true for the ability to remember color (the human eye can distinguish about 2 million different colors), texture, or anything else we experience. "Each of our senses gives us a part of the world. . . . [M]emories can be recalled from any number of sensory cues" (Ratey, 2002, p. 203).

Teachers who pay attention to aesthetics give the brain rich fare from which to build neural networks and memory. When Reggio teachers choose materials, they consider materials' individuality; unusual features such as shape, pressure, temperature; and the movements children must make to use the material. The word *aesthetic*

Figure 4.1. Detailing of the train corner at the MELC is subtle and pleasing with a soft lamp, shelves that exactly fit the trains, baskets to hold the tracks that also fit exactly, a book stand for a "train buff's" book, and large mirrors (across top of image) that cover the knee walls and extend to the ceiling. A small detailed mural of a scene with a train is mounted at floor level in the corner, with a mirror the exact size of the mural abutting the corner. The mural and its reflection provide a detailed three-dimensional context for the children's elaborate train constructions.

often means beautiful, but its shades of meaning also include delicate, as in a delicate balance, or well done, as in furniture that is nicely finished.

With young children, the most important reason for paying attention to items' aesthetic qualities is to encourage children to pay attention to detail. Items that are mainly plastic or predominantly six intensely saturated colors diminish what children can experience. The time when brain circuits are forming is the most important time to widen experience. Numerous, subtle, and pleasing items in good condition rouse children's interest, sharpen their perception, and color their memories with pleasurable emotional tones, textures, and numerous other qualities.

> **Key Point:**
> The items in an early childhood classroom *are the curriculum.*

Structure of Space and Time

The organization of the space, the use of time, and the role of the teacher provide the structure for an Open Flow classroom. In fact, the design of the environment is a direct result of what the teacher does, when it is done, and how the teacher orchestrates or guides activities.

Some believe that a classroom with "children's choice" is a laissez-faire free-for-all in which anything goes and the teacher plays no role. Just the opposite is true. An essential factor in an Open Flow day is how teachers orchestrate, that is how they

- guide children;
- help them choose activities;
- instruct them in skills;
- collaborate on projects;
- converse about ideas;
- help children learn the meaning of stimuli.

The teacher's role is complex (see Chapter 7) and changes as the children become increasingly self-regulated. Factors crucial to the success of Open Flow are (1) the selection of items that are available before children become self-regulated and (2) the timing of how items are increased as children become more self-regulated. A third factor, techniques teachers use with new children, is discussed at length in Chapter 2 and is reviewed briefly below in connection with both new and settled children.

Items Initially Available. A critical part of the teacher's role is deciding what to put in the classroom when the children are new to Open Flow and before they have developed respect for one another and the environment. In this early stage, the number of items on the classroom shelves is limited to time-tested staples that can be used meaningfully with minimal introduction:

- blocks;
- pretend area, such as kitchen or grocery;
- pencils, crayons, and paper;
- variety of puzzles and other tabletop manipulatives;
- LEGO;
- trains;
- light table with an assortment of translucent, transparent, and shiny objects;
- puppet theater and hand puppets;
- well-stocked library;
- listening area with books on CDs;
- live animal;
- variety of plants;
- one or more of the kinds of museum-type objects that originated in Reggio schools, such as a mirrored kaleidoscope, a square pyramid, a large periscope, or a structure specially designed to hold dress-up clothes. This structure is well-provisioned with hooks and other easy-to-use hangers, has a non-distorting mirror so children can check out the effect of their get-up as they add clothes, and has an opening placed so that children can make a dramatic or surprise appearance. Reggio educators call this a Disguise Closet.

Items Increasingly Available. Gradually, as children's self-regulation develops, teachers add an ever-increasing collection of materials, tools, and other items that they introduce in small-group lessons. These are

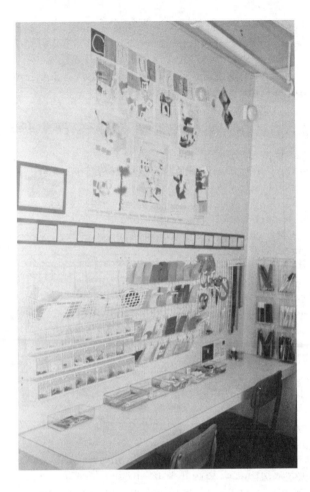

Figure 4.2. At the MELC, items in the Communication Center were added gradually. Children were introduced to each item and in time developed the self-regulation to use pencils, fine-point markers, scissors, hole punches, and other tools skillfully.

Key Point:
Group lessons are *not* the scripted, formulaic lessons found in Teacher's Guides that are part of published early childhood curricula. Rather, group lessons are discussions about care of the environment, conversations about friendship and other values, instruction on certain procedures (as above), and collaboration on projects.

- items that must be
  - handled in a precise way,
  - laid out in a sequence, and/or
  - cleaned up according to certain procedures;
- tools such as
  - wire cutters,
  - scissors,
  - hole punch,
  - stapler;
- materials with constraints:
  - ribbon that must be cut,
  - markers that must be capped,
  - wire that must be stripped.

Before putting such items on the shelf and giving children free access, teachers must be sure each child can handle them with some precision. Only when all children have been shown the procedures should teachers make such items freely available.

Teaching New Children. When children are new, one teacher is the Classroom Manager (see Chapter 2) who observes all the children not working in a small group with the teacher. In this stage of a class's life, managers are constantly on their feet, moving to different children who need guidance, and making notes so the teacher can see how children are using their time. Primary responsibilities are

- watching to be sure children are not running, shouting, disturbing others, or at loose ends;
- guiding children at loose ends to choose something to do;
- ensuring that children put their work away when finished and, if necessary, reminding them to do so or helping.

If most children are productively engaged, the Classroom Manager takes notes on who does what and for how long. If a child or children lose interest in their work but everyone else remains engaged, the Classroom Manager may gather the disengaged child/ren for a conversation, small-group work, a story, or other activity. As with all teaching, each moment is new, so each requires a reflective response in which a teacher brings together knowledge of the children, the environment, and everything taking place at a given moment.

> **Key Point:**
> It is easier to guide docile observers than out-of-bounds children. Let observers alone and concentrate on children with the least self-regulation.

Caution: There is a difference between children who are at loose ends and children who are observing others. Observing is a powerful way to learn. These children should be left alone to observe.

A Settled Class. Once all the children choose work and stay involved for long periods, the Classroom Manager, along with the teacher, can converse with small groups of children, read books, make music, or give lessons. To give lessons, Classroom Managers must be fully conversant with procedures for using things, and it is the teacher's responsibility to instruct the Classroom Manager. However, at any time that children become aimless, the Classroom Manager resumes overview of the class.

Children's activities result from a coupling of their own enthusiasm with a teacher who listens and reflects what she hears back to the children. The teacher does not know *what* will develop, but she trusts a process in which teachers and children together form problems and solve them with books, materials, and tools, and collaboration with other children and adults. In such a process, teachers' and children's minds develop.

> **Key Point:**
> Teachers who are open to possibilities will be comfortable using an Open Flow structure.

HOW OPEN FLOW LOOKS

As we look in more detail at an Open Flow day, keep in mind that Open Flow works because the children are self-regulated (refer to Chapter 2); the classroom environment is prepared as a "third teacher" (see Chapter 5); and teachers observe, reflect, guide, provoke, and converse (see Chapters 6 and 7).

Time Blocks

An Open Flow day moves like this:

7:30–9:00: Arrival. Children and teacher greet one another. Children hang their coats and put away their belongings, think about what they want to do, and get on with it.

Note: If children have breakfast at school, they take it on their own, eat with a friend of their choice, clean up when done, and get on with their work. If most of the children have breakfast, one teacher greets, and the other engages in conversation at the table(s) with the children while they eat.

9ish: Full-class meeting. The time can vary. If the teacher thinks that meeting is important first thing, she gathers the children. If the children are deeply engaged, the teacher may decide to hold the meeting at the end of the morning. Predictability is important, but so is flexibility. Determining the priority at any given moment is the art of teaching. In the MELC, we occasionally held a meeting early and at morning's end. Any full-class meeting may last from 5 to 30 minutes or longer, depending on the conversation.

As children leave an early morning meeting, they state what they intend to do. The teacher may
– let a child choose;
– suggest something;
– encourage a child to do a particular thing;
– ask a child to work with her;
– remind a child to continue a project.
End of meeting is a delicate time because there are many options and not all children make choices easily.

10:00: Snack. Food is set out, and children help themselves and clean up independently.

11:00 or 11:30–12:00: Playground and/or full-class meeting time, toileting before lunch. Children who are deeply engrossed may remain at their work, providing they do not disturb the full group. *Note:* Early childhood teachers may have to negotiate for playground time that does not break the Open Flow.

12:00–1:00: Lunch and preparation for nap. Toileting and hand washing may begin while the full group is meeting or a wrap-up conversation may take place during lunch. Teachers sit with the children, encourage them to eat, and engage in conversation.

Afternoon: As children wake, they resume the independent or small-group work they were engaged in during the morning and continue until the end of the day.

Anytime: Teachers read to small groups or sing with them any time during the day or full-class meeting. Often, children drift to a small group as a teacher reads or sings; children within earshot but working at other things listen or participate.

> **Key Point:** Time in an Open Flow day can be used in many different ways.

Barriers to Open Flow

Open Flow stumbles when time is consumed by teacher-conveyed information parceled out in unrelated bits and crumbles when 5-, 10-, and 15-minute transitions eat up time that children could spend working independently. Open Flow dissolves when a day is interrupted by specialists' classes (music, art, language, and so on). I advise bringing specialist teachers into the classroom. Those children who want to join, can do so. Those children in flow can continue their work and will benefit from listening. Try not to interrupt children who are engaged in concentrated activity for anything except a fire drill. If they want to continue working during the full-class meeting, let them. But be sure they put their work away when finished.

> **Key Point:** Children do not learn to concentrate if they are continually interrupted.

MOVING TOWARD OPEN FLOW

Pre-packaged curricula and interruptions undermine Open Flow. Consider these ideas for eliminating them.

Curricula

Curricula are often based on the kinds of scheduled lessons found in Teacher Guides. Most are constraining because they leave no time to explore an idea and considerable amounts of material must be "covered" in short bits of time.

A sign that a curriculum is in charge is a posted outline of the day's activities in 20- or 30-minute periods. Activities that change every 20 or 30 minutes break children's focus. Ultimately, learning to focus is more important than "covering" the content in a curriculum. Focus is the first act in learning anything; children who cannot focus cannot learn.

Topics in published curricula are often remote from young children's experience. Children's brains have no hooks for information that is not based on experience. If they have had no related experience, children are unlikely to be interested because lessons have no meaning for them. When not interested, children are unlikely to focus, especially if lessons are delivered by a teacher to a group or the full class.

> **Key Point:** Interest builds focus that is the basis for self-regulation that in turn is necessary for an Open Flow classroom to function.

Lessons for young children *must* be grounded in experience–where children have been, what they have done at school, what they bring up in their conversation. There are many ways teachers can stage Big experiences–a walk down a lane where tree branches meet overhead, padding across a moss-carpeted lawn, a fall frolic in piles of leaves. Such experiences abound in nature; they awaken all the senses and delight children. Teachers can also lead children from experiences to new endeavors–through conversation and books that stimulate new experiences. Pre-packaged curricula rarely include content that is experientially based, that flows from connected ideas, or that provides time for give and take.

Schedules

Joy rarely shows up on a schedule. Schedules are not likely to provide time to cover everything and still be joyful. Consider moving away from schedules in the following ways.

Learning Independence

Five- or 10-minute periods used for toileting, hand washing, or putting on coats are time eaters. Help children learn to do these activities independently.

For example, to make toileting independent, talk with small groups of children about toileting habits and preferences:

- Do they prefer to go alone or with an adult?
- Do they need help with clothes or wiping?
- How can they obtain help if an adult is not with them?
- How can they find toilet paper if there is none?
- When should they flush?
- How should they wash hands?

Work Out Systems. Some teachers put a bell in the bathroom for a child to ring if he needs help. If the classroom has no bathroom, some teachers hang necklaces on the doorknob to limit how many children can leave the room at once. Others have a buddy system so children are never in a hallway alone. If requirements say children must be accompanied by an adult, take small groups to minimize wasted time.

> **Key Point:**
> In an Open Flow day, there is time for teachers to work out procedures with small groups of children.

Children Have Many Ideas. As they discuss a process, children mentally enact it; with enough practice, it becomes habituated so they can manage on their own.

Learning Procedures

The immediate value of learning a procedure is that procedures foster independence. The transcendent value is that procedures "train the brain" to think in logical sequence. Logical thinking is a basic and essential cognitive function. In any discussion on a procedure:

- Raise the topic of the procedure.
- Have a free-ranging conversation about it. (Free-ranging means related ideas, not drifting into unrelated topics.)
- Record what children say, read it back to them, and discuss the matter further.
- Have children draw their ideas about the procedure.
- Practice the procedure.

For example, clean-up time can be eliminated by making clean-up integral to using everything in the classroom. Part of using an item is returning it to its place.

Discuss clean-up with small groups of children. Examine every item in the classroom. Draw out children's ideas about finishing each activity:

- Where do the items belong?
- Does the table need wiping?
- What work should be saved?
- Where does it go?
- What should be thrown out?
- Where does it go?

> **Key Point:** Children remember procedures they have helped to create.

The answer to each question is one part of a procedure. Working out procedures requires forethought. Children become engaged when their ideas are taken seriously.

Putting Procedures to Work

Often, all children eat snacks together, and everything else stops. An adult sets out and cleans up; sometimes children help.

An alternative is to put snack out for children to help themselves when they want. Children can manage snack procedures, including

- selecting a table;
- bringing a placemat and napkin;
- carrying snack to their place on a small tray;
- bringing beverage carton and straw or, if the procedure is to use a glass, pouring the beverage in the service area and carrying it carefully—one hand around the glass, the other underneath to steady it;
- cleaning up with table crumber, sponge, and basin;
- washing the glasses.

Having snacks when and with whom you want encourages children to act maturely and makes a significant amount of time available for work. A teacher wanted her children to have snacks independently, but was reluctant to give up the ritual of before-meal prayer. Her solution was coaching children to learn the prayer and say it with the friend(s) they chose to eat with.

> **Key Point:** Many negative behaviors disappear when children have real responsibility.

Sometimes children become so engrossed in an activity, they forget to have a snack. Or a child might be afraid to carry the glass, so finds someone to help. Occasionally, a child drops a glass. If it is restaurant stock, it is unlikely to break. If it breaks, there are clean-up procedures, worked out with the children—dedicated buckets, mops, and sponges for the floor, an adult's help with broken glass.

Young children have far more capabilities than they are generally allowed to use. In a mixed-age group, older children take responsibility for younger ones (sometimes against the wishes of a younger child). The key is for procedures to work, and each child to understand the procedures.

Transitions

Transitions kill time. Frequently, children sit and wait (or squirm or poke), while teachers help individuals with toileting, washing hands, cleaning up, getting snacks, putting on coats. The more independently children handle transitions, the more time there is for individual or small-group lessons, and activities with the entire class.

> **Key Point:** Conversation and activities with the full class, such as the Montessori line games described in Chapter 2, make transitions productive learning times.

CONCLUSION: DIFFERENTLY ORGANIZED DAYS

In an Open Flow day, most of the time is free for children to work or play. They do so on their own, with a small group, or with a teacher. Instruction is mainly one teacher with a small group or one-on-one teacher to child—individualized instruction. Subject matter is not predetermined but evolves from what is in the environment or from experiences that children have had at school with one another, with their families, or in the world outside the classroom.

Of course, Open Flow only works under certain conditions—when

- The environment has been prepared so that it is manageable, rich in potential, and enticing.
- The children have been taught procedures for putting things away independently, respecting others, walking, using quiet voices.
- Two teachers, for a period of time until children are self-regulated, have divided responsibilities: One manages the class while the other gives lessons to individuals or small groups.

The majority of early education centers use schedules. Montessori and Reggio schools are exceptions. One of the hardest changes for teachers who are inspired to use the Reggio Approach is to eliminate schedules and instead respond to what is happening as the stimulus for what will happen next.

Questions to Consider

1. What feelings does the thought of an Open Flow day provoke?
2. Can you envision yourself running an Open Flow classroom or working in one? Why? Why not?
3. What would be your first step to begin Open Flow?
4. What practices described in this chapter can you envision yourself using?

CHAPTER 5

The Environment
Is the Curriculum

WYSIWYG: What you see is what you get
(pronounced "wiz-ee-wig").

—Computer System Term

IN EARLY EDUCATION, the physical state of a classroom reveals a lot about the program. In a school I was asked to assess, the first classroom I visited made me groan. The room was cluttered, furniture cumbersome, storage inadequate, containers a hodgepodge. Materials were missing parts, some were dirty, others broken. There was too much plastic. Colors were overwhelming, a highly saturated palette of noisy primary and secondary colors that dominated the space. The effect was not restful. No single element was aesthetic. These conditions impact children's choices and therefore the ideas they can express and the connections they can develop.

Establishing an environment that expands children's thinking capacity involves teachers' consideration of

- what it means to be a designer;
- the art and science of design;
- how to develop or refine a sense of aesthetics;
- how to design (or redesign) an environment.

Studying the exemplary features of Reggio classrooms provides a lens through which to look at a classroom.

The most important idea is that design influences teachers' practices and children's behavior and cognition. At its best, design can:

- promote collaboration;
- encourage children to focus for long periods of time;
- reflect children's and families' interests, values, and culture;
- build relationships among children, children and adults, the environment, and ideas.

Each of these influences impacts brain development, which occurs *because* of these very factors—or fails to because these factors are not operative.

In this chapter, I describe designs that did not work, show Reggio designs that did work, and use a number of design principles to help you design or redesign your own classroom.

WHEN DESIGN FAILS TO SUPPORT CHILDREN

Design determines what relationships children can form with others, with the environment, and in their brain. What is in the classroom, where it is placed, and how it functions constrains or expands what the children can do because: *In the early years, the environment is the curriculum.*

Examples of Design Failure

A number of instances show how the design of a classroom space can unsettle the children. Some examples relate to the room's configuration, others to items in the room. In each, the problems can be overcome with little difficulty.

"Givens." In classrooms with "givens"—space differently configured from the norm—children failed to focus or collaborate as a result of how the space was used.

- The classroom was long and narrow, not the typical square. Children ran back and forth as if it were a racetrack. Their racing back and forth disturbed the focus of other children. Placing the furniture differently solved the problem.
- The classroom had an anteroom and two tables with manipulative materials that the teacher changed frequently. The small space became a noisy bottleneck preventing other children from moving in or out. Using the space differently solved the problem.
- The school was an old house with many small rooms. Each was bursting with a mishmash of toys, puzzles, and "outgrown" stuff donated by parents. There was so much—huge numbers of clothes in the dress-up corner—a child could not unbury a selection. Or there were so few materials—not enough unit blocks to make a structure with any complexity. Items were placed illogically, so children made few relationships among them. Weeding out much of the stuff and logically grouping the rest solved the problem.
- The oversize classroom felt institutional. To soften it, the room was decorated with fabric in a dark green. It covered windows, some walls, and a dominating sofa. The drapes stuck when pulled so they were usually shut. Lack of daylight and yellow-tinted fluorescents contributed to the oppressive feeling, an impact noticeable in half-dead plants and children's listlessness. Replacing the fabric, changing bulbs, and removing the sofa solved the problem.

Choices. A teacher's choice of items also influences children's behavior. In the following examples, children's ability to focus, make choices, or collaborate was hampered.

- The classroom had enough shelving and manipulative materials to stock several more classrooms. Shelf units were 24 inches deep, so materials were lost behind one another. Shelves were piled high with materials stacked from bottom to top, impossible to see or remove easily. Children rarely chose things from the shelves because the welter limited their opportunities to learn how to choose. Removing excess materials made selection easier.

Figure 5.1. A large space at the MELC is dedicated to a well-designed block area that includes a platform on which to build; silhouetted shapes to show where blocks fit on the shelves; a shelf full of matched baskets, each containing a different kind of item to use with blocks; large found objects on the top shelf; and other materials to augment block play nearby.

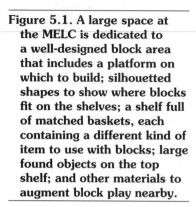

- Shelves were scattered around the room with no logic in which items were placed together. Thus, children did not see relationships between paper, markers, scissors, and tape, and as a result, missed opportunities to increase hand skills. Because cars, miniature people, houses, and trees were far apart, children did not use them together and thus did not expand their imagination by using a rich mix of materials. Reorganizing shelves and materials enabled children to make connections between items that go together.
- Art materials consisted of play-dough, crayons (almost 200 jumbled in a box), and 16 shades of liquid tempera, each in its own jar. Play-dough and crayons do not build hand skills as real clay and fine-point markers do. And ready-mixed paints do not build children's sensitivity to color gradations. The teacher learned how to structure paint mixing so children could do it independently. She kept small squeeze bottles for liquid tempera with primary colors and black and white. Children mixed colors by squeezing small amounts of tempera into empty containers. It wasn't a lesson on making green with blue and yellow, but a free exploration of creating color. Children learned through experience that mixing the three primary colors yields muddy brown.
- Books were displayed on a typical display unit that holds few books. There was no reading corner or comfortable place to sit with a book. Limited books and lack of reading space do not encourage children to use books. A multitude—with variety, access, and comfort—makes children book users. By removing the bulky display unit, the teacher made room for a small reading corner with large pillows and a bookshelf that held a plentiful number of books.

Detailing. Detailing means paying attention to every individual item—each game part, crayon, marker, and the contents of every container.

- In one classroom, I counted 20 different kinds of manipulative materials. One was missing the board for the pegs; another was missing pieces to complete a pattern; another had no pattern cards to offer novelty and challenge. The teacher had inherited the accumulation and did not know that she could remove any. On reflection, she realized that her shelf space could be put to better use.
- Another class had a large overstuffed couch with bulbous arms that occupied most of the library area, but contributed nothing to children. When the teacher brought a smaller couch with the same amount of seating but slim arms, the area accommodated the addition of two beanbag chairs, a bookcase, and a rack for headphones so listening to books-on-tape became an option.
- Another room had a great surplus of furniture. In a cheap plastic cabinet one drawer contained some broken crayons, another miscellaneous colored paper, a third was empty, and a fourth contained stray game parts. The teacher realized that neither cabinet nor contents contributed to children's activities and removed it.
- In the art area was a transparent plastic box, twice the size of two large shoe boxes, overflowing with crayons. Many were broken and, despite the huge number, there was little variety beyond the 12 standard colors. The teacher discarded everything that was broken and organized the crayons by color to fit in small matching clear glass jars.
- Another classroom's walls seemed to close in. Labels named door, doorframe, window, walls, each item of furniture, every piece of equipment, and materials. Beside the entry, the classroom sink, and over the bathroom sink were large posters with instructions on hand washing. Beside the entry and covering most of the front wall were notices about health practices, fire drill procedures, other safety-related bulletins, administrative memos, EEOC regulations. Lost in the jumble was a daily class schedule and a list of individual children with either postage stamp–sized photos or snapshots in which children could scarcely be seen. Children noticed none of it. The teacher decided to learn to document, so she cleared her walls, which gave her the space to mount panels.

> **Key Point:**
> Thoughtful design causes children to notice detail and also supports the development of self-regulation, concentrated work, and numerous physical, social, and cognitive skills.

Each problem had contributed to a cluttered, disorganized feeling and robbed children's experiences of meaning.

Who Really Influences U.S. Classroom Design?

Design of physical space is a science. People attend 4-year schools to learn design principles and techniques. But because "everyone knows" what a kindergarten or preschool room looks like, classroom design in the United States tends to be determined by decades of established practice. Actually, that look is determined by a huge industry. "The multi-billion dollar market for infant, toddler and preschool products represents one of the most dynamic and resurging segments of the consumer goods industry" (The U.S. Market for Infant, Toddler, and Preschool Products, 2003). End users, the children and teachers, have little, if any, influence.

The problem is more complicated than designing outside the established supply chain. Large corporate day-care centers, public school systems, and government-funded child-care programs have purchasing requirements that make it difficult for teachers to suggest what to order. Those who decide what to buy may be courted, wined, and dined by sales people. Cozy relationships may form between sellers and purchasers who place big orders.

Standard order forms constrict teachers to choosing mainly chalk, pencils, and paper. Most selections are made by someone in the central office who probably does not ask teachers what they need or prefer and may know little about early education. Teachers who want other things often spend their own money. This limits choices to small items because teachers do not earn enough to get a room painted, change furniture, or make major purchases.

Some schools have gotten around the supply-chain problem in several ways. Teachers have found that they need far less furniture (which tends to be oversized and bulky), so they eliminate many shelf units, tables, and chairs. Young children work comfortably on mats on the floor. Teachers buy lighter-scale furniture at places such as IKEA's "scratch and dent" area or Big Lots. They cut table legs to a lower height, find small chairs at inexpensive importers, and use smaller-scale, open, lightly colored shelving. Teachers also eliminate the noisy-patterned floor rugs in favor of neutral, patternless carpet. Some teachers find volunteers to build furniture to a smaller scale. Teachers appeal to parents or PTAs to fund their purchases. Some teachers change the look of their room simply by eliminating all commercially produced printed materials such as pictures, posters, ABC charts, number lines, and the like. In these ways, they make significant changes to the prevailing "look" of early education classrooms.

EXEMPLARY FEATURES OF REGGIO CLASSROOMS

In Reggio the idea of overriding importance in design is *relationships*: How will this arrangement, that experience, those materials encourage children to form relationships–with the space, the materials, with another child or a small group of children, with a teacher, with parents, with ideas between what they already know and something that is new?

Theory-Based Design

As I explained in Chapter 1, the socio-cultural theory behind Reggio's practices maintains that human development occurs as a result of the relationships each person forms with the environment and everything in it, especially the people. One way to think about a classroom is to consider what relationships children will be able to make. The mind can make an infinite number of relationships. No relationship is wrong. They differ because of people's different experiences.

Reggio educators design spaces so children can experience the texture of materials, the odor of different matter, dark and light, and black, white, or colored shadows.

They know that curtained nooks, platforms, and certain furnishings stimulate certain kinds of relationships. They know that tools and materials such as wire cutters, artists' low-fire clay, jars to mix paints, or fine-line markers stimulate other kinds of relationships.

The Reggio color palette is harmonious and soothing. Use of loud colors is limited to a small area to achieve a calculated effect. There are no commercial hangings. In this low-key surround, the children's work stands out.

Relationship-Based Design

Accounting for possible relationships in every aspect of a classroom means considering where items are stored, how they are displayed, how they might be combined with anything children might imagine. Loris Malaguzzi said, "An environment is a rich network of possible situations in which an adult envisions relationships that will facilitate children's work" (Lecture, Reggio Emilia, March 1992).

Reggio teachers consider every small detail–down to the color and shape of tiny beads. Teachers ensure that each item is attractive and offers children something to do that has meaning by itself or can lead to something related. Teachers' collaboration with children encourages them to build relationships. In doing so, they bring their experience as adults to analyze, interpret, and reflect with children, to provide them with a new perspective. Malaguzzi calls this a "loan of knowledge," especially when the "loan" helps children solve a problem they have set for themselves.

Reggio educators are proficient listeners and skilled observers. With a listening teacher, children's fleeting ideas become stable. With experience, isolated ideas form concepts (red, yellow, and blue become "color"); concepts are the basis for deepening relationships between mind and matter, place and person, home and community. As they observe the nuances in children's use of the environment, teachers look for potential relationships.

Key Points:
- An environment is a rich network of possible situations.
- To design a space means to envision the relationships children could have in that space.
- Children focus on the tiniest details, remember them, and draw on these memories to form relationships in their minds.

THINKING ABOUT DESIGN

The aesthetic of a Reggio environment is informed by centuries of good design as long ago as Roman times. Whether we think of clothing, cutlery, or cars, fashion, food, or furniture, Italian design excels. Here, I discuss how to develop a sense of design.

A Special Designer

For many years, I was privileged to work with a brilliant architect. T Meyer had the look and demeanor of Abraham Lincoln–tall, thin, and thoughtful. He listened intensely, asked penetrating questions, and when he spoke was magnetic. His particular genius was as a problem solver—building consensus among people, establishing aesthetic environments, coaxing workable programs out of gerrymandered spaces—in other words, making "silk purses out of sows' ears." He could make a church basement or a fire station social hall feel like a school or turn an old-age home into a children's museum.

T guided us, a group of intrepid parents, to expand a preschool into an elementary school, build our own building, and renovate a junior high school when our children grew older. At each juncture in endless meetings orchestrated by T, we laid out our vision. When I founded Capital Children's Museum, T was by my side, evaluating potential sites, considering how people might flow through different spaces, engaging in long discussions to extract exhibit and education programs as well as administrative, maintenance, archival, and technological requirements.

Twice, T left. When he announced he was leaving Washington, I doubted I could continue to run the Children's Museum, so much had I relied on his counsel from layout of spaces to choice of colors. After he left, I called him when situations demanded his particular wisdom. When he died of a brain tumor in 2005, our world went dark.

Design Principles

T's distilled wisdom and Reggio design inform some of the following principles. My own 3 decades of running schools and a museum informs others.

1. *Less is more.* In other words, create clarity, not clutter. You should be able to read what can happen in a room from its contents and how they are placed.
2. *Color calls attention to itself.* If you want people to pay attention to something, use color. Otherwise, keep it quiet, which means using soft, pale, neutral shades.
3. *The beauty of the environment* is spoiled if anything—furniture, rug, wall decoration—is not beautiful in and of itself. Eliminate it!
4. *Lighting* can be warm or cold, can make a space beckon or repel, can make someone look well or ill. Warm lights (there are many shades of fluorescent tubing) and an occasional small lamp make a space feel soft and intimate.
5. *Daylight* makes a dramatic impact on space; sun and shadow lines are important design elements.
6. *Artificial light*—spot lights, projector beams, floodlights—can make space look dramatically different, is easy to install and change, and is cheap.
7. *Repeated forms,* like containers of the same size, shape, and color, "go away" as visual elements. For examples, if you use identical straw baskets, the items inside will be more noticeable; if the chairs at a table are identical, they will not distract from what is on the table.
8. *Plants* add intrigue and variety, fill awkward areas, cover ugly spaces, and soften straight lines. Caring for them builds children's appreciation for living things.
9. *Getaway or private spaces* offer a respite from too much stimulation. They provide rest for individuals or foster relationships among two or three children.

Figure 5.2. Light from a small lamp softens the housekeeping corner at the MELC, where furnishings are realistic, a mirror stretches along the sink side, appliances are real but small, cupboards hold real (empty) canned goods, the refrigerator is stocked with realistic meat, cheese, fruits, and vegetables. Dishes are china, and the table can be laid with different cloths, napkins, candles, or flowers to make the setting beautiful.

10. *The weight of furniture* determines whether children can move it to form large or small groups and different configurations.
11. *Modular furnishings* that fit together in different patterns make space interesting and flexible. For example, two trapezoid-shaped tables form a hexagon, two rectangular tables a square, two triangles a diamond or a square.
12. *Movable partitions,* shelves on wheels, ceiling mounted screens, or hanging panels make space easy to vary and determine how children can move through the space.
13. *Simplicity and complexity* serve different purposes. The environment should be flexible enough, the materials rich enough, to enable children to transform a simple space into a complex space (complex does not mean cluttered).
14. *Reflective surfaces* (mirrors, Mylar, polished metal) surprise children and provide complexity.
15. *Colored filters* (see-through colored Plexiglas, theater gels) used judiciously add elements of transparency, surprise, and transformation.

16. *Natural materials* such as wood, cotton, hemp, or straw (as opposed to plastic and other synthetics) add the beauty, variety, and warmth of nature. They are rich without being intrusive, and their subtlety invites reflection.
17. *Storage* holds the raw ingredients that determine what experiences can take place, as a pantry's ingredients determine what can be cooked.
18. *Storage systems* that are not easy to use become spaces where junk accumulates. Reggio educators make many storage systems in the classroom so children have ready access.

Key Points:
- The environment is the curriculum.
- Design is a science and an art that can be learned.

DEVELOPING AN AESTHETIC SENSE

Classroom design grows from a teacher's personal sense of aesthetics. "But I don't have one!" wails a young teacher. The good news is that an aesthetic sense can be developed.

Teacher as Designer

Teacher/designer can be thought of as a teacher in two ways. One is her responsibility overall–for curriculum, the flow of the day, parent involvement, assessment, everything. The other is her responsibility for the aesthetics–the look, organization, and function of the classroom's physical aspects, those things you see, touch, sit on, store in, or divide with, and the individual items children use. These elements of design stimulate children to interact with objects and one another or adults. I consider these aspects of aesthetic design next.

Considering How Aesthetic Issues Affect Children

Begin the process of developing an aesthetic sense by looking at how the classroom environment impacts the children. Each decision about an aesthetic issue has an effect on children:

1. Will colors, materials, and finishes appeal to children's visual, tactile, auditory, and olfactory senses? Will an object's attributes entice, repel, or over-stimulate children?
2. For many people, the visual sense is dominant. What in the classroom appeals to children visually and why?
3. Do certain spaces and materials appeal to children who enjoy painting? Drawing? Clothing themselves? Making fantasy spaces? Arranging things such as the "house" or "store"? These children are sensitive to visual/spatial aesthetics.
4. Are there certain places where children particularly like to be? What about them attracts the children?

5. Are there opportunities for children to play with a range of colors, sounds, textures, and smells? To arrange and rearrange them? To change them?
6. Are the children drawn to particular images? Are the design elements (line, shape, pattern, color, rhythm) in these images strong or subtle? What do the children say about them?

> **Key Point:** Answers to these questions show which senses a classroom arouses, and what opportunities are present for visual, tactile, auditory, olfactory, gustatory, or haptic (touch and movement combined) perception.

Awakening an Aesthetic Sense

To take the next step, determine what you like, organize your ideas, awaken or sharpen your design sense. Focus first on developing a visual aesthetic by clipping images of appealing environments, like a gardener clips pictures of plants, patios, pathways. Include every kind of natural and man-made environment—home, office, private space, public square, classrooms, windows, lighting, surfaces, textures, storage. Do not eliminate something because it might be too expensive. This exercise builds visual perception; it is not a purchase list.

Find images everywhere—the Web, magazines, advertising. Take photos of environments, including other classrooms. Even if only one element is appealing—a storage system, a wall display—photograph it. It may be difficult to find classroom images because classrooms are rarely displayed as examples of good design. Occasionally, a high-tech grad school gymnasium or modern elementary school is featured. But mainly, schools have suffered from decades of sameness.

This is less true in Europe. Websites may offer examples of Scandinavian, Dutch, or French schools. North American Reggio Educators Association (NAREA) has a website with images of Reggio-inspired schools that members can browse. Reggio Children, the international association of the Reggio Preschools, has its own website and several publications with photographs of their environments. Study them and scan images for your collection. (This is permissible if you do not use the images commercially.)

Jot down what is appealing about the images—layout, color, light, texture, rhythm, repeated forms, one-of-a-kind arrangements, juxtaposition of items, mixture of elements. Then organize the images according to what is appealing to you, and create an Environment Notebook. There is no right or wrong organization. Categorizing reflects *your* mind. As the collection grows and becomes organized, the clippings become an index of your aesthetic taste.

Expanding the Aesthetic Sense

Museums, art galleries, paintings, and sculpture offer endless ideas about the use of shape, color, texture, space, composition, contrast, and other elements that define aesthetics. Books of artists' work—or any book with awe-inspiring images—build an aesthetic sense. The work of nature photographers Ansel Adams and Elliot Porter comes foremost to mind, as does artist Andy Goldsworthy's sculpture. In analyzing images, state precisely what is appealing. These exercises train the aesthetic sense and develop the ability to look at a classroom with new eyes. Knowing what you like and thinking about why you like it builds trust in your own eye.

It may take a year or more to inform your aesthetic sense. The process is engaging and may become a lifelong habit. If your colleagues take part, you can exchange ideas. Explaining choices to others clarifies one's own thinking. That is the purpose of this exercise.

Key Points:
- An aesthetic sense can be developed.
- Pay attention to what appeals to you.
- Index your taste.
- Trust your eye.

DESIGNING OR REDESIGNING A CLASSROOM

Questioning the design of a classroom and photographing it are two ways to clarify how the classroom functions for children and whether it builds their aesthetic intelligence.

Questioning the Current Design

Analyze these questions to determine whether your classroom appeals and the design is functional for you and your children.

- Do you and the children look forward to arriving and feel reluctant to leave at the end of the day?
- Does anyone enjoy arranging, straightening, and organizing materials on the shelves?
- Are there comfortable places for children and adults to sit?
- Do particular places in the classroom make the children calm or anxious?
- Is there a "nook" where one or two children can be away, alone, and quiet?
- Do children run, skid, or slide around the classroom? In particular places?
- Do children fight over who can use materials? Which ones?

List features of your classroom that are favorable and those that are constraining, that prevent you and the children from doing things. If you have seen a classroom you think is ideal, consider what you liked, why, how children behaved in it, and whether you could incorporate some of its features.

You may want to do this analysis with another teacher. You and someone you trust can analyze one another's classrooms. Or, you may want to work alone, or in secret!

Photographing

Before changing anything, photograph how the classroom looks and how the children behave. Once change begins, it is difficult to remember how things were. The scientist Jared Diamond (2005) calls this "landscape amnesia" (pp. 425–426).

Take overviews of the room from every perspective and take photos of each area, shelf unit, the individual items, and children using them. No detail is too small to overlook because every detail is subject to redesign! As the classroom changes, then/now comparisons help you see how far you have come. Remember to continue to document because a classroom, like a living organism, changes throughout its life.

> **Key Point:** Your photos will be the history of your growth as a designer and of the impact of your design on children.

The Design Process

After the analysis, begin the actual design. The following process is one way to go about the design or redesign of a classroom.

1. List activities you want to take place. Title it "Essential Areas."
2. Some teachers are required to remove everything from the room over the summer. Some schools move to new buildings or pack up during renovations. This gives teachers a blank slate to change layout, storage, wall displays, and placement of materials.
3. Study the space: Where are the windows in relation to the sun's changing light? Where are the electric outlets? Where are water and toilets? Where are built-ins? Where are doors?
4. Draw a simple diagram of the room. It need not be to scale but helps to draw on graph paper. Make several copies. Save the original.
5. Important Step: Linger over this one. Using a sharp pencil and an eraser that really works, pencil in a circle for each Essential Area. At this stage, there is much erasing. Do several "block" layouts–rough sketches of where each area might go. Study the sketches–sometimes called "bubble diagrams." Think about:

    Traffic: How will children move from area to area without disturbing others? Are doors blocked?

    Calm: In which areas do children most need quiet and to be out of the traffic flow? How can the layout discourage running?

    Storage: Where will clothes, cots/mats, supplies, work products be stored? Which do children need regular or immediate access to? Are these things accessible?

    Activities: How much space do children require for full-class meeting? Blocks? Dress-up? Manipulative materials? Library/books? Housekeeping (or other imitative play)? Writing? Art? Other?

    Flexibility: How easy will it be to change the layout and for children to regroup movable items?

    Small groups: What arrangement is most likely to support small groups of children working together or with a teacher?

    Light: What are the lighting requirements for particular activities? Are windows close to art or other activities that children will find more appealing in daylight?

    This is the conceptual stage, the time to think about every classroom you have seen, what you like, your ideas, children's preferences, accessibility of materials. Don't rush the process!

6. Measure the classroom. Floor tiles, usually 6-inch, 8-inch, or 12-inch, are handy for approximating size. Round down to the nearest foot. Example: If your classroom is 32 feet, 8 inches long and 25 feet, 3 inches wide, ignore the inches and multiply 33 x 25. The classroom is about 825 square feet.

7. Count out the size in squares on the grid paper to draw an approximate scale plan—32 squares in one direction, 25 squares in the other if you use one square per foot. For now ignore small irregularities such as niches and jogs. Show doors, windows, closets, and large areas that alter a rectangular space.

8. Now the fun! Cut small pieces of paper that approximate the size and shape of the furnishings for each Essential Area to see how they "feel" in your floor plan(s). Note: Place largest items first.

9. Make many layouts, switching the placement of elements until there is a plan you like.

10. Pick the design you like best. If circumstances (relocation, renovation, cleaning) cause you to empty the room, celebrate! It is an opportunity to lay out the classroom in masking tape. Yes! "Build" the room by putting masking tape on the floor to represent what is on paper. Walk around, sit in the spaces, imagine each filled with furniture and children. It is easier to remove masking tape than to move objects. If you are purchasing any large new pieces, it is cheaper to test their bulk in masking tape. Change the masking tape until the room feels right. If you are unable to empty your room, the paper plan will help to determine where to move large objects before placing smaller ones or individual items.

11. When the layout pleases you, put the furnishings in place. Remember: You do not have to bring back everything you took out or, if you left everything in the room, you do not have to keep everything. This is the time to weed out what is ugly, bulky, or dysfunctional.

12. Study the room. Make adjustments. The goal is clarity. Children should be able to read the space, to know from looking at the room what activities will take place and where they will happen.

This process is not a gospel. You or a colleague may prefer another process. The goal is to improve the classroom's functioning and aesthetic quality. The rest of this book will help you determine whether the redesign has achieved these goals because everything that children do depends on the environment. The process never ends. Once you learn to look critically, you will continue to do so.

Caution: Don't change things so often that children become confused! If possible, talk with children about impending changes. Elicit their ideas. When Reggio children were asked what they would tell children new to their school, they gave very detailed accounts of the physical space; they could not have done this if the space changed continually. Among hundreds of comments, they said:

> A door in the classroom opens to the mini-atelier: There you'll find the containers, a sort of plastic box where you can put your toys you bring from home and anything you wish. . . . In the mini-atelier you'll also find all materials required for molding clay, painting, working with paper, paint, brushes, wire . . . ; then you'll see a shelf with the finished works on it, some toys that have been lost, some sheets. It's nice. It's for keeping nice things on it. (Bondavalli, Mori, & Vecchi, 1990, p. 14)

> **Key Points:**
> * Analyze your space.
> * Photograph before you change anything.
> * Play with your ideas on paper. (It is cheaper than buying the wrong items!)

What to Do First

A starting point in implementing your design is to eliminate items you do not like. T often said, "The temporary becomes permanent." So the carpet squares that give children their own place to sit during full-class meetings have become soiled or ragged. Throw them out now! Alternatives are discontinued rug samples sold in carpet stores for $1 (sometimes free to teachers) or plastic tape to mark a space for each child. Better is an ellipse made of tape (see Chapter 4). For an easy way to draw an ellipse, see http://www. mathopenref.com/constellipse.html. Sitting on an ellipse rather than facing the teacher makes conversation possible. If children sit on chairs on the ellipse, they tend to wiggle less.

> **Key Point:** Eliminating something you have never liked is like having fresh air in a stuffy room.

CONCLUSION: A NEW TAKE ON ENVIRONMENT

In their introduction to the book *We Write Shapes That Look Like a Book,* Reggio educator/authors say:

> Words and images interweave to make the educational approach visible and perceptible. This is a new, hybrid language based on competencies unknown in traditional training for teachers. . . . [These] new forms of knowledge declare and underline the importance of an aesthetic dimension in teaching and learning. (Cavallini, Filippini, Transcossi, & Vecchi, 2008, p. 2)

Reggio educators view all aspects of their work through a lens focused on aesthetics and they define aesthetics philosophically, that the principles of beauty are basic to many other principles. For me, aesthetics provides the subtleties that enliven the senses. Aesthetics means not only how something looks and functions but its potential to shape experience, and in doing so, to shape the mind.

> **Questions to Consider**
> 1. Are you comfortable with yourself as a designer? Why or why not?
> 2. What specific tools or ideas in this chapter do you find useful? Why or why not?
> 3. What aspects of your classroom encourage children to form relationships?
> 4. What have you learned in this chapter about aesthetics that will help you evolve into a better classroom designer?

CHAPTER 6

The Art of
Meaning-Full Conversation

A riddle, a riddle as I suppose
A hundred eyes and never a nose.

—Mother Goose

WHEN YOU CONSIDER how much children must know to solve riddles, it makes the acquisition of language all the more remarkable. Conversation is, possibly, the single most important way the brain learns to use and understand language. In this chapter, I explain Meaning-full Conversation, describe a project driven by conversation, lay out techniques to engage in focused conversation, and show the impact of conversation on projects.

DEFINING CONVERSATION

What is conversation? What is it *not*? And why? Conversation is the focused and extended sharing of a particular thought. Conversation can take place between two people; among several; in a large group where few know each other, like a town hall meeting; or in a small group where everyone knows everyone, like a classroom of children and their teacher. In a conversation, each participant

- maintains a focus on one topic and ideas related to the topic;
- communicates particular meanings;
- builds on a train of thought so that ideas extend one another; and
- exchanges information or solves problems.

Conversation is important because it prepares children to think logically, and builds vocabulary so children can understand content. When children understand content, they can form concepts. For example, hard, bumpy, and scratchy are content; the word *texture* is a concept. Concepts exist in the mind, not in reality. When you know concepts, your thoughts flow more easily.

Conversation requires children to speak fluently. Fluent speech is evidence of a brain that is processing rapidly. The essential precursors to reading and writing that conversation develops are focusing, exchanging information, communicating meaning, thinking logically, enlarging content knowledge, expanding concepts, and processing meaning.

Conversation Is Not

Using the definition, consider the following example that *is not* a conversation:

> TEACHER: Who's not at school today?
> JIMMY: Jeffrey's not here; he's home sick.
> TEACHER: Right!
> SHAMEKA: Janine's not here.
> FRANCO: Juan's with his aunt today.
> TEACHER: Who else is not here today?
> CHORUS: [So many voices call out names that they cannot be distinguished.]

This example is *not* a conversation because the children do not

- expand on their single-phrase answers;
- comment on others' answers;
- provide evidence;
- ask for evidence.

The problem of knowing who is in school was not solved in the exchange with children because after group time the teacher takes attendance using the class list in her Record Book. It does not seem that the teacher intended to have the children determine who was absent because she solved the problem herself later. Such interchanges merely fill time. Worse, they convey to children that the activity is unimportant or that they, the children, are incapable of solving the problem. Activities like this waste time.

Conversation Is

The next example *is* a conversation because the teacher

- intends to solve a problem;
- pursues a train of thought with each child; and
- requires evidence.

Notice how the teacher states the problem, announcing what she wants the children to focus on and challenging their brains to figure something out. And notice how the children listen closely enough to adapt each other's forms of evidence. For example, Michael adapts Shameka's statement that a coat is missing.

> TEACHER, *alerting the brain with the words "let's figure out"*: Let's figure out who is at school today.
> JIMMY: Derrick isn't here; he's home sick.
> TEACHER, *asking for evidence*: How do you know that?
> JIMMY: We went by his house and he didn't come out.
> TEACHER, *pursuing logic*: Did he know you were there?
> JIMMY: He comes out every day, but not today. He sick.
> TEACHER, *encouraging the child to describe his thought process*: How did you know he was sick?

JIMMY: My auntie called his momma on her cell. His ear hurts. He's going to the doctor.

TEACHER, *moving the conversation ahead*: Who else is missing today?

SHAMEKA: Janine's not here.

TEACHER, *requesting evidence*: How do you know?

SHAMEKA: Her coat's not in her cubby.

TEACHER, *seeking precision*: How do you know?

SHAMEKA: Her cubby's next to mine, but I saw her coat isn't in it.

MICHAEL: I didn't see Stephon's coat in his cubby.

DONALD: I saw Stephon in the bathroom; he's wearing his coat.

The children continue considering who is there and provide supporting or contradictory evidence either spontaneously or in response to questioning. After about 15 minutes, the teacher reads a checklist accurately reflecting what the children know about who is at school, thus proving to themselves that they solved the teacher's challenge: "Let's figure out . . ."

As I explain later in the chapter, certain techniques enable a teacher to hold conversations with children. You can think of these techniques as a Conversation Tool Kit. The *Kit* is not a bunch of "stuff"; it is teaching strategies. The strategies are rooted in socio-cultural theory, which emphasizes the central role of relationships with other people as the most important factor in human development and as the spur to language development (Vygotsky, 1934/1986).

> **Key Point:**
> Every verbal interaction is *not* a conversation.

HOLDING FOCUSED CONVERSATIONS

Conversations knit the community together and build children's facility for language. Conversation expands children's reflective capacity as well as many other brain functions.

Conversation in Action

In focused conversation, a teacher has an intention. It may be to

- expand children's memory;
- extend their focus;
- encourage them to support statements with evidence;
- enlarge their content knowledge;
- challenge them to form concepts;
- build their understanding of context;
- give them practice making logical connections.

Each of these acts is a process the brain uses to comprehend, enlarge, store, or in other ways manipulate information.

Below, we listen in on a focused conversation with a teacher named Gerry who

- is *intentional* because she announces her goal to alert everyone that something important is about to happen: "We are going to have a conversation about *planes*."

- conveys *meaning* as she addresses Eddie by relating the topic to something he said: "Do you remember, yesterday you asked why planes had such big wings?" Eddie nods enthusiastically.

Gerry alerts the brain by focusing on something she knows is fascinating to children—size: "Do you want to find out how *big* wings are?" Eddie, wide-eyed: "Yeah!"

Gerry has given meaning to Eddie's remark in two ways: by causing him to tap into his memory to recall something he said and by telling him he will be engaged in finding answers to his own question. Watch how Gerry's serious consideration of a child's seemingly casual remark leads the children to explore a host of *transcendent* ideas. Transcendent ideas build relationships in the brain.

> GERRY, *continuing to emphasize size and engaging the brain's movement centers, asks Eddie*: Can you *show* us how big the wing was?
>
> EDDIE, *standing, arms out, and roaring to make the sound of a plane taking off, "flies" to a near wall in the classroom, then responds*: This big!
>
> GINA *offers*: I seed an airplane that's bigger, *and she "flies," silently, the length of the classroom.*
>
> GERRY *asks a question about wings to maintain the focus of the conversation*: Has anyone else seen an airplane's wings?
>
> *A chorus of "yeses."*
>
> GERRY *sustains the focus of the conversation on the concept of size by asking*: How big were those wings?

Many children express ideas—as big as the classroom, as big as the whole school, as big as the Empire State Building, as big as 50 billion million, outdoing one another with their impressions of bigness.

Gerry took their ideas seriously. In the ensuing weeks, she carefully selected ideas to pursue that would enlarge the topic, ground the children in reality, and challenge them to provide evidence for their statements. Ultimately, the five children who were most interested visited a small airfield, interviewed an equipment maintenance worker, and embarked on a long project making an airplane wing so large they had to build it on the playground. These Big experiences provided a context for children to learn about size as it relates to airplane wings. Experience is a powerful way to put ideas into context. For young children experience may be the *only* way they can grasp meaning.

What began as a conversation focused on something one child had said tapped into a deep interest—children's fascination with the size of huge objects. The initial conversation—with the teacher's thoughtful listening, reflection, and orchestration—became the springboard for several challenging related projects. At the start of each project and at every juncture, conversation drove the next step and enabled children to understand the meaning expressed by themselves and others. Meaning is content, the "stuff" we think about. As Seymour Papert, MIT mathematics professor and inventor of the LOGO computer language, said, "We can't think without thinking about something" (1979, Lecture).

> **Key Point:**
> "Whether the interaction is successful in enabling the children to practice linguistic, discursive, and cognitive skills depends largely on the teacher's reactions" (Dickinson & Tabors, 2002, p. 10).

Conversation and Literacy

To be literate, a child must speak, read, and write. These acts require the following:

1. Mastering sets of specific skills such as:
    *   recognizing the meaning of spoken words;
    *   retrieving words from your own brain's memory centers;
    *   vocalizing the words you retrieved;
    *   recognizing that particular letters stand for particular sounds and hearing meaning in specific combinations of sounds; and
    *   decomposing words that you hear aloud or in your head and shaping them with a writing instrument so they are visible.
2. Understanding the content, concepts, and context of what you hear, say, read, or write. Together, content and context comprise meaning. Conversation helps children *construct* meaning by:
    *   expanding their vocabulary (content and concepts);
    *   building increasingly complex sentences;
    *   extending a train of thought;
    *   finding relationships among thoughts;
    *   using your own knowledge or a group's collective responses to share premises and solve problems. (When we read, we share premises with an author.)

The content/context aspects of literacy make it possible for 5-year-olds to laugh at a statement like, "The hair on the hare is hairier than the hair on the cat here." Five-year-olds have a large enough vocabulary to make the different meanings in homonyms seem funny and their grammar is strong enough to understand that the word ending "-er" makes a comparison. Two-and-a-half-year-olds giggle at "the dish ran away with the spoon." Toddlers know dishes and spoons can't run and find it funny to hear something that so outrageously contradicts the reality they have recently figured out. A 4-year-old, looking out the window in the front car of a subway train, says, "The night is swallowing the light," using a powerful metaphor for a visual experience. Using homonyms, humor, and metaphor are essential reading skills that depend on understanding content and context.

> **Key Point:**
> Conversation is a vital tool to build literacy skills.

Conversation and the Brain

When children listen, speak, read, or write, many parts of the brain's executive attention system function virtually simultaneously. For example, the brain

*   maintains focus on a train of thought;
*   controls behaviors so children do not interrupt, talk out-of-turn, or poke others;
*   makes relationships to the topic being discussed;
*   accesses one's own "mental dictionary" (Pinker, 1994, pp. 323–324) to find the words needed to understand and speak meaningfully;
*   manipulates and coordinates motor areas such as the tongue, lips, vocal chords, and diaphragm to produce specific sounds of human speech;

- logically relates prior and next remarks;
- enjoys the unique human ability to share ideas;
- builds cognitive capacity.

Cognitive capacity builds in a "progression from understanding the content of experience to the formation of concepts" (Feuerstein, Feuerstein, & Falik, 2004, p. 19). Lacking the capacity to form concepts, the brain stumbles at performing mental operations that take place at still higher cognitive levels.

For example, *content* means knowing feelings such as hot, cold, warm, and so on, or things such as circle, square, and so forth. *Concepts* mean knowing that feelings like hot and cold are all called *temperature* or that things like circle and square are all called *shape*. Ideas such as color, temperature, and shape do not exist in the world but are ways the brain organizes information so that humans can think efficiently.

Once you know a concept, you can use higher-level thinking such as analogy: Blue is to sky as white is to _____; metaphor: as hot as the sun; and inference: If I lengthen two opposite sides of a square, it will become a rectangle. Children can learn these forms of thinking through conversation.

Mastering the brain functions required by conversation demands practice. Children must converse *repeatedly* in order to speak articulately (good pronunciation), grammatically (correct word usage), fluently (continuous flow of ideas), cogently (ideas related to one another), and succinctly (knowing when to stop). Cogently also means using more and more complex brain functions, for example:

- making comparisons;
- categorizing;
- seeking evidence;
- performing transformations;
- building relationships;
- summarizing so that others' attention does not shut down or wander.

These complex brain functions can only be acquired through practice. When children use these functions, their conversation is meaning-full.

Figure 6.1. Children at the MELC have transformed natural objects into a tree, bird, flower, branch, and butterfly. In doing so, their brains have formed many relationships among the shape, size, and appearance of a number of life forms.

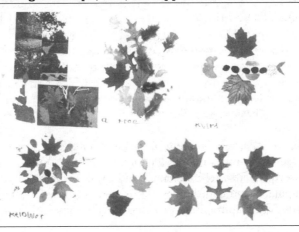

Key Points:
- Conversation is the focused sharing of ideas that relate to one another.
- Conversation builds children's vocabulary or content knowledge, expands what concepts children know and their grasp of context, and gives them practice using language to convey meaning.

CONVERSATION PUNCTUATES A PROJECT

Conversation played the key role in a project involving four children at the MELC who had a Big experience making self-portraits in five different media. The teacher's *intention* was to help them learn that there are many ways to explore and to show variation. The *meaning* was each child's interpretation of what a portrait is. The *transcendent ideas* were that faces have both differences and commonalities and that ideas can be transformed into different media.

Years later, Jennifer Azzariti said, "During our years at the MELC we were all so young and Reggio practices were so new." Only years later, as our experiences broadened, did we use words like *intention, meaning,* and *transcendence.* The words come from Reuven Feuerstein's theory of mediation that explains how to make adults' interactions with children effective (Feuerstein et al., 2006, pp. 71–75).

Did we know these things intuitively so many years ago? The MELC teachers were unusually attuned to observing children. Interwoven in the following story of self-portraits is what I would do today, given what we now know. The now and then are clearly identified.

Initial Conversations

The experience began with a conversation with the full class about portraits but grew from other experiences: All fall, the children had been exploring materials in the Studio, making collages, and discussing the content of their family photographs (see Chapter 3). As the teachers later discussed children's comments, they noticed that four children were particularly interested in the discussion about portraits, so chose them for the project.

Noticing Same/Different. As the project began, the children and the teacher looked at themselves in a mirror and had a conversation about what they saw. Sonya focused on each part of the face, including the hair in the nostrils. Today, I would emphasize looking for things that are the same and different on one's own and one's friends' faces by touching one another's faces to *feel* the differences. And I would enlarge children's familiarity with the context in which portraits are found and how they are made. I would extend the idea of same/different and enlarge the context by orchestrating experiences, such as:

- collecting portraits, realistic and abstract, in many different media, and engaging the children in seeking same, different, and similar, and in expressing degree of difference;
- discussing how the portraits were made—brush, chisel, mold, camera, film, pencil, and so forth;

- adding books with portraits to the classroom library and the Studio;
- encouraging the children to pore through magazines, cut out portraits, and categorize them by the sameness and difference they perceived;
- visiting museums to see portraits.

In fall 1993, we were already researching in books and magazines and taking field trips to enlarge our knowledge of whatever topic we were investigating. Today, I would more pointedly engage the brain functions of comparison and categorization and would encourage the children to develop criteria for how to sort the images—by facial expression? Medium the artist used? Facial decoration? Feelings the faces evoke?

Same/Different and the Brain. When children analyze the ways in which any two things are the same or different, they engage three cognitive *functions*:

1. Comparing
2. Summarizing differences
3. Defining relationships

Every object—a tree, a shape, an animal, a nose—exists in, so to speak, its own universe. In noticing anything, the first thing we do, unconsciously, is determine what it has in common and how it differs from something else—its defining characteristics. We make ourselves conscious of an object's properties. This creates a mental construct.

No relationship exists between an eye and a nose until I bring them together and categorize them: What is the same? Both occupy adjoining real estate, perceive the world, inform the brain. Both are oriented in a forward direction (unlike the ears). I link them as part of the larger category *parts of a face*. What is different? The eye perceives color, shape, form. The nose perceives odor—smoke, gardenia, toast. The eye may be blue, green, brown, black, or some other color. The nose may be flat, pointed, hooked, delicate, or some other shape. Comparative behavior elicits constructs that do not exist but that are totally a product of the human mind. The significance is:

- Once a relationship has been made, it can be transported to find commonalities and differences in a variety of other objects.
- The categories of difference can be used to compare very varied objects.

Distinguishing same/different is one of the most basic cognitive operations. It is present in the simplest creatures and developed early in the evolution of life on earth. Noted psychologist/biologist Robert Ornstein (Ornstein & Thompson, 1984) supposes that organisms could not have survived without this ability, that anything that could not distinguish same from different could have eaten itself! Children who have difficulty noticing same/different will have trouble recognizing letters as they begin to learn to read.

> **Key Point:** The power of best practices is that they bring meaning to experience.

Deepening Conversation

If we were carrying out the self-portrait project today, I would deepen the conversation by asking children to analyze the elements of a portrait—how they knew a picture was a portrait, the fact that someone must create a portrait, the tools a portrait-maker can use. I would enlarge children's vocabulary by using words like *complexion, shade, oval, broad, elongated, wiry, smooth.* Children soak up words like dry sponges soak up water. They learn words such as *analyze* and *categorize* as readily as they learn words such as *circle* and *square.*

I would focus more on how the children's faces differ from one another, encouraging them to look at overall shape, color, hair texture, and distinctions in individuals' eyes, nose, mouth, forehead, cheekbones. In 1993, when the MELC teachers had not even had a year's experience using Reggio practices, the children spent a long time looking in each other's mouths and counting their teeth.

The children were becoming familiar with the properties of different materials. Today, I would spend far more time before they began their portraits analyzing what materials they would use. Which materials lent themselves to different features of their portraits? What was best for hair? Twine? Yarn? Raffia? How does each feel? Soft? Stiff? Silky? How does *your* hair feel? Which material is most like your hair?

I would allow more digestion time between experiences. Before beginning the portraits, I would quote from prior sessions any of the children's words that showed subtlety in their analysis of materials. In other words, I would slow down.

In 1993, it took 2 days to finish the first portrait, a collage of found objects. Jennifer had each child make four more portraits each in a different medium—charcoal, pastel, fine-line black marker, and #2 pencil. Their portraits were richly detailed, unique, and resembled each child. If Jennifer and the children conversed about the different mark-makers, the conversations were not recorded or are lost. It is ambitious to have children transform an idea with 5 media; it is impressive to succeed. Today, I would record children's comments, read them back to the children, and in conversations encourage children to analyze what they said.

Jennifer asked, "Why it is important to draw ourselves?" Quatesha replied, "Because it's beautiful" (Lewin-Benham, 2006, p. 110). Quatesha's remark is full of emotion but is a missed opportunity to ask her to elaborate on her meaning.

Comparison and Cognition

Psychologist Reuven Feuerstein says that making comparisons is one of the basic elements in cognition. Comparison requires the brain to:

- focus on detail;
- draw on schemata (the brain's organization of concepts);
- express conclusions (Feuerstein, Feuerstein, Falik, & Rand, 2006).

If children's responses are anemic, it means they lack the ability to elaborate, a mental function that reflects what "verbal concepts are part of an individual's repertoire . . . [and can be] mobilized at the expressive level" (Feuerstein et al., 2002, p. 139). If their responses wander, it means they cannot pick relevant stimuli or they fail to make connections. As children gradually learn to stay on topic, they enlarge their vocabularies and become more fluent. They also use more accurate and complex grammatical construction. Conversations in the MELC from 1992 through 1996 show these changes. They reflect the increasing skill with which the teachers orchestrated conversations (Lewin-Benham, 2006).

Key Point:
Through conversation, teachers can hear some of the brain functions children use (or fail to use).

Figure 6.2. Children have represented themselves in words, collage, tempera paint, fine-line black marker, #2 pencil, and pastel. Teachers added a photo and small mirror.

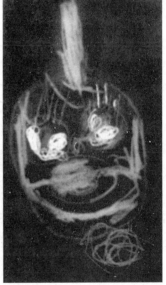

Rationale for Focused Conversation

Conversation exists because of humans' innate and unique language capacity. "Language, the primary cultural tool used by humans to mediate their activities, is instrumental in restructuring the mind and in forming higher-order, self-regulated thought processes" (Berk & Winsler, 1995, p. 5). Conversation is a powerful cultural force in which group activity profoundly influences individual development. "All higher mental functions have social origins that are eventually internalized" (p. 5).

Focused conversation is *not* greetings, directions, passing asides, or remarks about behavior. Research shows that teachers' talk to young children is mainly casual and consists primarily of directions or corrections (Shin & Spodek, 1991). School time may lack the kind of focused conversation as described in this chapter. Moreover, children's TV time, parents' cell phone time, today's hurried pace, and extended school days have lessened family conversation time. The 3-year-old is a "grammatical genius" (Pinker, 1994, p. 280), but *only attains this proficiency through frequent experience using language in conversation with others.* Conversation builds many different brain functions, among them those that are necessary to write and read. When used in intentional, meaning-full, and transcendent ways, conversation is the social spur to using language fully. As the relation between conversation and brain function becomes better understood, it may fall to the school to ensure that Meaning-full Conversation occupies a substantial amount of time in young children's day.

> **Key Point:**
> Holding conversations with young children is *the* essential prerequisite for their developing fluency in spoken language *and* fluent speech is an essential precursor to reading and writing fluently.

TECHNIQUES IN THE CONVERSATION TOOL KIT

The Conversation Tool Kit is a large number of related techniques that a teacher can use to build children's capacity to hold conversations. Techniques include

- choosing the best times to hold conversation;
- selecting the topics most likely to encourage extended conversation;
- getting the conversation started;
- helping children learn to focus;
- asking good questions;
- listening acutely;
- keeping records of what children say.

These techniques can be learned using the conversations in this book or those from your classroom as study examples to analyze the flow of a conversation:

- Do the ideas follow one another logically?
- Exactly how does each idea relate to the topic of the conversation?
- Does the conversation lead to the solution of a problem? Expand an interest expressed earlier? Or provide a context for an isolated thought?
- Does a child's remark convey a transcendent idea?

Figure 6.3. Conversations among small groups of children with or without a teacher took place continuously throughout the MELC.

At the MELC, we improved our techniques as we listened to tape-recordings of our conversations. At first, they were rambling and unfocused. But as we overcame the awkwardness of listening to ourselves on tape, we learned to analyze whether a conversation had *meaning.* This analysis was an example of teachers' *intention,* a word we did not know then but which has since come into vogue. When we looked for bridges to future projects, we were using transcendence, ideas that relate the present to the past or future.

We integrated conversation into all classroom activities. As we became more adept, saw children's attention increase, and heard their vocabulary grow, we learned to use conversation before, during, and after every full-class, small-group, or individual activity. This put enormous emphasis on speaking. The emphasis gradually encouraged language to blossom. As a result, the thinking skills that are the basis for literacy grew—larger vocabulary, standard grammar, and logically related thoughts.

Each class has different challenges: In the MELC, we had children who spoke non-standard English and had limited vocabularies. If children come from homes that encourage speaking, some of those children may dominate a conversation, may tell entire stories instead of picking a point that relates to the conversation, may digress, or may interrupt. As children practice focused conversation, these behaviors fall away. Children become less egocentric and their remarks become more targeted. They direct responses less to the teacher and more to one another.

> **Key Point:**
> With practice, children engage in reciprocal speech, which is the hallmark of conversation.

Managing Conversations

How do experienced teachers get conversations started? What behaviors do they model to encourage conversation? When do they hold conversations? How do they select topics?

Getting Started. Teachers in Reggio preschools typically begin their conversation with the words, "*Alora! Attenzione!*" "Now then! Attention!" At the end of the morning, Lisa, an experienced early childhood teacher, gathered her full class and announced: "We are going to have a conversation about what we did this morning." They sat in a circle so everyone could see the teacher's and each other's faces. The two teachers, their intern, and a visitor joined the group. The teaching staff settled themselves next to children who had difficulty behaving. Lisa knew that her initial remarks would alert the brain, like a bugle call: "Get ready! Focus!"

Modeling Behaviors. Lisa began: "William, tell us what you did this morning." The teachers listened intently by turning toward William, focusing their eyes on and inclining their posture toward him as they would toward any speaker.

> WILLIAM, *pleased to have been selected*: I worked on the blocks. I made, uh, uh, a
>   road for a dinosaur.
> LISA: Did anyone work with you?
> CHUCK: I did. I got Tyrannosaurus rex.
> WILLIAM: And it chased a brontosaurus up and down the road.
> LISA *gave both boys serious attention, neither commenting on nor laughing at their idea of
>   dinosaurs running on roads. Then, noticing Daniel's keen attention to William and
>   Chuck*: Daniel, what did you do this morning?
> *Gradually,* LISA *called on each child. She suspected that this conversation would be full of
>   non sequiturs because they had been involved in diverse activities, but dinosaurs were
>   rippling through many brains.*
> JOEL: My daddy gonna take me to buy some dinosaurs at Toys-R-Us.
> LISA, *ignoring Joel's non sequitur and matter-of-factly refocusing him on the question
>   under discussion*: Tell us what you did this morning, Joel.

Lisa was intentionally modeling:

- how to give uninterrupted attention to the speaker;
- how to keep a question in mind;
- how to respond to questions.

She made notes of digressions, like Joel's, that might be fruitful to pursue in a conversation at another time.

Times for Conversation. At many times during the day, Lisa used conversation:

- in full-class meetings;
- in transition times–between activities, before meals, nap, or dismissal.
  Conversation turned empty times into focused activity.
- during work time by gathering children–like William, Chuck, Daniel, and
  Joel–who were all interested in the same thing. "I found a great new book
  on dinosaurs. Would you like to look at it together?" Lisa took the boys
  to a table where they could comfortably discuss the book, knowing that
  the illustrations would spark extensive conversation. She gave them her
  undivided attention as they commented, questioned, and discussed whatever
  caught their attention in the book.

- during work time by gathering children at loose ends, finding a comfy place, and asking what they would like to talk about. If they were silent, which happens when children are new at conversation, Lisa used notes of what they had previously said to launch the conversation: "Joel, the other day you said your daddy was going to buy you some dinosaurs. Would you like to tell us more about that?"
- as she introduced any new experience;
- as she concluded an experience. At these times, Lisa encouraged the children to summarize the experience and to transcend to related ideas by asking questions such as, "How could we learn more about dinosaurs?" Or, "What do dinosaurs remind you of?"

A word about fostering attention: Every behavior involves movement. Because humans learn by observing and imitating, a teacher who wants children to behave in a particular way can teach them to do so by how she herself behaves–or moves. Children under age 4 or so pay especially close attention to movement.

Selecting Topics. Topics mean the content of conversation. Lisa conversed about, literally, anything, but knew that subjects of interest to children are most likely to hold their attention. For example, Lisa used:

- comments of what children have previously said that she recorded: "John, yesterday you told us you found an incredible picture of a train in the new book. Would you like to describe it to us?"
- children's talk about superheroes, TV programs, or toys: "Raymond, yesterday I heard you talking about Spider-Man. What would you like to know about Spider-Man?" Or, "Matthew, last week you made a construction with the blocks and called it an alien space station. What do you remember about it?" What the child remembered was the basis for the conversation.
- photos of children engrossed in activity. Children like being asked to describe what they were doing, especially when each child in the photo has a chance to comment. A different photo of the same activity can spur more conversation: "Adele, what were you doing in *this* photo?"
- pictures in books: "Brenda, let's see if this book has pictures that will answer your question."

Using a wide variety of books with realistic photos or drawings broadens children's understanding of the topic under discussion and builds their ability to find transcendent ideas. Books can be used to extend children's remarks: "Harry, here is a book that might have something about that. Let's find out." Or, "Nan, do you think this book might have something about that?" Or, "Maybe this book will." Or, "Can *you* find a book that does?" Or, "Do we need to find more books? Where could we look?" Lisa also had conversations about why a book lacks answers.

The public library near Lisa's school allowed teachers to borrow many books. Her library also sold de-accessioned books for 10¢ each, and she requested donations of high-quality magazines through bulletin boards, Craig's List, or newspapers.

> **Key Point:**
> A teacher can practice the different techniques to manage conversations so that the techniques become second nature.

Lisa took advantage of the fact that children who have taken part in the same experience have similar memories and thus share a context for conversations. Shared experiences prepare them to consider questions such as: "Where can we find out more about . . . ?" Or, "What made you think of . . . ?"

Maintaining Focus

Knowing that focus is *the* most important thing young children can learn, at the MELC we emphasized building focus. First, we concurred among ourselves on the behaviors that define focus and agreed to practice those behaviors during conversations with the children. They included:

- not interrupting a conversation to ask a child to focus;
- refocusing a child who interrupted with gesture: extending an arm, hand up, palm forward toward the child, a gesture that firmly says "Stop!" or facing the child with an expression (no words) that clearly said "Stop!";
- sitting a hitting or kicking child on a teacher's lap, or holding her around the waist. Before our children could regulate their own behavior, a teacher might actually hold two or even three children;
- agreeing among ourselves in advance on the eye signals to ask another adult to attend to an unfocused child;
- ignoring children who interrupted while someone was speaking. We did not want to interrupt the flow of the conversation to correct behavior! Immediately after, we would call on the interrupting child: "Jim, what did you want to tell us about cats?" Or, "Sharine, did you have something else to say about painting?" The purpose was to sanction the child's desire to join the conversation, not to punish the child for interrupting or lecture the child on her behavior.

Conversation with the full class was an ideal time to model focused behavior and to reinforce the behaviors that encourage children, gradually, to learn to self-regulate.

Key Points:
- The techniques necessary to hold a focused conversation can be learned.
- Initial techniques are selecting the topic and choosing the time and particular group, then alerting children's brains with a good question or statement.
- Later techniques are modeling behavior and ensuring that children remain focused.

THE IMPACT OF FOCUSED CONVERSATION

The story that follows shows focused conversation in action in a series of projects at the MELC that we called "Pollution."

A Story: The Context

One winter, the water in Washington, DC, became too polluted to drink. The MELC children were gravely concerned, and over many days we conversed frequently about pollution. Several projects emerged.

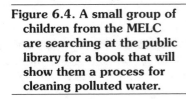

Figure 6.4. A small group of children from the MELC are searching at the public library for a book that will show them a process for cleaning polluted water.

Key Point:
The teachers did not solve the problem but allowed the time necessary for the children to come up with a solution.

In one project, the children polluted water, then tried to clean it, but failed. After 2 weeks of trying everything–white paint, dish-washing liquid, other cleansers–and after waiting, observing, and more trials, Galeesa suggested checking the dictionary. The children did so with great excitement. But the dictionary offered nothing. Then, "Renée figured out that we could go to the library and we did . . . and then we look [sic] in the books!" (Lewin-Benham, 2006, p. 127).

When the children first tried the research books, they were no help. After more days, and more conversations, they concluded that they needed to search further. On the *third* library visit, they found what they wanted–a diagram of a simple filtering system.

The Role of Conversation

Because conversation took place throughout the project, with teachers using the techniques described above, the children began to:

- wait their turn to talk;
- listen attentively;
- focus on the substance of what each speaker said;
- make appropriate responses;
- stay on topic;
- interrupt less, and eventually, not at all.

With teachers' consistent attention, the children also stopped hitting, poking, or otherwise annoying others. With teachers' encouragement, children began to use a great variety of books, magazines, dictionaries, and reference books spontaneously to find answers to questions that arose during their conversations.

Key Point:
Teachers who use the Conversation Tool Kit are intentionally making conversations the basis for literacy.

CONCLUSION: CONVERSING TOWARD LITERACY

Psychologist Jerome Bruner (1996) said, "Learning, remembering, talking, imagining: all of them are made possible by participating in a culture" (p. xi). Stories are the meat of culture. A story is a train of thought told so that members of a culture learn or remember something. Stories are made accessible through words, and are reconstructed whenever they are told or read. Stories contain things commonly known in a culture—word meanings, concepts, and the context of an experience (like what you eat at a ballgame or how you dress to attend one). Stories show you what a culture stores and shares and what the brain processes and recalls. Stories are shared through conversation and children who converse are telling stories.

As children's ability to converse grows, they become focused and able to restrain inappropriate behaviors. They learn to enjoy the sociability of conversation. They develop the habit of finding information in books, magazines, and on the Internet. Their ability to form concepts increases. As children feel more competent in their own ability to navigate ideas, they become less dependent on "superheroes" and their talk about superheroes and TV diminishes. As they acquire more skills and become involved in mind-absorbing problems, children become less interested in the mindlessness of TV. They talk more about the whys and wherefores of the world, and ask increasingly meaningful questions.

The Conversation Tool Kit costs nothing and requires no materials or equipment. You may already use many of the techniques; if not, they are easy to learn. Topics of conversation can be aligned to curriculum and assessment. Books, which are important to support conversation, are available from libraries, and high-quality magazines can be obtained free. The Internet is a source of abundant information and provides teachers with opportunities to help children learn search skills and to identify responsible sources of information.

Perhaps the most important benefit of conversation is the increased likelihood of children's school readiness in the all-important areas of early language and literacy because they have learned how to focus, to listen, to find relationships among divergent ideas, and to remember, talk, and imagine.

Questions to Consider

1. What are two or three topics of interest to specific children in your class that might appeal to all the children at a full-class meeting?
2. What sentences could you use to attract children's attention and alert the brain to attend?
3. How do you handle children who disrupt conversations?
4. What could you do to the environment to increase its support for conversations?

CHAPTER 7

Intentional Teaching

Jeremiah, blow the fire,
Puff, puff, puff!
First you blow it gently,
Then you blow it tough.

—Mother Goose

IT IS THE INTENTION to do something that makes things happen. The word *intention* is sweeping early education. It refers to *how* a teacher teaches. Yet, outside Reggio Emilia, I seldom see teachers who act with intention.

Reggio educators have created a tapestry-like alignment of their beliefs, practices, and roles. Weaving together these elements has created a platform for intentional teaching. The alignment of why teachers teach, what they teach, and how they teach represents a new structure for early education, a paradigm shift. We see the shift in how parent involvement is integrated (Chapter 3), how Open Flow works (Chapter 4), how the environment is prepared (Chapter 5), and the use of Meaning-full Conversation (Chapter 6), as well as the nature of intentional teaching and other topics covered later in this book.

In this chapter, I explore what the words *intentional teacher* mean, examine techniques of intentional teaching, and explain intention in terms of the multifaceted roles that Reggio teachers play.

WHAT IS INTENTION?

Intention means acting with authority. Authority is the midpoint on a continuum that at one end is permissive and at the other authoritarian. Permissiveness gives children a degree of control they are unable to handle; authoritarianism imposes an adult's will on children arbitrarily ("Do it because I say so."). Authority, on the other hand, is based on listening and communicates respect (Baumrind, 1967).

Recognizing Intention

Teachers can communicate intention both verbally and nonverbally and do so when they speak with authority, engage children's eyes, incline their body toward children, and watch children closely. Teachers' intention:

- communicates what they aim to do;
- conveys their determination;

- sets limits;
- marks when something begins;
- has fixedness of purpose;
- suggests that there is a goal;
- shows resolution to adhere to the goal until the end;
- casts aside doubt or hesitation;
- demonstrates resolve.

The word *intention* describes teachers' *presence*, not *what* but *how* they do something. Intention refers to bearing, demeanor, and manner. Intentional teachers make us aware of their presence by their concentrated facial expression, determined carriage, decisive tone of voice. Intentional teachers attract students and influence their behavior by the authority they convey.

When teachers are intentional, children hear far more than words: They read teachers' body language, tone of voice, and attitude. They know if teachers mean what they say or if they can be played or disobeyed. Intentional teachers have a purpose, are prepared, and communicate certainty to children. They *expect* that children will cooperate.

> **Key Point:**
> Teachers' intention determines what children's response will be.

Intention and Emotions

Intention reflects teachers' affect. How do they feel about what they are proposing? Do they have the resoluteness to pursue their proposal? Are they positive? Serious? Committed?

From birth, and before children acquire language, they read parents' and caregivers' affect, their nonverbal cues. Do parents have the energy to interact with the infant, the desire to sing, the disposition to play, the inclination to read to the baby? To fetch the crawler? To chase the runner? As Stanley Greenspan explains:

> The child's moods respond to seeing the gleam in a parent's eye or the nodding approval for something well done. She's learning what respect feels like—as well as what humiliation feels like when she's done something she shouldn't. All these patterns are learned in the second year of life and before language comes in to a significant degree. (Greenspan & Shanker, 2004, p. 61)

Infants become experts at reading adults' intention. As words are the coin of the adult's world, emotions are the coin of the infant's. Adults use words to try to mask emotions. But adults cannot hide their emotions from children because as infants

Figure 7.1. Examples of words that show whether teachers' requests to children are intentional or not.

INTENTIONAL		NONINTENTIONAL
Definitive		Vague
"Let us . . ."	OR	"Will you . . ."
"Put it away now, please."		"Do you want to stop?"
"Are you going to use blocks or puzzles?"		"What would you like to do?"

children learned to read adults' emotions. It is no wonder, with two different languages being spoken–words and emotions–that contests of will occur between young children and adults.

> **Key Point:**
> Recognizing the emotional factor in one's behavior is essential to being an intentional teacher.

Communicating Intentionally with Children

Intention is a way for teachers to speak the child's language. Cathy, who teaches toddlers under age 3, is a highly intentional teacher. She pays attention to children's demeanor–their tone, facial expressions, and body language–as clues to what their words and behavior mean.

Steven grabbed the spoon Denise was using in the housekeeping corner and ran off with it to the blocks. Denise bawled! Cathy quickly assessed the situation, saw that Denise wasn't hurt, observed that Steven had the spoon cantilevered between two blocks. Cathy observed that Denise calmed herself enough to run to the block corner, presumably to take back the spoon, but became fascinated by Steven's construction, which he was trying to use as a catapult. Denise settled in to watch, mesmerized along with several other children.

> **Key Point:**
> Intention requires that an adult be conscious of both the affective (emotional) and cognitive consequences of responding to children.

Had Cathy intervened immediately, she might have nurtured Denise's hurt feelings. Denise would have learned that bawling is effective in grabbing adults' attention. Cathy's intentional observation gave Denise time to calm herself–an important step toward self-regulation–and to see how Steven built what became the classroom's favorite device.

Intentional teachers use their cognitive ability to stifle the emotional impulse to react immediately. They pause and observe before intervening and carefully determine whether or when to intervene. Children's tears do not automatically cause a teacher to step into a situation.

INTENTION IN REGGIO TEACHERS

Reggio teachers' role is complex and marked by intention. The roles are:

- designer of the classroom environment;
- researcher, who listens, observes, records, and hypothesizes;
- orchestrator;
- collaborator;
- documenter;
- mediator.

The rest of this chapter explores the intention in each role.

Designer

In Chapter 5, I showed one aspect of teacher as designer–determining a classroom's aesthetics. Here, I use the word *design* very broadly to refer to all aspects of a teacher's actions, for example:

- how time and space are used;
- whether a teacher talks or listens;
- the kinds of lessons teachers design;
- the design of teacher/aide role sharing.

Each aspect is influenced by the teacher/designer's intention. A classroom's tone is the sum of all a teacher's choices.

Scheduling Time or Detailing Space

Time and space are the crossroads of experience. Everything we do occurs at a specific space and in a precise time interval.

Consider Time. It takes time to document—to observe children's actions, listen, record pivotal comments, photograph key moments, interact, collaborate, and select key vignettes from documentation to put on panels. A teacher cannot do all this and also adhere to a schedule of preplanned, predetermined activity!

> **Key Point:**
> Teachers whose intention is to "get through" a day or accomplish preset plans will not have enough time also to orchestrate experiences with as-yet-undetermined outcomes.

Notice the thickness of textbooks and Teacher's Guides. The time required to present the material leaves little, if any, time to have conversations, explore materials, or undertake projects that sprawl over days or weeks. Preplanned lessons leave little time for listening. As we read in Chapter 3, teachers with their own answer in mind cannot hear children's ideas. When intentions conflict—use the textbook versus base activities on children's interests—teachers must choose.

Being an intentional teacher/designer requires making choices that intentionally allocate the time to plan, to practice intentionality, to gather evidence of children's competence, and to stifle the impulse to "do for" children in order to give them time to become independent.

Consider Space. If you are engaged in lessons with a group of four children, what will the rest do? One of the greatest stumbling blocks to working with small groups or providing individualized instruction to a single child is teachers' fear that the rest of the children will climb the walls. They will if the space is not designed with intention.

If children can engage in vigorous movement (remember the tumbling mats and ropes in Chapter 2?); if every area is richly detailed with challenging materials; if children are allowed to observe other children, listen to a CD of their choice, snack with a friend, play all morning with blocks or LEGO; if children can draw to their heart's content (what *they* want to draw), they will not be bored. Having such options available makes the environment the curriculum. And if, in small groups, teachers regularly engage children in talking about rights and responsibilities in using the environment, children will learn to maintain the order by themselves.

> **Key Point:**
> Teacher/designers *intend* that the environment will be the curriculum.

Talking or Listening

To become literate means to speak, write, and read with increasing fluency (see Chapter 6). As we learned to hold conversations at the MELC, we redesigned our

Figure 7.2. Typical flow of teacher/child exchanges contrasted with exchanges that typify reciprocal conversation.

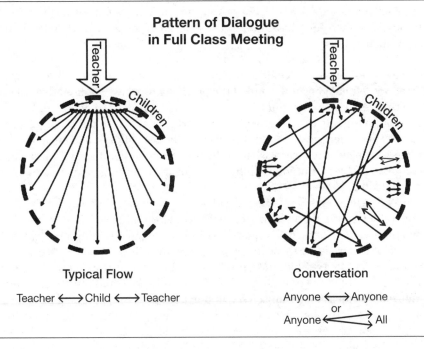

role, changing from providing information to listening to children. For example, in whole-group meetings in typical classrooms, teachers note who is in school, "do" the calendar, have show-and-tell, sing, do finger play, or use a flannel board. Talk between teachers and children tends to be formulaic: Teacher asks, child responds, teacher rephrases what the child said, and moves on to another child. The pattern of talk is mainly teacher/child/teacher.

In contrast, we intentionally designed conversations so that:

- anyone, not just a teacher, could initiate an interchange;
- conversations would stay focused on the chosen topic;
- teachers would listen to children's ideas, not convey information.

"Designing" how we wanted conversation to flow changed our behavior. We became orchestrators of conversation—encouraging children to maintain focus on the speaker, to listen to each other, and not to disrupt the flow of the conversation. To do this, we intentionally listened far more than we talked.

Routines like "calendar" fell away as focused conversations grew in length and complexity. The children's increasing ability to stay focused on a topic carried over to conversations among small groups with a teacher or among peers so that, in time, the children's interchanges with one another lasted for 20 to 30 minutes. Interchanges also became increasingly conversational, a sign of self-regulation, respect for others, and increased language capacity (see Chapter 6).

> **Key Point:** Teachers can design their role to become listeners, not speakers, if they focus conscious intention on doing so.

Designing Lessons or Designing a Process

Our intention at the MELC was to use children's interests as the basis both for project work and for what children chose to do on their own while teachers worked with small groups.

To realize this intention, we had to change how we "designed" lessons. Full-class meetings, for example, could not follow a list of lessons, but had to follow a list of what was left hanging at the end of the prior day or week. We used that list to encourage children who had not finished an activity or a project to continue. We used notes of their comments to remind children of what they had been doing or to renew or stretch their interests. We used records of activities children had engaged in to determine who needed to learn what skills. So, for example, if scissors were being used competently by all but four children, we engaged those four in an activity requiring scissor skills.

We became highly intentional in learning how to observe and listen to children, how to determine the meaning of their behavior and remarks, and how to connect our observations and their remarks with the design of small-group lessons and the choice of materials for those lessons. For example, if we observed that the same four boys always played Spider-Man, we would bring them together as a group to ask what they wanted to know about Spider-Man, how we could find out, and then would follow up on ideas the group agreed to pursue. Our lesson planning became a process in which we hypothesized what kinds of experiences might encourage children to pursue their interests, an approach to lesson "design" that is entirely different from a Teacher's Guide.

We also became intentional in listening to parents' remarks. For example, after our oldest six children "graduated," parents told us that 1st-grade teachers expected children to know their letters. Consequently, we significantly increased our work with letters. Specifically,

- We encouraged children to seek and photograph objects shaped like letters.
- We asked parents to cut individual letters from printed matter and, as letters that parents found poured into school, we added them to the message-making area—each letter of the alphabet in its own jar—for children to use in their messages.
- We increased use of the Montessori sound game, sandpaper letters, and movable alphabet.
- We involved children in writing to one another, to parents, or to others whose involvement with the school occasioned a letter. One recipient of letters, written by many children and discussed by the whole class, was the turtle the children had released from its classroom home to the pond at the Arboretum.
- When children spontaneously used computer, typewriter, or pen to write letters, names, or phrases, we used their writing as the focus of a panel on writing.
- In full-class or small-group conversations, we read (or, if they could, had children read) what they had written.
- We added pencils and fine-tipped color and black markers to areas throughout the school and encouraged children to use markers—to draw,

Figure 7.3. At the edge of the pond at the Arboretum, the MELC children are leaving a large collection of messages they have written and pictures they have drawn for their turtle.

write words, send messages—as part of whatever work they were doing. Around age 4, children tend to make writing-like marks. The ready availability of pens and pencils that make attractive marks fostered the tendency.

In short, because we believed parents' concerns were legitimate, we focused intentionally on designing many ways to engage small groups of children in experiences that expanded their interests and directly or indirectly built literacy.

> **Key Point:** Because our intention was to be responsive to children's tendencies and parents' concerns, our planning process changed.

Redesigning Teacher/Aide Roles

Redesigning the aide's role involves issues about salaries, credentials, and feelings of professionalism. At the MELC, we redesigned the role because, in order to help the children become self-regulated, it was necessary to have each teacher play a different role—one to teach, the other to manage (see Chapters 2 and 4). The teacher's responsibility was to give small-group lessons; the aide's role was to oversee everyone not involved in a lesson with the teacher.

Following Reggio practices, we became aware that two people can listen better than one. At first, we asked our aide to take notes of children's activities while the teacher was engaged in small-group work so teachers would know what children outside the small group had done. The aide welcomed the responsibility and took excellent notes. Gradually, we redesigned the relationship to be collaborative, for teachers and aide to be co-equals, and after a year we changed the aide's title to teacher. Thus, our practice morphed from separate roles to any adult playing either role.

Fostering Children's Independence. I have worked with aides and teachers who resist redesigning the aide's role. Some aides are unable to foster children's independence and cannot resist putting on children's coats for them, cleaning up instead of encouraging or helping children do so themselves, writing children's names instead of finding ways for children to do so, pouring their juice, and the like. This infantilizes children. Even if aides' roles are not redesigned, teacher and aide must support the same goals. An intentional teacher makes those goals explicit and instructs an aide in how to achieve them.

Playing Roles Flexibly. If the intention is to have an Open Flow classroom, adult roles must be flexible during the period when children are becoming self-regulated. Without self-regulation, children cannot work independently so the aide must oversee work time. But once children are self-regulated, the aide can also give lessons, although the aide's first responsibility remains keeping an eye out for children who require guidance to settle into concentrated work. Being flexible means knowing when to play which role.

Enabling children to act flexibly is an important goal of teaching. Flexibility requires that children make conscious choices and that they engage both emotional and cognitive thought processes in whatever they do. This, in turn, requires that teachers intentionally model flexibility. For example, when Nan was 3, she strongly resisted wearing a sweater or coat on chilly days. Following her teacher's example, when Nan was 4 her teacher heard her say, "I don't like my coat but I know I must wear it to go out." Or, Robbie at age 3 was very resistant to being shown how to do anything. A year later, his teacher saw her intention reflected as Robbie approached Steven, a new 3-year-old, and said, "Now, Steven, I know you want to do this yourself, but if you just watch, you'll see how it goes. Then you can do it yourself."

Helping children become flexible is the part of the teacher/designer's role. Years later, Jennifer would say that one of the most important things the teachers learned was that organization and flexibility are not incompatible, that in fact, organization is the foundation for flexibility. Only when your environment is thoughtfully built can you use it as a solid platform on which to perform spontaneously—for therein lies the art of teaching—the ability to perform and at the same time observe yourself critically so that the next performance will improve.

> **Key Point:**
> Intentional design is a lens through which to examine every aspect of teaching practice.

Researcher

The role of teacher as researcher is multifaceted; it requires listening, recording, and hypothesizing. Next I describe the teacher/researcher role with examples from the MELC.

Listening and Recording

Sonya is at a table with four children, pencil in her hand, notebook close by, recorder on the table. Wendy is in the library conversing with five children, clipboard in her hand. Jennifer and MELC teachers Genet Astatke and Deborah Barley are in different areas, also taking notes. After school, the five teachers huddle together, listening as each reads her notes. They are bent on grasping what children mean by the remarks each teacher diligently recorded. When the teachers determine that the children are interested in their heights, they make these two hypotheses. Children can

- recognize that their heights differ from one another;
- determine the relationship between height and measurement.

The teachers decide that Sonya and Wendy should hold conversations with the children most interested in height and test these hypotheses: Will children recognize that their heights differ? Will they determine how to measure heights? Beyond these questions, the teachers do not script what they will do.

> **Key Point:**
> Teachers who intend to be researchers listen, record, and hypothesize.

Wendy Listens. Wendy began by gathering Michael, Courtney, Garry, and Rochi and reminding them: "Two days ago, Courtney said, 'I'm taller then Michael.'" Then, with the intent of reigniting their interest in height and comparison, Wendy said: "Choose someone from the group and tell me what is the difference between the two of you."

MICHAEL, *to Rochi*: Her teeth are missing.
COURTNEY, *to all*: Hey, Michael, she got more hair than you.
GARRY: Rochi is a girl, and Michael is a boy.
ROCHI, *to Garry*: And you got big hands.
WENDY, *wondering if the hypothesis was wrong or if the children will return to their interest in height*: Something else is different.
MICHAEL: I don't know.
COURTNEY: Garry doesn't have earrings on his ears, and he has boy's tennis shoes on and I don't.
WENDY, *probing*: Is there something else?
COURTNEY: He's a boy, and I'm a girl.
WENDY, *suggesting*: There is something else.
COURTNEY: I am 5, and he is 5.

Through a page of single-spaced remarks, the conversation rambles as children talk about age, hair length, skin color, eye color, drawings of themselves, details of their clothing.

COURTNEY: I can reach the paper towels in the back bathroom now. Diara, Mark, and Carmen still can't.
WENDY, *recognizing an opening*: Why can't they reach the paper towel rack?
COURTNEY: 'Cause they are still little.

The conversation turns to taller, age, being bigger than last year, birthdays. A page and a half of conversation follows, with children talking about what they can do when they are bigger.

GARRY: Hey, Michael, I bet you I am taller than Bud.

The conversation stays on the topic of finding out who is taller. The children decide they can do so by standing beside each other. They continue to focus on the relation between age and height:

GARRY: Look, Rochi. I am taller than you.
ROCHI: So! 'Cause you are older than me.
WENDY, *intending to introduce a new idea*: There is another way we can find out about height and something we can use.

Finally, the conversation moves from height to measurement.

GARRY: Jennifer got something.
MICHAEL: The big ruler.

And the group goes to the Studio to find the yardstick.

Sonya listens. Sonya began her conversation with five children by asking each: "How old are you?" Then she reminded the group that Stephon (age 6) is taller than Kriston (age 4), and with the intention of focusing on height, asked the five: "How can we tell that Stephon is 6 and Kriston is 4?"

The children mentioned birthdays, where they lived, physical features, size of clothes, color of hair and eyes, and honed in on clothing sizes, as Stephon said: "He might be a larger medium, and she might be a smaller medium, and I'm a large."

After a long conversation (five and a half pages of notes), the children came up with the idea of standing next to each other to see who is tallest and lined themselves up in that order. Sonya, with the intent of inducing them to think about measurement, asked: "How can we tell exactly how tall we are?" Kaila, right on spot, responded: "Use a measurement."

After about the same amount of conversation as Wendy's group, Kaila and Stephon together say: "Jennifer! We can go to the Studio."

Hypothesizing

Hypotheses are a way that teacher/researchers plan what to do and carry out the plan. In the 2 groups the children's remarks about height began with different questions, rambled, and touched on many topics. But because the teachers had made hypotheses and intended to test them, they had a focus. After a 30- to 40-minute conversation, both groups worked their way to the same place—using a yardstick in the Studio to determine their height.

Listening with intention raises teachers' consciousness of what children say. And listening as a researcher

> **Key Point:**
> With the teacher's intent to have a conversation about height and measurement, children connected the ideas of their different heights and a tool to measure the differences.
>
> *Note:* At this age, most children are unable to use yardsticks, rulers, or other standard measures. Although children this young rarely know how to use measurement devices, if rulers and the like are used in their homes or school, children are aware of the devices' existence, know the context in which they are used, and can identify situations in which to use these tools.

takes teachers' focus off what they themselves have in mind, prevents them from seeking one right answer, and precludes them from doing most of the talking. Hypothesizing keeps teachers from imposing predetermined outcomes and instead has teachers focus on what children do and say by taking notes. From this information in their notes, teachers can address gaps in children's knowledge.

> **Key Point:**
> Hypothesizing, as researchers do, clarifies teachers' intention.

Orchestrator

As orchestrators, teachers manage the flow of the day, determine which children are most likely to benefit from a project, ensure that projects progress, seize opportunities to involve parents, and in other ways move activities along. Sergio Spaggiari (2000), director of the Reggio Emilia Schools, said:

> The most important ability of a teacher is knowing how to capture those vital and significant events, as they appear, around which the teacher's intervention should be organized; . . . to structure the educational experience primarily *as* it evolves, not just beforehand. (p. 8; emphasis in original)

Structuring experience "*as* it evolves" is the essence of the Reggio Approach and therefore is a prime example of intention. Remember the tumbling children, the boys seemingly at loose ends, and the vigorous toddler play (Chapter 2)? All showed teachers' intent to help children develop self-regulation.

Reggio teachers' work as orchestrators is not often visible because:

- We are not in their classrooms for the extended periods over which activity is orchestrated.
- Few of us speak Italian.
- We miss subtleties—the interactions of children with one another, the substance of conversations among teachers and children that emphasizes what has happened and what could happen next.
- We overlook understated interactions—hands demonstrating a tool, fingers pinching to glue two objects, mere glances.
- We translate what we see through an American lens.

From limited observations, we cannot grasp the structure. Nor are we present to observe the "grooming" of the environment. Have you visited a magnificent garden, marveled at meticulous beds, manicured edges, sculpted hedges? Buchart Gardens (Victoria, British Columbia) and the Japanese Garden (Portland, Oregon) make visitors gasp. But in visitors' few hours, they see neither the constant work that produces the effect nor what came before or will follow. So it is with visiting Reggio classes: Teachers' intentional orchestration is essentially invisible.

Orchestrators *dis*pose more than they *com*pose. The word *dispose* means placing people and things "in relative positions for mutual cooperation or support on an extended scale" (Fernald, 1947, p. 66). So, with intention, the orchestrator disposes the children to

- reconnect with the group they worked with yesterday;
- work with an assortment of new materials on the light table or a new board game;
- paint together with a friend on the easel that today stands in the courtyard;
- join the teacher to begin a new project.

> **Key Point:**
> Orchestrators *intend* to launch experiences, converse about them, reenact or expand them, make some *thing*, transform what has been made into another medium.

Just as symphony conductors are aware of everything, teacher/orchestrators are aware of the potential direction children's actions might take, the flow of the day, how long what looks like disarray can continue. They are astutely aware of which of their multifaceted roles they are playing.

Collaborator and Documenter

Collaborators and documenters observe activities as they take part in them. They are simultaneously *in* the situation and listening to it. Three words are often confused: *interference, interruption,* and *intervention.* The first two have negative impacts—imposing a teacher's will, disrupting children's activity, disturbing their concentration. Intervention is neutral. It merely means to interact. Observing and listening, which rarely precede interference and interruption, are an essential part of intervention. Intentional teachers monitor their own actions to eliminate interference and interruption, and instead work to intervene.

Collaborators. Teacher/collaborators intervene as a member of a small group of children, as they

> **Key Point:**
> Knowing how powerful intervention is, collaborators intervene delicately; they intentionally avoid overriding children's initiative.

- take part in the experience;
- negotiate first steps and next steps;
- lend expertise and know-how;
- facilitate children's intentions.

Collaborators sit among the children—who are constructing the dinosaur, lining up to compare their heights, shaping the clay model of a Ferris wheel—and intentionally bring an adult's experience to problems.

Documenters. Teacher/documenters capture an experience in writing or image, preserve, and use records of the children's experiences. Along with their colleagues, documenters

> **Key Point:**
> Documenters' intentional recording makes it possible to reflect on past experiences, to extract meaning, and to project the meaning onto future experiences.

- select pivotal records for children and teachers to reflect on;
- make panels as a vehicle for reflection;
- collaborate in interpreting panels with peers, children, parents, or visitors.

Mediator

The word *mediator* is the crux of psychologist Reuven Feuerstein's theory (2006) of human development that says mediators

- have a clear intention;
- convey specific meaning;
- generalize to related experiences (transcend).

Intention drives mediation: I *intend* to believe in children's competence. I *intend* to listen and observe before I intervene. I *intend* to convey meaning. I *intend* that you succeed.

I watched as Giovanni Piazza, *atelierista* at La Villetta, a Reggio school, observed three boys making a complex construction. The boys were struggling to cut the wire and after numerous attempts were unable to do so. Giovanni's intentions were (1) for the boys to succeed in making their construction, (2) to help them master a skill needed for the construction, and (3) to demonstrate a skill that would be useful in the future. Silently, Giovanni took the cutter, held it where the boys easily could see the angle, made the cut, and returned the tool to them. It took a few seconds, not a word was exchanged, but the boys' attention was riveted on Giovanni's movements and they made their next cuts easily. Later the boys remembered how to use the tool.

Mediators have a meaning in mind that they intend to convey in words, actions, facial expression, tone of voice, or any of the other numerous ways humans communicate.

> **Key Point:** When teachers consciously combine the roles of designer, researcher, orchestrator, collaborator, documenter, and mediator, they become intentional teachers.

CONCLUSION: THE TEACHER'S ROLES IN ACTION

The orchestrator stages a firsthand experience: We'll visit the Arboretum. The mediator sees a meaning: Fall colors are at their height. The designer knows the classroom has dozens of materials and tools with which to expand children's use of color.

At the Arboretum, the researcher observes the children, listening to what they say. Back at school, the teachers collaborate, mining what the documenter captured as the children ran, played, and talked. As researchers, their intention is to determine what most interested the children. As mediators, their intention is to encourage the children to build relationships between this experience, other things they have done, and what they could do.

The orchestrator initiates a conversation with the full class. The collaborator interacts with the children to determine the level of their interest in what the researcher selected. The mediator encourages children to pursue a particular meaning.

The researchers heard from children's conversation that they were curious about the path leaves take when they fall. They hypothesized: The children will express their ideas about falling leaves by representing leaves as they fall and will do so in several different ways. The orchestrator oversaw the flow of the experiences; the collaborator worked alongside as children represented falling leaves in various ways; the designer ensured that materials were at hand.

It sounds as if there are six teachers present. In fact, each role is a different aspect of intentional teaching and intentional teachers learn all the roles. What makes Reggio teachers unusual is how masterfully they play all these roles at once, all the while conscious of which role to emphasize at any given moment.

Questions to Consider

1. Do you see any of the teachers' roles in the following Reggio vignette?

   A small group of children are engaged in outdoor shadow play. As they try to cover their shadows, they have the following conversation:

   - "We could try to cover the shadow with a gigantic rock."
   - "With lots of little stones, lots and lots. . . ."
   - "Why don't we try with a sheet? Let's go and get one!"
   - "It won't cover up! Mine's here and so is Veronica's!"
   - "Maybe if we tape it. . . ." (Sturloni & Vecchi, 2000, pp. 34–35)

2. In the above vignette, can you find the designer, researcher, orchestrator, and documenter? The answer is on p. 200 at the end of the Glossary.

CHAPTER 8

Materials and Human Development

If all the world were apple pie and all the sea were ink . . .

—Mother Goose

MATERIALS SURROUND US; always have, always will. Materials spurred the growth of culture. They make up the substance of our body, food, clothes, shelter, possessions. Materials motivate children from birth to explore and to build relationships among everyone and everything.

The 1-year-old who strokes mother's fur collar and says, "Kitty!" and the 2-year-old who makes digging motions with a block are using materials to make relationships. Reggio educators use the word *materials* broadly, including symbols, spoken and written language, and metaphors. When Reggio educators say that children *speak* "100 languages," they are referring to the numerous relationships children make with their world and the role that materials play in those relationships.

When parents ask why children are messing around with paint or glue instead of working on ABCs or 123s, the answer is: Using materials builds young brains in ways that enable children to be better thinkers:

- to understand the ideas expressed in ABCs;
- to see the relationships among numbers;
- to develop the abilities to recognize letters and write words;
- to understand meaning;
- to form thoughts and act on them.

In this chapter, I explain the "language" of materials, the role of materials in brain development, and how to use materials to establish basic cognitive functions. The most important idea is: Materials are a primary means through which perceptual systems (seeing, hearing, touching, tasting, smelling), motor systems (grasping, walking, wielding tools), language systems (listening, speaking, writing, reading), and neural networks in the brain form connections. As they make and shape things with materials, children develop increasingly higher-level thinking skills.

THE "LANGUAGES" OF MATERIALS

Materials define epochs and cultures–the Stone Age, the Bronze Age, the Iron Age, the Industrial Age. The word *material* means a critical factor, determining, anything composed of matter (Fernald, 1947, pp. 249–250). We speak of "material difference" to distinguish two things we do not want to confuse. Judges require "material evidence," meaning some thing or person that is a crucial factor in the outcome of a case. Reggio educators have evolved a robust philosophy around the idea that every material has its own "language."

"Reading" a Culture's Materials

Throughout history, materials have shaped entire epochs. The earliest age—Stone—lasted two or more million years. We know Stone Age people by the stone chips, adzes, chisels, and other tools they used to shape materials. Changes in how materials became tools and in how tools shaped materials mark the rise and fall of prehistoric human groups. In fact, the groups we know about are those that left material traces.

The renowned neurologist/author Oliver Sacks (2002) describes his visit to the pre-Columbian cultural museum in Oaxaca, Mexico:

> There are great funerary urns . . . [a]nd exquisite jewelry and ornaments made of metal—gold, silver, copper, and alloys of these—and of jade, turquoise, alabaster, quartz, opal, obsidian, *azabache* (whatever this was), and amber. Gold was not valued by the pre-Columbians as such, but only for the ways in which it could be used to make objects of beauty. The Spanish [conquerors] found this unintelligible, and in their greed melted down thousands, perhaps millions, of gold artifacts, in order to fill their coffers with the metal. . . .
>
> In another case we find small mirrors made of pyrite and magnetite. How is it that while these Mesoamerican cultures appreciated magnetite for its luster and beauty, they did not discover the fact that it was magnetic, and that, if floated in water, it might act as a compass? Nor the fact that, if smelted with charcoal, it would yield metallic iron?
>
> How strange that these brilliant and complex cultures, so sophisticated in mathematics and astronomy, in engineering and architecture, so rich in art and culture, so profound in their cosmological understanding and ritual—were still in a pre-wheel, pre-compass, pre-alphabet, pre-iron age . . .
>
> But there is no linearity in . . . evaluat[ing] a society, a culture. We can only ask whether there were the relationships and activities, the practices and skills, the beliefs and goals, the ideas and dreams, that make for a fully human life. (pp. 150–151)

> **Key Point:**
> Materials are so intimately bound to human existence that the very meaning of the word *material* is: important; the essence of; so much a part of an item that it cannot be separated in the mind or in actuality.

If our society were excavated millennia hence, what materials would be left? How would they be interpreted? What would they tell future archaeologists about our ideas and dreams?

Learning the "Languages" of Materials

To Reggio educators, "100 languages" means the multitude of ways—far more than 100—in which children can learn to express themselves. Every "language" requires children to increase their skill in using specialized tools to shape, form, or fashion particular materials.

In Reggio practices, materials have two lives: The first is an exploration of the properties of a material. The second is learning to use the material for some purpose beyond exploring its properties.

Words are defined by meanings; materials are defined by their attributes, functions, and potentialities, properties that determine what you can do with a material. You would not use a tapered glass sliver as a toothpick, send a letter on a plank of wood, or carry water in tissue paper. Before age 4, most children know such things. By exploring materials with a thoughtful adult, children develop firsthand knowledge of materials' characteristics, how they behave, and what they can be used for—in other words, the materials' "languages."

When the MELC children wanted to represent the path of a falling leaf, they decided to use wire and thread it with strips of fabric. They knew which wire, from various rolls in the school, would be pliable enough to bend and had holes large enough to thread fabric in and out, yet was firm enough to retain its shape. They chose chicken wire, not hardware cloth.

Relationships between materials' properties and uses are not always obvious. Some take us into the higher realms of biology, chemistry, and physics. For example, mounting evidence suggests that food additives, coloring, and pesticides might increase the likelihood of cancer and autism and that synthetic hormones might alter normal development of the reproductive system. Arguments about the evidence rage between those who promote healthful eating and food-industry representatives. Separating fear from fact will require years of research that will push our understanding of nutrition, the science where biology, chemistry, and physics intersect. At the basis of our understanding will be knowledge of how materials that enter or make up our bodies behave at the molecular level.

> **Key Point:** Knowing how to use materials gives children control of their world. In the words of psychologist David Perkins (1995), they learn to "know their way around" (p. 262).

When we nurture young children's desire to use materials, we acknowledge that understanding materials is basic to thinking. Children who master materials' properties and become passionate about materials offer hope that, as adults, they will penetrate complex relationships that govern the universe and thus be better stewards of our own fragile planet.

Introducing Children to Materials

Young children have innate and powerful drives to explore materials. This gives teachers opportunities to

- introduce a greater *variety* of materials than are typically used; variety develops different pathways in the brain.
- encourage children to build *competence* in using materials with their hands alone or with specialized tools; building competence stokes children's appreciation of themselves and others.
- share with children the amazing *stories* of the invention or discovery of any material they use; because stories describe what others have done, they stretch children's imagination about what they themselves might do.

Take Paper . . . Paper is so widely used in our culture that we overlook its potential as a means of developing the brain's eye/hand connection. Consider the different shapes your hand can form or actions it must take to fold, crush, crease, smooth, tear, soak, bend, pleat, curl, shred, strip, mold, stack, roll, or burn up paper. Then, consider a few of the innumerable kinds of paper: parchment, copier, cardstock, gift wrap, brown bag, lightweight cardboard, tissue, foil, newsprint, chrome coat, waxed, construction, woven, waterproof, laid, linen, rag.

Now play this game: Shape your hand to apply each action, one at a time, to a piece of foil: fold, crush, crease, smooth, etc. Then apply each action to a piece of cardstock, then to a piece of tissue paper, and so on. Describe your hands' actions. As you do this, think about:

- what your eyes are doing;
- how your hands are behaving;
- the analyses your brain is making in planning what to do first, next, and after;
- what each result is;
- how each outcome makes you feel.

Once you have done this yourself or with your colleagues, do it with children. There are enough papers and actions to spread experiences over a year or more.

Recall Chapter 6, how anything you do with children begins with a conversation. Begin a conversation about one particular kind of paper and:

- provide the precise name of the paper you are introducing;
- elicit what the children know about it;
- ask them *how* they know it, what experiences they have had with it;
- encourage them to describe how the paper behaves and why;
- challenge them to predict what might happen if . . .

Let the children's responses germinate for a day or more, then repeat the conversation, but this time encourage the children to perform one of the actions. Demonstrate if necessary and discuss what happens. Read back to the children what they thought might happen. Compare what they predicted to what actually happened. Do they want to make new predictions and do it all over again? If you multiply the kinds of actions, the kinds of papers, and the opportunities for conversations, there are hundreds. And you will have used only your hands, perhaps some water, perhaps fire (the teacher only, of course). You will not have brought scissors, glue, coloring, or markers to help you alter the paper. Through such activities, children learn the *language* of each material.

With Toddlers. Alexa taught toddlers. When she engaged small groups in learning the language of paper, she described reactions. For example, when she tore silver foil, she said it lacked tensile strength. When newsprint soaked up a puddle of water, she said it was absorbent. When cardstock did not crumple easily, she said it was resistant.

When a teacher aligns an experience with a precise word for what is happening, she "trains" the brain to observe, compare, and describe. These are three of many lower-level brain functions that provide the essential foundation for more complex thinking, such as making syllogisms, permutations, and transformations–higher-level thinking capacities that will only be facile if basic functions are sturdy.

Other Materials . . . It is easier to see potential in some materials rather than others: Ribbon, for example, comes in great variety–under one-quarter-inch wide or over 4 inches, pliable, wired, shreddable, stiff. It can be dotted, striped, shiny, luminous, gauzy, curly, satiny, made from natural or man-made material. How many actions can you list that alter ribbon?

It is harder, perhaps, to see the potential in markers until you consider the nib's material (felt or metal). Nibs differ in thickness, angle, degree of saturation, the kind and amount of ink they hold. Then, think of possible colors: The human eye sees 2 million colors.

I gave my grandson, age 7, a felt pen that made a metallic silver mark. It became a treasured possession and stimulated him to make the drawing in Figure 8.1. (The beauty does not show in black and white.) Nibs and colors combine in almost endless ways.

> **Key Point:** Discovering materials in the early years sparks interests that can last a lifetime.

Slowing Down

Allow time to learn the language of one material before combining it with other materials or with tools. The reason is not some authoritative hierarchy of experience. Rather, it is the opportunities that a material, in and of itself, affords to children's development. Making eye, hand, and brain work together takes years; artists, musicians,

Figure 8.1. Special writing implements, such as the magic marker with silver ink used in this drawing, inspire children to draw with detail.

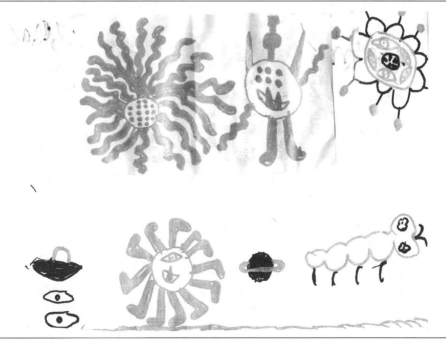

surgeons, and engineers hone the eye/hand/brain nexus throughout their lives. Using materials straight away for a predetermined end or to do a project lessens the likelihood that children will explore the inherent possibilities in any one material.

Children who have folded, crushed, smoothed, and performed many other actions the hand can make to change paper will never look at paper in the same way. Their brains will have developed neural networks–to shape the hand and handle objects–that can be used in other actions with other materials. Moreover, when they do use paper for purposes beyond exploration, they will be more likely to select paper that serves their purposes and will know why it is suitable.

Shallow experiences narrow the numbers and kinds of connections the brain can make. Learning different materials' languages opens up the world, deepens children's familiarity with it, makes them knowledgeable about what is common and curious about what is uncommon.

> **Key Point:**
> We rush children:
> "Here's the paper,
> here are the crayons,
> now draw!"

Knowing materials builds children's ability to focus with specificity rather than perceiving in broad and sweeping ways. Intently focused attention is essential to write, read, and organize any activity, whether simple or complex. By exploring materials, children learn to focus, enlarge their vocabulary, and develop concepts–all essential for later success–not only as readers and on test scores, but in life.

MATERIALS AND BRAIN DEVELOPMENT

Young children are drawn to materials like bees are drawn to honey. We literally create ourselves by using materials. Skilled hand use, focused attention, pride in accomplishment, and imagination all develop by using materials.

Materials and the Hand

Think about a 6-month-old's hand and how it learns to grasp by having some *thing* to grasp–or not to grasp:

> Baby sees and reaches for
> A beam of sunlight on the floor
> Tries to catch and tries to clasp
> But smiling it eludes his grasp.
> He's too young to understand
> You can't hold sunlight in your hand
> And while his busy fingers play
> The sunlight winks and slips away. (Ann Lewin-Benham, unpublished)

An infant's first tool is the hand itself. Infants initially watch their hand, accidentally catch something with it, and soon begin to grasp intentionally at anything within their reach. Humans are called "toolmakers" because early on we took advantage of the thumb's unique opposable structure and turned what we found–stick, rock, shell, bark–into something useful. When we engage young children in using a rich array of materials, we tap into our species' dim beginnings and the evolution of human/tool relationships.

Humans' progress using brain/hand/material to create increasingly complex cultures parallels the progress of an individual infant/toddler/child using materials to wire increasingly complex neuronal connections. Both in evolutionary terms and in each individual's growth, our development is inseparable from our use of hand/material/tool.

> **Key Point:**
> "It is in the child's earliest experiences in practical physics—watching, locating with both hand and eye, and then intercepting moving objects—that the nervous system builds its own unique library to the computational problems presented by coordinated movement" (Wilson, 1998, p. 103).

Materials and Feelings of Competence

At every age, the hand's links to brain development are underexploited in the classroom. Teachers of young children undervalue their competence, so they do things for them that the children could learn to do themselves. In a 4-year-olds' class, the teacher decided that four children would prepare food. She seated them around her as she carefully cored an apple, peeled it, and cut a segment for each child. She kept firm control of corer, peeler, and knife as eight eyes watched hungrily—not for a bite of apple, but for the experience of preparing the fruit. As she finished, the teacher handed each a plastic knife to cut the segment into bits. The experience was frustrating because the plastic barely cut the firm fruit.

Most children know when they are being infantilized—denied the opportunity to learn a skill because an adult does not think they are competent to handle the tool. Long before age 4, most children understand that some tools can be dangerous. Most children heed words of caution and are responsive to lessons in how to use tools properly. With a misplaced sense of safety, we deny children opportunities to develop skills during the period of life—birth to age 6 or 7—when they are receptive to being shown and eager to please, two traits that predispose them to handle potentially dangerous implements with great care. By age 3 or younger, children can be taught to use peelers, corers, and even metal knives that cut rather than plastic knives that mush.

Being able to do something builds a child's sense of self. All educational standards include some version of "takes pride in himself" or "takes pride in her work." Yet schools offer narrow opportunities to develop a sense of pride. Young children's pride develops into older children's self-confidence, so a lot is at stake when early experiences provide only limited ways to feel proud. At age 7, my grandson Shep switched schools in the middle of 2nd grade, leaving a school he had attended for 3 years. When I asked about his new school, he responded, "Nobody here knows me. In my old school everyone, even the bus driver, knew I made the best paper airplanes in the whole school."

> **Key Point:**
> The work of their hands gives young children a sense of pride and identity.

Materials That Challenge

As I observe classrooms for toddlers, I note whether there are challenging things to do with the hand. Are there small objects to be picked up, making thumb and index finger work together? Are there tweezers or other grippers to lift tiny objects? Are there liquids to spoon into increasingly small-necked containers? Are there eyedroppers? Are there scissors with sharp enough blades to cut? Wire cutters to slice clay? Gripping small objects, pouring into small-mouthed containers, spooning, and other challenging fine motor skills engage concentrated attention from the age of 12 months or so to about age 2 or 3. Later, even though a child may pour or spoon, the tasks will not be compelling. For children over 3, are there wire strippers to peel coatings off wire? Real food preparation implements? Needles to thread and cloth to sew?

Children who have been in school as infants and toddlers lose interest in typical sand/water toys by age 3 or 4 (see Chapter 4). These toys are too imprecise to challenge children to improve the hand/brain connection. In building hand/brain connections, we do not do enough early enough. "So what?" you ask? It is the hand/brain connection that enables children to perform the physical act of writing, a task demanded of kindergartners as a measure of school readiness.

Beyond school readiness, hands that are competent enable people to engage in meaningful activity throughout life. We measure milestones in infant development as much by what the hand does—get into the mouth, hold a bottle, pick up a Cheerio—as by language, crawling, and walking. Facility, or lack thereof, with one's hands can determine a life's course. Auto mechanic, jeweler, pianist, puppeteer, ball player, dentist, surgeon, and scores of other professionals make a living because of *hand smarts*. Each of these occupations involves the hand's precise use of highly specialized tools or equipment, mastery of specialized techniques, and skill in manipulating challenging interactions between tool and material.

> **Key Point:**
> Using materials requires combined use of all the intelligences that Howard Gardner (1983) identifies.

"FRAMING" AND THE BRAIN'S ATTENTION SYSTEMS

Neuroscientists have identified several systems in the brain that they call the *attention system,* complexes of neuronal networks located in different areas of the brain that alert, focus, and sustain attention. Framing means alerting several of these brain systems to get ready for an experience.

Infants' Attention

For infants, everything is new and whatever they do builds brain networks. An adult covers his face with a piece of paper, draws it slowly over his face, reappears, and says, "Peek-a-boo!" The infant laughs uproariously and wants to play again . . . and again, and again. The adult tires first! Why?

Peek-a-boo offers high-level perceptual and cognitive challenges at the age when the skills required to meet those challenges are high on an infant's agenda, driven by innate structures in the brain. Playing peek-a-boo fulfills maturational imperatives present in the first year of life:

- learning what is part of what—Do voices, smiles, and eyes remain with the person even when the person disappears?
- determining what is constant—Do facial features stay in the same place?

In psychologists' words, infants are establishing an understanding of *object permanence.* In addition to the high-level challenge (for its age) of object permanence, infants enjoy the entire milieu of the game—the attention, repetition, and reciprocity with an adult. Greenspan says that as infants feel sensations, they "code" or store them with an emotion, and thus, "emotions organize intellectual abilities and indeed create the sense of self" (Greenspan & Shanker, 2004, p. 56).

Framing for the game of peek-a-boo is an unconscious adult reaction–adult and infant co-regulating their actions in seamless back-and-forth exchanges. The framing is evident in the adult's smooth movements that cannot be disaggregated–leaning toward the infant, giving total attention, engaging the infant's eyes. These complex actions alert infants, who match their intensity to the adults'. The game builds trust, pleasure in relationships, joy in discovery, sense of humor, and understanding of give and take.

> **Key Point:** Materials as simple as a single sheet of paper can be used to arrest infants' attention.

Toddlers' Attention

You have some elaborate tale in mind: "Johnny opened the door and saw a lion . . ." So you begin, "Johnny opened the door . . ." As you look at the toddler's face, he is enraptured. A 2-year-old has not learned that lions do not wait outside doors, so the statement "saw a lion" would not seem unreasonable. You realize you do not need the lion; the mere act of opening the door is excitement enough at age 2. Simply opening the door builds expectation. It frames the plot of the story.

When you gather the group (or approach a single child), when you make the offer (Now we will . . .), when you command attention (Heads up!), when you present a material (Look at this!), you are alerting the brain, literally pulling it from whatever it was doing to what you are about to do, and building expectation. In some classrooms, children are alerted and then asked to attend to a boring lesson.

> **Key Point:** Brains that are alerted and not engaged learn to ignore the alert.

Paying Attention

Research describes what happens in the brain and body when we are alerted: The vestibular system, located in the inner ear, is called into action. Its main function is to send signals to neural structures that control eye movements, and to muscles that keep us upright.

> [It] plays a vital role in maintaining head posture and balance, as well as producing compensatory eye movements in response to head activity in order to maintain a steady visual input. . . . [The system] has profound effects on head and body posture as well as on the control of eye movements. (Cartwright & Curthoys, 1996, p. 485)

In terms of brain/body response, framing an activity means, literally, to create a condition in which the head can maintain an upright position on the neck and torso and stay erect so that the eyes can focus. When teachers alert the brain by framing an experience, they stimulate children's curiosity. The process triggers a readiness to focus. Focus is the next stage in paying attention. As children focus, other clusters of neurons fire and other neuronal systems are active.

Each new material or each new use of a familiar material alerts the brain anew. When we frame how we offer the material, new connections form between neurons. When we use the material repeatedly, neurons wire together, and with repetition, children build new skills that are the basis for procedural memory (Kandel, 2006).

> **Key Point:**
> Using materials helps children learn to pay attention and stay focused.

Educators are fortunate that research from the 1990s on has provided images of what goes on in the brain and between the brain and other parts of the body. The research helps us understand why activities that require coordinated hand actions have positive impacts on brain functioning.

TRIGGERING VISUALIZATION AND IMAGINATION

Telling young children stories about materials connects them to the chain of human invention that made our lives possible. The materials used in early education have antecedents we know dimly, if at all. When original inventors are unknown, beginnings are mysterious. I looked up some beginnings on the Internet. If the stories catch your imagination and spark your children's interest, you can easily find more. Stories transcend immediate experience, incite wonder about long-ago times, and stretch children's understanding of human capacities.

Record-Keeping

The earliest record-keeping, by clans long extinct, may have marked space: What is the route to the water? How can we recognize the berry patch? Or time: How many suns have risen since the men left? How long has it been since it rained? Traces of record-keeping have been found on every type of material—rock wall, stone, bone, stick, fiber, hide, and the earth itself. Traces have been made by and on every natural substance—stone honed chisel-like to carve information in hard surfaces; clay shaped into wedges to impress marks on soft materials; bark singed to become pliable as a writing surface; reeds beaten and boiled; hides split and softened.

The Inca empire in Peru and its predecessors, 5,000 years ago, stored information in knotted fiber called *khipu,* believed to be "one of the world's oldest complex recording systems" (Mann, 2005, p. 1008). Khipu are huge bundles of cotton cord tied in long strings that hang off a main cord according to a complicated system. Only 600 khipu exist today. Most khipu—many thousands—were burned when the Spanish conquered Peru. We know something of how the counting system worked but not what was being counted. A teacher might ask: "Can you imagine a way to 'count' that no one can read?" Or, a teacher might suggest, "When *you* grow up, maybe *you* will solve the mystery of what the khipu count!"

> **Key Point:**
> Rousing children's imagination about materials gives them keys to the universe of human accomplishment.

Paper

Over 4,500 years ago, paper began to evolve. Around 2500 B.C., the Egyptians invented a complex process for stripping the center from a wetland reed, then abundant, called papyrus. More than 2,000 years later, the Greek's invented parchment, made from animal skin (circa 200 B.C.). In the same era (circa A.D. 105), the Chinese invented a secret process to make the first papers from cloth, bark, or vegetable fibers. It took over 1,000 years to spread to Europe. Using the extensive ancient trading routes, the Arabs brought paper to the Middle East (circa A.D. 795). Paper eventually made its way to Europe (circa 12th century A.D.). Had there not been paper, the printing press (invented circa A.D. 1450) would have been useless. (Printing presses were adapted from the widely used grape presses common in wine making.) The printing press was successful commercially only when there was an adequate supply of paper and ink.

In our culture, uses of paper have expanded greatly—wrapping, storing, and fashioning everything from toy airplanes to model yurts. Trashy books of the early 1900s were called "pulp" fiction because they were printed on quantities of cheap paper. It is impossible to conceive of handling today's information without paper. Computers, which were predicted to make work paperless, actually have generated more paper. "Laser printers in North America alone are churning out 1.2 trillion pages annually. . . . Just ten percent of office documentation was in digital (paperless) form as of the mid-1990s" (World Resources Institute, 2001).

Paper and Infants. Gently sweep a sheet of shiny paper across an infant's visual field, and the infant will respond with rapt attention or palpable glee. A 6-month-old will be enthralled for 5 to 10 minutes by the simple act of tearing or crumpling a sheet of paper. Watch this happen on YouTube; enter "Why buy expensive toys."

Reggio teachers, working with artist Alberto Burri, made two mats about 6 feet by 8 feet, from varied materials, including many kinds of paper. One mat was in shades of white, the other in shades of black. A lengthy project began in which babies explored paper in every imaginable way (Reggio Children, 2004). The teachers' goals were "to increase their own awareness of how children explore, to learn more about what makes children curious, to observe what processes build children's knowledge" (Lewin-Benham, 2010, p. 124).

Paper at the MELC. As the MELC began to use the Reggio Approach with 3- to 6-year-olds, Jennifer provided simple geometric shapes—circle, square, and triangle—about 4 to 5 inches wide, cut from black construction paper. Children cut their shape into small random pieces, each child's distinctly different from any other's. Then children glued down their cut pieces to make a new arrangement of shapes. Jennifer varied the activity by having children tear the shapes.

In a different exploration, Jennifer provided long, thin strips of colored paper, about 12 inches long x ¼ inch wide. By gluing both ends onto stiff paper, children made an assemblage of bridges. Jennifer prepared accordion-pleated paper strips, about 1 inch wide by 8 to 10 inches long, for children to glue. Children joined the ends of inch-wide strips of computer paper to make hoops. They pleated, folded, bent, or curled other strips, then glued them to a black background. To this study

Figure 8.2. Children were asked to select a geometric shape, cut it however they wanted, rearrange their pieces into a new design, and glue them down.

Figure 8.3. Children collaboratively bent and curled thin strips of paper and glued them onto a backing board to make this 3-D collage.

in black and white the children added a few colored "bridges." As Jennifer became more experienced, she used paper alone, introducing glue or scissors only *after* the children had learned the language of paper.

Key Point:
The ultimate versatility of paper provides endless opportunities for exploration. For inspiration, visit this website, where you will see amazing folded paper constructions, some of which undulate when moved: http://www.youtube.com/watch?v=kLXl2lZ5Yk8&NR=1

Glue

The desire to attach one thing to another is almost as old as the desire to record information. Various archaeological methods, some recent and computer-assisted, enable us to learn amazing historic facts. We now know that glue was used 10,000 years ago.

Ancient Uses. The earliest evidence of glue is from the Lascaux (France) cave paintings where glue was mixed with paint to help keep the moisture in the cave from destroying the colors. Evidence from 4000 to 3000 B.C. comes from burial sites where clay pots were repaired with glue made from tree sap. Hairs from furniture found in Egyptian tombs suggest that glue was made from animal hide. The technique was confirmed by stone carvings that show the process of gluing different woods. Other paintings depict the use of glue to make papyrus. Ancient Greeks made furniture with adhesives made from egg whites, blood, bones, milk, cheese, vegetables, and grains. The Romans used tar and beeswax for glue. Throughout their ancient histories, Greeks and Romans made extensive use of glue in mosaic floors, tiled walls, and baths, which are still intact (Bellis, 2009).

Modern Glue. The first patent for glue was issued in Great Britain around 1750 for a product made from fish. Shortly after, many patents were issued for glues made from natural substances such as rubber, animal bones, starch, and milk protein, called casein. Today, every American uses an estimated 40 pounds of glue annually in furniture, plumbing, construction, cars, books, shoes, and clothing.

Today's glues are still made from natural products but a multitude of new, powerful glues are made from chemicals. Among the first was Hot Glue, invented in 1940 when chemical engineer Paul Cope was trying to improve water-based glues that melted in hot, humid climates. Krazy Glue was first discovered in 1942 when its inventor, Dr. Harry Coover, was trying to make a clear plastic; he rejected what would someday be called Superglue because it was too sticky. Nine years later, he rediscovered it with Dr. Fred Joyner when they were trying to make a heat-resistant canopy for jet airplanes: Two materials he was testing stuck firmly together! Eight years later, in 1958, the Eastman Company packaged Superglue as a product; its first name was #910 (Bellis, 2009). A web resource on what will attach anything to anything is This to That (2010).

Glue and Youngsters. Glue is indispensable for school projects. Jennifer uses glue with 12-month-olds. As soon as their hands are strong enough to squeeze a bottle, she shows them how to put drops of white glue on paper. Most play with the substance, testing how it feels, surprised by its stickiness. (A few find the stickiness unpleasant.) When their fascination wanes, she gives them paper to explore what happens when paper and glue meet. She may use attractive scraps saved from what they cut. By age 2, children realize the power of glue and fetch it themselves when they want to attach things.

> **Key Point:** Fastening things together is an integral part of using materials.

Scissors

Scissors are so common it is hard to imagine a time when they did not exist. In fact, their first use is ancient.

Origins. In 1972, French architect Jean-Claude Margueron (2003) led a hurried archaeological expedition to learn about Emar, the ancient Syrian city (14th century B.C.), which was about to be flooded by a dam project. In the ensuing years, examination of Emar's household goods revealed the first confirmed use of scissors.

It is suspected that scissors were used in Egypt as early as 4,000–3,000 B.C., although there is no specific reference to an artifact or image. The earliest scissors were forged by fire, the two blades heated then shaped and sharpened. A curved spring-like piece to open and close the blades was attached opposite the point. Sheep clipping shears still work this way.

Modern scissors were first made in 1761 by Robert Hinchcliffe of Sheffield, England, who used a recently developed technique of pouring melted steel into molds (*Scissors*, http://en.wikipedia.org/wiki/Scissors#History).

Children's First Uses. Scissors can be used with children as young as 16 to 24 months. Begin by having the child grasp one handle in each hand, pull hands apart to open the blades, and push hands together to close them. At this stage, it is not necessary to cut paper. Merely opening and closing is fascinating.

When the action ceases to amaze, begin to cut some *thing.* Insert a strip of cardstock (sometimes called oaktag) about an inch wide between the blades so the child can cut snips off. Some children's first attempts to cut look like fringe. Occasionally, place the scissors in correct cutting position in one hand as a gentle reminder. All early scissors activities are done with teacher and one child. Children learn to cut with one hand at very different times, some as young as 2, others not until after 4.

Because it is frustrating to use a tool that does not work, I recommend Friskars. Their scissors have sharp blades that are rounded at the end. Important lessons are:

- *Carrying.* Clasp a hand firmly around the closed blades and put your thumb over the end.
- *Handing them to someone.* Offer the handle end, not the blades.
- *Moving.* Walk *slowly* with scissors in your hand.

> **Key Point:**
> It is as essential to learn about the tools that shape materials as about materials themselves.

CONCLUSION: THE ROMANCE OF MATERIALS

Children's romance with materials continues age-old uses. Prehistoric peoples adapted what was readily available. In ancient times, sophisticated processes for making bronze, iron, and glass were developed and then lost, and have never been rediscovered. Since World Wars I and II, entirely new materials have been synthesized from chemicals.

Tales of human endeavor have important meanings. What clans learned before there was writing was carried from one generation to the next by storytellers who guarded, preserved, and transmitted the information essential to survival. Storytellers were the carriers of the culture, as important as the keepers of flame who preserved warmth and warded off darkness.

"Goldilocks" and "The Three Little Pigs" have their lessons. Stories of the origins and uses of materials are not as well known or widely told as traditional children's stories, but their lessons are at least as important. Materials rooted in humans' earliest days have future uses that we cannot predict but our children will invent. Children who are well versed in materials' languages and stories will use materials in ways that are beyond any we can conceive.

Questions to Consider

1. Observe infants at 3-month intervals from 3 to 15 months. Record what their hands do. What conclusions can you draw from your observations?
2. Perform an action with paper and describe it. What movements did your hands make? What words did you use?
3. Introduce to children the action you performed for the exercise in Question 2.
4. Find stories about a material not described in this chapter. Tell the stories to children. Observe their reactions.

CHAPTER 9

Materials and Relationships

The world is so full of a number of things
I'm sure we should all be as happy as kings.

—R. L. Stevenson, "Happy Thought"

ISITORS TO THE MELC were astounded at how many materials we had and amazed that most came from children's homes. Free materials are everywhere! Yet, many classrooms lack materials or have too many that are the same—puzzles load shelves but people, animals, and houses are lacking to use with blocks; crayons abound but there are no fine-point markers.

In Chapter 8, I explained what it means for a material to have a life. In this chapter, I explore why materials matter, how to find good materials, and the kinds of thinking that develop as children learn to use and care for materials. What is a *good* material? Consider this example: In Chapter 2 we saw four boys in a Reggio classroom who, at first unsettled, became engrossed for most of the morning in making a complex construction. One reason for their long engagement was that the boys were able to invest the materials with their own interpretations. So, a length of shiny, filmy gauze became a diaphanous roof over their construction. The gauze could have served as readily as a costume for dress-up, raw material for weaving strips, an unusual background for fabric painting, a prop for dancing, a covering in the housekeeping area—anything where the gauze's particular properties fit a purpose a child had in mind. Such materials require children to exercise judgment in selecting them. Making judgments means continually weighing pros and cons; it accustoms children to establishing a reflective mindset and handling complexity. Thus, such materials keep the brain "on its toes," alert, and engaged.

WHY MATERIALS MATTER

Simple materials can spur mind-expanding work. That knowledge drives Reggio projects.

Problem: What Relationship?

At Anna Frank School in Reggio Emilia, I observed two 5-year-olds use their 8-inch clay sculpture to create a still life on a mirror. Nearby stood a flashlight, blank paper, two jars with many fine-line colored markers, and a small pine branch they had stabilized with a half-sphere of clay. Also nearby was their drawing of the still life.

The children were deliberating this problem: how to place the branch so, when they shined the flashlight, the figure reflected in the mirror would appear to be standing in the branch's shadow. The materials were common and cost little; what was uncommon was the relationship the children had established among them.

> **Key Point:**
> The materials in a classroom determine what relationships children can make.

Learning "100 Languages"

As referred to throughout this book, the phrase "100 languages" reflects the fact that humans can communicate—receive, send, preserve, and alter information—in limitless ways. In their first months, infants use facial, hand, and body movements; sounds; and emotions to engage caretakers in interactions that psychologists call "co-regulated." The pair adjusts to one another's rhythm and emotional state. Early interactions set the stage for communication that becomes increasingly rich and varied throughout our lives. Greenspan says these early emotional interactions play a "vital role . . . for forming symbols and higher levels of reflective thinking abilities" (Greenspan & Shanker, 2004, p. 31).

> **Key Point:**
> By the time children leave Reggio infant/toddler centers and enter the 3- to 6-year-old schools, they have well-educated hands that are ready to operate increasingly complex tools and make new combinations from expanding collections of materials.

Reggio educators have shown that 4- to 6-month-old infants are capable of using paint, clay, paper, shadow, markers, books, and other media. At first, much of what they do is for the pure pleasure of moving. But movements become increasingly purposeful in expressing what children intend to convey.

Well before age 3, children in Reggio infant/toddler centers are given clay-shaping and cutting tools; scissors; glue; wire; leaves, bark, and seeds. One of the teachers' intentions is to choose items that will cause hands and fingers to assume many different grips—spherical, two- or three-finger pincer movements, claw (as in unscrewing wide-mouth jar tops), pliers. After age 3, the range of tools and materials broadens to include looms, light, extensive collections of natural objects, expansive arrays of man-made materials. In Chapter 8, I showed how many hand movements "operate on" paper.

Putting Languages to Work

Building children's capacity to speak "100 languages" means helping children learn to use increasing numbers of materials facilely and ultimately to use materials to express big ideas. First, children cut, glue, weave, string, pile, and attach materials, thus building a vocabulary of actions. As they educate their hands, children undertake increasingly challenging endeavors.

As one of the American educators who studied the Reggio Approach in the mid-1990s, I was agog at a project called "Amusement Park for Birds." On several trips, I saw children in the process of conceiving, studying or drawing plans, making models, and creating working attractions for birds that included a water wheel, various fountains, and bird observatories. And I saw the finished park. In progressing from conception to working device, the children transformed their ideas from one "language" (or medium or material) to another. Altogether, they used many kinds of paper, markers, cardboards, clay, wood, plastic tubing, bricks—more than four dozen different materials to transform their ideas into increasingly functional constructions.

My translation of the idea of "100 languages" is simple: the increasingly facile use of varied materials and tools to express whatever the mind conceives. Artists, engineers, inventors, technicians, architects, scientists, and manufacturers also make increasingly facile use of varied materials and tools.

> **Key Point:**
> It is through the use of materials that young children and people of all ages reinvent their world.

FINDING GOOD MATERIALS

At the MELC, we collaborated with families to enlarge the collection of materials. We asked ourselves:

- What materials are readily available at no cost?
- What relationships could children make among the materials?
- Could the materials stimulate collaboration among children and/or between school and families?
- How can we help families understand why we want materials and how we use them?

An abundance of man-made and natural materials makes a classroom rich. But not an abundance of just anything!

Man-Made Materials

Americans accumulate ever-increasing amounts of stuff. Much has no relation to the life of the mind, but is instant gratification–point-of-purchase trinkets, souvenirs from trips, gadgets from catalogues–none essential. But with thoughtful selection, some can be *repurposed* for classrooms.

Packaging—Closures, Cushioning, and Compartments.

- *Twist ties* that fasten plastic bags could attach small objects to sculpture, mobiles, or weavings.
- Rectangular *plastic bag–closers* and milk cartons' *inner sealing rings* could be used in small-scale collage, as dangling objects on weavings, or could be decorated and attached to other constructions. The secret is having *lots*! A small pile of any item is trash; a large jarful of one kind of item is treasure.
- *Net bags* (natural or synthetic) that package fruits and vegetables are textural and colorful for many uses.
- *Cardboard* of all kinds can be used to back or hold other objects or can be shaped in its own right.
- *Sturdy cardboard rolls* from paper products can be used with blocks, flimsier ones in 3-D sculptures.
- Soft, scrunchy *shredded papers and straw* are textural. The MELC children formed a nest from hardware cloth for a fanciful bird they had made. But, worried that the stiff metal would hurt the bird, they wove in shredded packaging to make the nest comfortable.

- Foil and decorative *candy wrappers*–a commercial art form in Italy, many with elegant miniature engravings–are treasures; Reggio teachers smooth and store them by color for projects or reflective arrangements on mirrors or light tables.
- *Ribbons* that are not too holiday-ish can be sorted by color and are beautiful in weavings, collage, or imaginative structures.
- *Boxes* ranging in size from jewelry to shoe boxes make housing for collage or small-scale tableaux, ramps and garages for vehicles, or cityscapes.
- *Compartmentalized box liners* from candy boxes, fruit or preserves, or beverage cartons are lightweight, decorative, plush, or sturdy; different liners suit different projects.

MELC children collaborated on making a sculpture by rolling lengths of corrugated cardboard to fit into a cardboard box separator. The effect was striking. The children had to determine:

- how large a roll would fill the space;
- how to cut corrugated material so it would fit;
- how to keep the rolls tight while fitting them into the compartments.

The work required judgment and hand skills.

Sewing.

- *Fabrics*–lace, leather, linen, tulle–have many uses, like the cottons, wools, and synthetics that made the leaf sculpture (Chapter 8). Colors are pleasing, patterns eye-catching, and textures appealing.
- *Trims*–riff-raff, pom-poms, tassels, fringe, gimp–add unique touches in constructions, collages, weavings, sculpture, and more.
- *Yarn, raffia, thread* and string-like materials have numerous uses.
- *Elastic* or stretchy materials can determine the success of a mechanism.
- *Buttons and beads*, sorted by color and/or size, are inviting.
- *Novelty items*–feathers, glass "stones," or jeweled pieces have many uses.

Anything shiny is valuable in children's eyes–sequins, bugle beads, metallic trims. Much like magpies, children are drawn to glitter.

Office. Recently, office items have been manufactured in luscious colors:

- *Paper clips* or brads in gold, magenta, turquoise, mauve, or other unusual tones.
- *Rubber bands, binder clips, push pins, and paper clips* have different shapes and colors. Important for their designed purpose, they have other uses as well– arrays of clips fastened along the edges of cardboard strips, arrangements of colored pushpins on a thick square of cork, rubber bands stretched over small, sturdy forms. Effects are striking and items can be reused.
- *Envelope liners* made of foil or shiny paper can be removed and used wherever high-quality paper is needed. Paper in various colors and finishes from these

liners, as well as from other sources, and cut into pieces about 3 or 4 inches by 4 or 5 inches is attractive for children's messages to one another.

- *Envelopes*, small and gently used, can transmit children's "private" messages.
- *Advertising promotions* may be printed on expensive, heavyweight paper; the paper can be reused or large letters cut off and saved for children to use to form words.
- Some *postage stamps* are works of art and can be cut or steamed off envelopes.
- *Return address labels* (received unsolicited) may have appealing pictures that can be cut off and used as stickers.
- *Embossers*, such as wax or notaries' seals, are unusual tools.

Hardware. Kitchens, tool rooms, and garages offer troves: corks, bottle tops, clamps, dowels, nuts and bolts, washers, small ceramic tiles, copper, tin, string, rope, wood remnants, springs, hooks, old keys, key chains, wire, burlap, cheesecloth, small screws, bits and pieces from abandoned projects, extra hardware left over after product assembly. Uses are unlimited.

Miscellaneous. Great finds are:

- Broken *game pieces* or parts from old games like the metal Monopoly pieces (before plastics).
- Broken *jewelry*, single earrings, other jewelry parts, and belt buckles are treasures.
- *Tinsel* cut into small bits and sorted by color has the sparkle children love.
- *Artificial flowers*, petals and leaves cut from stems and sorted by color or texture, add interest to many projects.
- *Sample-size bottles* from condiments, hotel shampoos, or cosmetics hold many items or themselves become projects. A windowsill in the MELC held a collection of small clear glass jars—cylindrical, square, and conical—filled with colored waters mixed by the children. In the sunlight they shone like jewels. Colored foils folded into tiny bits and stuffed into small jars glitter like gems.
- *Colored and transparent materials* for light tables come from boxes, cellophane, and plastic. Sharp edges of thick broken glass can be smoothed in a rock tumbler for light tables and other uses.
- *Broken china and pottery*, if the edges are smoothed, make 3-D mosaics or collage.

> **Key Point:** There is no limit to the possible uses and creative potential of objects.

These are short lists of what teachers can ask families to send. Because each home's needs and interests differ, homes yield unpredictable materials. Moreover, you cannot specify in advance where an item might be used at school.

Natural Materials

Nature yields a great bounty of a different sort, but remember never to pull up or pick any part of a living plant. Do not take bark from a tree or seeds from a flower. Only take things from the ground that the plant has already discarded.

Caution: Learn the poison families–ivy, oak, sumac, castor bean, poinsettia, and so on–in order to avoid them.

Plants' roots, stems, flowers, leaves, fruit, seeds, and trees' twigs, branches, and trunks provide infinite variety, as do fungi (don't eat!). Every season, even winter, offers its own free and renewable harvest that differs in every climatic zone.

Seeds. Every plant produces seeds, although not many as dramatic as the huge coco-de-mer palm that can be seen on the website Wayne's Word: An On-Line Textbook of Natural History (1996). Common seeds in the United States include those from all species of evergreen trees, acorns from all oak trees, maples that produce what children call "helicopters" or "whirligig" seeds [*Samara*, http://en.wikipedia.org/wiki/Samara_(fruit)], and the sweet gum that produces spherical seeds, about an inch in diameter, covered with short spikes.

The larger a collection of seeds children make, the richer their experiences will be. Save all the seeds from several gathering trips and engage the children in sorting and classifying them. Children may not classify as botanists would; the purpose is to encourage children to make relationships based on their own observations, not (at this stage) to adhere to standard classification. Once children have familiarity with seeds they themselves have collected, enlarge the experience by bringing many books about seeds into the classroom and browsing a website such as Wayne's Word. This site has amazing images, including photographs taken through microscopes. Seeds vary from the enormous 12-inch-long, 3-foot-circumference, 40-pound coco-de-mer palm seed to the infinitesimally small seed–several fit on one grain of salt–of the Coralroot orchid that can only be seen through a high-power microscope. Such images enlarge children's content knowledge and convey the virtually endless variety of seeds that can be found in nature. Another site with a host of excellent seed images is http://search.aol.com/aol/image?q=seeds&v_t=keyword_rollover.

As seeds are classified and children do research by poring over images of seeds, encourage them to compare the seeds and engage them in conversation about what they notice. I have heard children describe seeds' color, size, smell, texture, hardness, taste, sound, how seeds roll, pour, mound, layer, or spill. After long exploration and many conversations, ask children what they could do with *their* collection of seeds. I have heard children decide to wash seeds, weigh them, use them as food to cook, serve, or store in a housekeeping area, make designs (especially satisfying if there is a flat mirrored surface), cut them apart (a whole new chain of explorations), pulverize, plant, paint, or glue them.

Bark. Bark is equally varied. The knobby ridges of the hackberry protrude like the knuckles of an old person who has done hard labor all her life. The birch tree has papery bark. The crepe myrtle's bark is more like a cardboard roll–sometimes shed in pieces 3 feet or longer. Barks enrich collections of natural objects. Treat bark the same as seeds–collect, classify, compare, discuss, research, and eventually talk about what to do with the bark, then through conversation hone in on something specific to do.

Stories. Learning the stories of natural materials can spark interests that turn into lifelong hobbies or passions, greatly enriching one's leisure hours, vacation time, and an antidote to mindlessness. A powerful way to find stories about natural objects is through their names. Some names are merely descriptive, like the Lilac Bush, named for its beautiful color, or the Smoke Tree, so named because from a distance its enormous clusters of fuzzy brownish-white flowers resemble clouds of smoke, or the Golden Chain Tree whose sprays of bright yellow flowers cascade like chains. (*Caution:* All parts of this tree are poisonous.) Asking children to observe a plant carefully then come up with a name for it, or asking them to hear a plant's name then consider why the plant was so named stimulates children to observe carefully and to make connections between what they observe and what they know. In addition, it stirs imagination. The goal is not to memorize botanical or common names of plants, but to develop children's power of observation so that they do not walk right by but instead wonder at the world around them.

The names of some plants contain interesting bits of history and their stories can lead children's minds along many different avenues. For example, the name dogwood goes back to 1614. One theory is that the name derived from the word *dag* because its slender stems of extremely hard wood were used to make daggers (dag/dog) [*Cornus*, http://en.wikipedia.org/wiki/Cornus_(genus)]. Or, the Horse Chestnut's name was once thought to have originated from the belief that eating the tree's nuts would cure horses' chest ailments! (*Aesculus hippocastanum*, http://en.wikipedia.org/wiki/Aesculus_hippocastanum). The story of the dagger appeals to children's love of gore and danger; the story of the horse chestnut tickles their sense of humor.

Trees' growing habits are diverse and, if told as stories, can capture children's imagination. The Bald Cyprus tree, common in the south and southwest, grows best in water. Children find it funny to learn that the tree has "knees" and that children who live near a Bald Cyprus play on the knees. Challenge children to imagine what the knees are for, why the tree is called "bald," or to copy the tree in drawings, clay, paper, wire.

> **Key Point:**
> Every natural object has its own life story; learning these stories develops children's awareness of nature and their sense of wonder and builds a store of content knowledge they can draw on for the rest of their lives.

The Joshua Tree grows only in arid desert plains. This tree was named by Mormon settlers as they crossed the Mojave Desert in the mid-1800s. The tree's shape reminded them of Joshua reaching to the sky as he prayed (*Yucca brevifolia*, http://en.wikipedia.org/wiki/Yucca_brevifolia). In this short description of an unusual looking tree, there are several stories: about deserts, Mormons, westward treks, settlers, Joshua, or prayer. When teachers use stories to spark curiosity, children learn to make relationships among different ideas.

Using Natural Materials. Inspired by fall materials they themselves had collected, a few children at the MELC created small-scale impressions of fall inside cardboard boxes (see Figure 9.1). Boxes were the size used for jewelry, cosmetics, or shoes.

Equally striking were selections of fall objects inside transparent pockets, sometimes large, as in Figure 9.2, and other times small, as in pages that hold 35mm slides. Children filled the individual pockets with miniature drawings, paintings, and collages that copied or incorporated fall, winter, or spring objects. The intriguing detail in each pocket resulted from working in small scale.

The Reggio Children (2004) traveling exhibition, "The Wonder of Learning," shows a series of projects by 4- and 5-year-olds who collected a huge range of natural materials. On school grounds and at a nearby park, in a project called "Natural Materials,"

Figure 9.1. This small-scale environment was created in a shoebox from drawings that were colored, cut out, arranged, and glued inside boxes as a miniature fall tableaux.

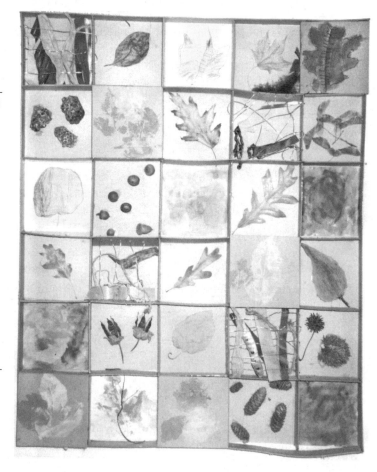

Figure 9.2. This striking piece, mounted on a 24" by 30" piece of cardboard, is titled "Fall in Different Languages." It incorporated different techniques and materials. Children made collages, weavings with wire and natural materials, prints, and watercolors of leaf drawings, then arranged their works in a cardboard grid construction prepared by the studio teacher.

the children rummaged around the environment hunting for materials, observing tiny details, surfaces, colors, changes of light and shadow, experimenting with the softness of a carpet of leaves, crumbling seeds looking for material inside other material, mixing sand and dust, testing, looking, observing, enjoying. The ordinary everyday things of the park revealed in all their extraordinariness. (p. 83)

The projects concluded with children's taking the materials they had collected, sorted, categorized, crumbled, pulverized, and mixed back to where they were collected. There, they made small works of art by scattering, mounding, mixing, and layering the materials into crevasses and pockets in the ground and onto plants, bark, moss, and earth, turning nature's spaces into 25 subtly textured canvasses. The works were left where the children placed them, photographed, and the story and photos are part of Reggio Children's second large circulating exhibition. No one who sees the photos will ever look at nature in the same way and will be equally awed at the collaboration among children, teachers, and materials.

> **Key Point:** Children experienced in using materials transform natural objects in diverse, original ways.

Children's Attraction to Materials

> **Key Point:** Materials powerfully stimulate the hand to acquire skill and the brain to make relationships between what children think and do.

Shep, at age 8, took his 5-year-old twin cousins to my attic to fill bags from the materials I save. You would have thought the twins' bags were filled with gold; they would not let them out of hand or sight. Wondering what was so precious, I peeked in. There were small tinfoil packages from individual tea bags; ends of leftover shelf paper rolls; fluted papers from boxed candies. The items were so specific and the bags so important, the twins clearly had plans.

From under 3 to about age 7, children have intense relationships with materials. With scissors, hole punch, and fasteners—tape, glue, rubber bands, string, clips—they make endless things. I have seen vehicles, traps, furniture for dolls, string toys for cats, cages for birds, helmets, swords. Children's ideas are endless. Children are not concerned if the "product" bears no resemblance to what they name it; they embed their creations in stories, explaining the creation as they make up the story.

Gathering Materials

Children who learn to see possibilities in materials can introduce their families to scavenging. Every outing is an invitation to gather, every material an opportunity for a conversation:

- Is it living?
- Is it from a plant or an animal?
- How can you tell?
- Why was it on the ground?

Children's natural curiosity drives the questions. Teachers' saying, honestly, "I don't know," and asking, "How can we find out?" stimulates action. When adults do not have answers and collaborate with children to find them, children learn to do research.

Figure 9.3. The teachers selected four children and 22 small jars, each containing a different collection of intriguing tiny objects. Children chose objects they found appealing and collaborated on using the objects to make a collage.

> **Key Point:**
> Gathering and using materials opens children's eyes to what is around them and their minds to new questions.

At the MELC, objects, some from homes, some collected by children, were stored in several dozen large and small glass jars (see Figure 9.3). The teachers selected 22 of the small jars from which children chose tiny objects to make a collage.

ASKING FAMILIES TO HELP

Initially afraid to ask poverty-stressed parents for anything, the MELC teachers gradually learned:

- Rich or poor, the U.S. home is full of junk mail, packaging, and "stuff."
- When parents understand the purpose of requests from school and are welcomed as important partners in children's education, they respond to requests wholeheartedly.

Families' eager responses to the request for photos (see Chapter 3) surprised the teachers. It taught them that *how* they asked determined what the response would be.

The Process of Asking

An outline of how teachers ask families to help would look like this:

1. Begin with children's interests. The initial idea may be a teacher's or child's. Consider: Does the idea capture children's imagination? If so, they will

enthusiastically generate ideas for what's next. If not, back off because you will have to lead, urging, cajoling, overriding collaborative activity, or dominating the project.

2. As projects begin, think deeply with your colleagues about opportunities for family involvement.

3. When you are sure a project will emerge from initial conversations, write a letter telling parents "what's up!"

4. Involve children in developing the letter:
   - Use their voices—quotes of what they said from your notes.
   - Read them the first draft, note their reactions closely, and edit the letter with the children to include their ideas.
   - Let the letter sit. Then, reread it with the children. With time to digest, their ideas will evolve. The purposes are to get information to parents and to involve children in an exchange of ideas.
   - When everyone is satisfied with the letter and copies for each family have been printed, ask the children to decorate the copies however they want—drawings, words, letters, marks. Invite the entire class to decorate, but only involve children who really want to. Otherwise, the activity will be forced.
   - Read the final letter and show it to the full class so their excitement will spread to their family.
   - Converse with the children about how their parents might react.
   - When a family responds—even just one—immediately act on it as the teachers did with Galeesa's photo (see Chapter 3).

The danger in using a list is that it becomes formulaic. The collaboration I describe is not a recipe but a structure for give and take. There is a general direction, but because each project is new, the structure should be used flexibly.

> **Key Point:** Structure serves as a guide to help teachers respond to changing situations.

Collecting with Families

After holding conversations in school about what to look for at home and why, the MELC children became better scouts. They looked for materials that varied in color, texture, size, weight, see-through-ness, stretchy-ness, bulk, float-ability, tear-ability. They even wrote to their families to ask for letters of the alphabet.

Letters to families explained what was needed and why (see Figure 9.4). Generating the letters was a lengthy process with lots of conversation. The result? Children knew everything that was in the letters:

- what was being asked of their family;
- why they needed what they were requesting;
- the purpose for requesting *many* varieties of material;
- *when* materials were needed;
- which children decorated the letters.

If parents had questions, children usually knew the answers.

Sometimes the school requested materials from indoors, sometimes from outdoors. The importance of the request was evident: Along with the letter, a bag for collecting was sent home, carefully prepared with the child's name and symbol.

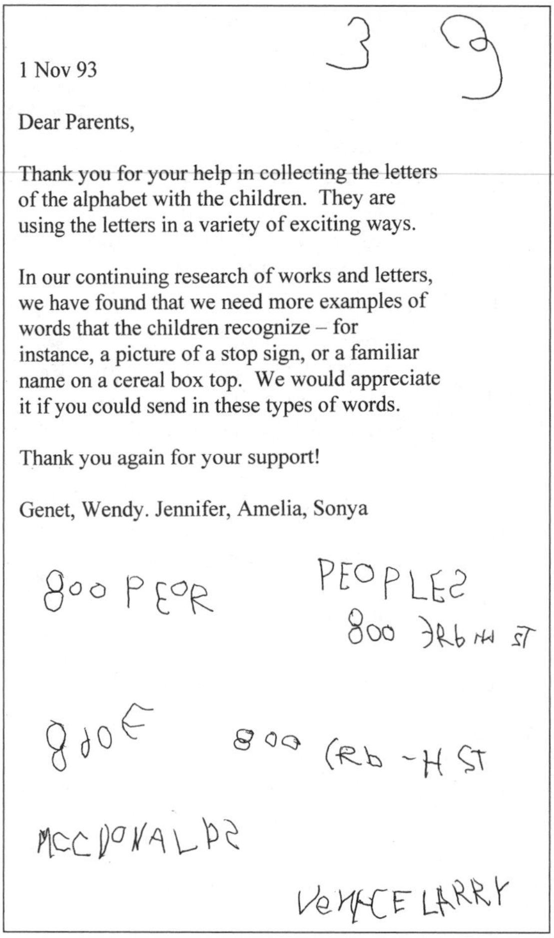

Figure 9.4. Children drew letters and numbers on a request asking parents to send letters cut from sources such as newspaper, magazines, junk mail, packaging, and flyers.

---

1 Nov 93

Dear Parents,

Thank you for your help in collecting the letters of the alphabet with the children. They are using the letters in a variety of exciting ways.

In our continuing research of works and letters, we have found that we need more examples of words that the children recognize – for instance, a picture of a stop sign, or a familiar name on a cereal box top. We would appreciate it if you could send in these types of words.

Thank you again for your support!

Genet, Wendy. Jennifer, Amelia, Sonya

Because great thought went into how to ask parents to participate, parents returned overflowing bags. Children's self-esteem increased because they knew their parent was involved in an activity that was important at school. Seeing their parents' bags valued, and knowing that their families can contribute, shows children that *they* are valued. Children love to use materials donated by their families.

The minute that bagsful of materials were returned, a project began as teachers gathered small groups of children, emptied materials in a big heap, and began to study them. Object by object, each child chose something to discuss: What is it? Who found it? Where? What color? How does it feel? Is it soft? Crunchy? Damp? How does it smell? What else looks the same? Collections were huge and sorting was exciting–handling each item, sharing observations, classifying, and eventually storing things that the children deemed went together.

Children remembered lots about what they gathered: "That seed from off the big tree over by Derrick house." "This seed little! That tree *big*!" Teachers don't know what experiences are fastened in children's memories until they hear such comments. Then, teachers realize children have made a relationship: Something little comes from something big. Making relationships is a cognitive act.

> **Key Points:**
> • Gathering materials brings children *in on the ground floor* of materials' life at school.
> • When children need materials for a specific purpose, they know what is suitable because they have requested, gathered, discussed, sorted, and stored everything.

MATERIALS AND COGNITION

A nursery rhyme goes:

> For want of a nail the shoe was lost.
> For want of a shoe the horse was lost.
> For want of a horse the rider was lost.
> For want of a rider the battle was lost.
> For want of a battle the kingdom was lost.
> And all for the want of a horseshoe nail.

The power of cascading events is nowhere as great as in the brain. Were materials to be used widely in U.S. schools in the ways they are used in Reggio schools, it could cause a cognitive revolution in the business of education. Consider the relation between materials and the cognitive acts described below. These are merely four of numerous cognitive acts that could be influenced by reflective use of materials in a bottom-up curriculum.

Transcendence

Children's comments give teachers openings to introduce what psychologist Reuven Feuerstein calls *transcendent* ideas–something at hand and something remote that somehow relate to one another (Feuerstein et al., 2006). Children understand: Looking at the acorn and recalling the huge oak tree, Michael comments: "That like when we put a picture and turn on the projector and it get big!" Same idea, little turns to big, even though the examples are entirely different. A teacher can exclaim, "Excellent analogy!" and explore children's other ideas about little things becoming big.

Experiences provide the basis for making relationships. At the World Bank Children's Center, toddlers watched as objects placed on the projector bed filled an entire wall! "The instant he saw the shadow on the wall, Reginold [age 2] tried to match the object, quickly figuring out what was making the shadows, intentionally placing objects so they would project, and checking back and forth from object to wall" (Lewin-Benham, 2010, p. 154).

Relationships are rooted in firsthand experience. If children make a small/large relationship, they can segue to blowing up balloons, baking cookies, growing plants, the change in size from infancy to now. There is no end to the relationships the brain can make.

Transcendent conversations–what happened/what could happen–encourage children to:

> **Key Point:**
> Transcending the immediate expands what is possible.

- make analogies;
- test their ideas against others' opinions;
- build relationships among dissimilar things;
- expand their knowledge base;
- enlarge their vocabulary.

These are acts of a brain that is thinking and learning. Collaboration, conversation, and using materials provide the structure in which relationships form.

Classifying and Observing

Conversations about sorting materials engage children in classification activities. Classifying materials challenges every naturalist; they must know plants'

- defining characteristics;
- reproductive habits;
- geographic niches;
- growth patterns;
- life expectancies.

Children develop personal classification schemes based mainly on sensory perceptions—what is an object's color? Size? Texture? Shape? Odor? Hardness? Sheen? Color, size, and shape predominate as children's bases for classifying. The MELC children's choices resulted from a process: observe, compare and contrast, explain, and justify. If children's budding interests turn to passion and they ultimately become botanists, traveling the planet in search of rare species, they would use the same process: observe, compare and contrast, explain and justify, although the knowledge base for the process would enlarge significantly. Neurologist Oliver Sacks (2002) says humans have a "primordial need to identify, to categorize, to organize. . . . How much [he asks] is such categorizing hard-wired in the brain? How much learned?" (pp. 58–59).

The MELC children were learning to observe. Teachers encouraged them to draw the objects they were gathering, sorting, or storing. The children noticed how many things were round and brown. They separated long pieces of knobby gray bark from paper-thin white bark. They separated objects from home by color and size; transparent, translucent, shiny, and spherical materials were favorites. Based on what they observed, they grouped items for storage. Teachers and children discussed characteristics, sources, potential uses, what an item reminded the children of, whether something else was similar, the amount of difference that necessitated placing objects in separate containers.

> **Key Point:**
> Commonalities and differences form the relationships necessary to examine any object.

Drawing

Observation is the basis for drawing. Reggio educators place great value on drawing because it reveals:

- what children have observed;
- details that children find important;
- the children's hand skills;
- each child's personal "vocabulary of lines and forms" (Gardner, 1980, p. 11);
- if a child is "at promise" graphically.

> **Key Point:**
> When teachers engage children in discussing, classifying, storing, and drawing materials, children become masters of the materials in their classroom.

Gardner (1983) defines the "development of knowledge as a building up of more elaborated and increasingly flexible skills. . . . It is my guess that once human symbolic functioning [such as drawing] has become a reality, the motor system becomes forever altered" (pp. 221–222).

Forming Judgment

Materials must be seen, not jammed in a box, crammed on a shelf, or out of sight (see Chapter 4). Where to keep particular materials is a matter of judgment: In the Studio? In the Storeroom? On a low shelf? Why? Such questions are good topics for conversations to have with children (see Chapter 6):

- How much might this be used? Every day? Once a year?
- Will we need immediate access?
- How can we identify objects easily?
- Are the shelves too deep to see these items? Too high?

As they come to value materials, children take such questions seriously and have thoughts and opinions based on what they know about the classroom, each material, their activities, their own and their friends' preferences.

Teachers know that a project can depend on having access to a critical material at an essential juncture. For example, when a turtle arrived unexpectedly at the MELC, had there not been an ample, sturdy box, they might not have been able to keep the animal. Or, if there had been no soft materials, the children would not have been able to make the comfortable bird's nest described earlier in the chapter.

Making materials accessible requires judgment—what to keep, where to keep it, how accessible to make it. At the MELC, as they discussed where to store things, the teachers heard what children valued. A child might want the buttons to be stored at the front of the shelf because he liked to string them on wire. Another might want transparent objects at the front because she loved to use the light table. Every child might have a good reason to want materials for his or her favorite activity close at hand. Shelves may not have enough frontage. The problem requires more conversation and probably negotiation.

> **Key Point:**
> When asked to exercise their judgment, children develop problem-solving skills such as planning ahead, comparing alternatives, predicting consequences, and envisioning outcomes.

Storing materials accessibly so you know where they are and can get them easily can be a big problem. Solving it requires give and take, empathy, and logical reasoning. The more a problem grows from a real-life situation and the more children are involved in solving it, the more responsibility they feel for the classroom and one another.

CONCLUSION: FINDING RELATIONSHIPS

One of the most important skills anyone can master is using what you know to find solutions to new problems. This involves seeing relationships, figuring out what information is available, what is missing, and how to find missing information.

Establishing relationships requires many mental functions:

- focused and sustained attention;
- comparison of two or more things to note obvious similarities and subtle differences;
- finding salient clues;
- understanding spatial relations–behind, near, over, alongside;
- understanding temporal relations–now, soon, later.

These cognitive skills are essential to every thought process and are the basis for higher-level thinking such as permutations, analogies, seriation, and transformation, all acts that are based on forming relationships.

For children between the ages of 3 and 6, materials provide powerful ways to build relationships. What children do with materials–whether blocks, mark-makers, dress-up clothes, bark, or seeds–shows teachers how they are thinking–whether they make comparisons, classify information, use symbols, make analogies, or engage other thought processes. Teachers who have a hugely varied assortment of materials can use them to see what children are thinking, to hook children's interest, to stimulate conversation, and to engage children in increasingly complex thinking.

Questions to Consider

1. Thinking about Chapters 1–9, what do you consider the most persuasive evidence that materials build thinking skills?

2. List your classroom's natural and man-made materials, and consider how you could enlarge the collections.

3. With other teachers, make a random choice of any three materials—for example, a branch, a ball of clay, and a book. Keep the materials in front of you on a table while each person thinks of relationships among the three. Once all have had a chance to think, each person explains the relationships he or she has made. When all have explained, discuss the similarities and differences among the relationships that have been made.

4. Ask children: If you could have whatever you want to make things at school, what would you want? Converse over many days about their ideas. With the children, hone their ideas to lists and discuss where or how they could find or acquire what they want.

CHAPTER 10

Documentation

White horse, white horse,
Ding, ding, ding,
On my way I'll find something

—Mother Goose

DOCUMENTATION DOES NOT leave it to chance that something will turn up. Just the opposite. It is an *intentional* collection, teachers' way of recording and preserving evidence of children's activities and passions. Teachers select from the records to make large panels, 3 feet high by 4 feet wide, that contain photos, text, children's words, perhaps a teacher's statement, a child's work, or an object from a Big experience. Some panels tell stories of Significant Work children have done. Others show moments of discovery or exploration of . . . an onion, a statue, their own face, wire, clay, or other materials. As explained in Chapter 3, such panels are a hallmark of Reggio schools.

In other schools, walls may be covered with commercial materials–cutouts of people or giant-sized crayons; banner-like renditions of forests, sky, or sea. Some are cartoon-like, bulbous, unrealistic shapes. A set of posters contains community helpers, reminiscent of Dick and Jane characters, helpers still at work after 70 years, the same except for skin colors, now brown, yellow, and red, not just white. Walls pulsate with highly saturated colors–reds, oranges, yellows, greens, blues, purples. The vendors' booths at early childhood conferences are a sea of sameness.

Documentation can be considered a Declaration of Independence. It releases walls from the burden of displaying commercial materials. It releases teachers from filling bulletin boards with ready-made borders, charts, calendars, posters, and other things suppliers think appeal to children but children rarely study, if they notice them at all. It releases children from the sameness of mass-produced images and the noise of loud colors.

Instead, you can see on panels children's explorations and investigations: What makes pollution? How do birds' wings work? How do fountains spout? Trees sprout? What is drought? Can a clay bridge span a wide table? How does the rain cycle work? Where do rainbows come from? No topic is beyond consideration. Young children are curious about everything.

Parents ask eagerly: "What did you do in school today?" Children answer: "We had juice and cookies," or "Nothing." Children may not remember enough to provide a narrative; or may not have developed the skill to relate a sequential account of their day; or may not know the names of activities. Or, they may be tired and want to leave school in school. (Many adults have this reaction to their workday.) So parents

141

have little idea what goes on at school. Panels change that because they show parents what children have done.

In Chapter 3 I described the documentation of the family photo project. Here, I describe the inseparability of documentation and children's work, in other words, how documentation can be used to shape the curriculum.

WALLS AS CURRICULUM

Walls that document enable teachers to enlarge and take children's interests in new directions. Documentation is a way to help children form relationships between what they know and new ideas. Forming such relationships is the essence of thinking. Children's ideas become the content for what happens next in the curriculum. In classrooms with documentation panels you typically see:

- children clustered around a panel, exclaiming about what happened, telling one another the story of the experience;
- a single child absorbed in studying a panel;
- small groups of children with a teacher discussing what they did, what it means, and how they might continue;
- a parent pulled to a panel by an eager child who wants to share the excitement of an experience;
- parents studying panels to learn what their children are doing;
- visitors intently analyzing panels, engrossed in the story of classroom work.

These kinds of engagement provide the basis for what happens in the classroom. Various names are given to curricula that grow from experience: emergent curriculum, negotiated curriculum, bottom-up, project-based, process-oriented learning. The basis for Reggio work is the listening and reflection that are the core of the process.

Caution: Without reflection, documentation panels have little more meaning for children than the commercial decorations.

Documentation as a Reflective Process

Walls occupy the largest amount of a room's space, second only to volume. What walls contain can open minds or shutter them. Using walls for documentation panels can help to realize the following goals:

- Spur children to form relationships with the physical environment and with others.
- Strengthen or increase the brain's networks by children's reflecting on the meaning of what they themselves have said and done.

Here's what happens when children use documentation:

- *Children are compelled to look* because panels contain photos, carefully selected by teachers to excite children: "That's me! And there's Yeshie!" "I see leaves! Leaves twirling!"

- *Children remember* because teachers carefully select words that stimulate their memory: "Pollution is everywhere, on houses, cars, in water." "We couldn't see nothing. The clouds made everything go away."
- *Children's attention is alerted* by headlines teachers read. The headlines are panel's titles; the words may be children's short statements or questions: "Gerald asked why colors were not on the floor."

The panel is the story of children's experience and teachers read what is on the panel to the children who were involved. The story consists of photos of the children; the text is the children's words or a teacher's brief statement. Like the opening statement in a news article, the statement conveys succinctly the who, what, when, where, why, and how of an experience.

Hearing the story is a lively process with the teacher reading, questioning, pausing, and children chiming in. Teachers reflect along with the children, encouraging them to remember, analyze, interpret, project, laugh, enjoy, and think: What next? The process of studying a panel in collaboration with a teacher involves children in using many different brain functions:

- *Recall*–"Do you remember what we were doing here?"
- *Visualize*–"What were we looking at so intently?"
- *Listen carefully*–"Did John say he found the book in *our* library or at the public library?"
- *Reason logically*–"What must we do next to take care of the seedlings?"
- *Plan*–"How can we find out how to use artificial light?"
- *Expand vocabulary*–"The seedlings we planted are lemon basil."
- *Reflect*–"What does this experience remind you of?"
- *Hypothesize*–"If we find a bird's nest . . ."

When teacher and children reflect, ideas bubble like vigorously boiling water, and with the teacher's collaboration, ideas gradually congeal so that the work continues or new work, that somehow relates, begins.

> **Key Point:** Documentation is the basis for the development of curriculum.

Cognition and Panels

Thinking involves numerous kinds of cognition. One is pattern seeking. As they reflect on a panel, children often identify something similar to what they already know: "That went 'click' just like a clock." The brain uses what it already knows as a hook to grasp something new. Relationships may be simple–"They both red" (a same/different *comparison*). Relationships may be complex–"When I mix red and white, I make light red" (seeing colors as a *series*). "When I mix red and yellow, I make orange" (a transformation). "When I mix red and lots of white it is like sound getting quieter" (metaphor). Such statements reveal different cognitive functions that the brain is using. Reflecting on panels builds cognitive functions. Panels remind me of words in a Hebrew prayer book:

> **Key Point:** Documentation panels offer teachers many handles with which to spark children's minds.

Wisdom and wonder,
Passion and instruction,
Stories and symbols. (Central Conference of American Rabbis, 2007, p. 33)

DOCUMENTATION OF AN EXPERIENCE

At the MELC, Alonzo had a Big experience. He made an amazingly detailed drawing of a large piece of sculpture. To the children, the sculpture resembled a dinosaur. It was about 3½ feet high by 5 feet long and was covered in pieces of green glass, their sharp edges embedded in a matrix of cement. It was sculpted by Nek Chand, a folk artist from Chandigarh, a northern India city in the Punjab.

A "Dinosaur" Sculpture

Jennifer had borrowed the sculpture from the storeroom of the Capital Children's Museum. The museum and MELC were part of the same organization housed in the same rambling buildings. The children knew the sculpture well because many of Nek Chand's similar pieces stood on an overpass that they walked under daily. Because the sculptures were part of their experience, when a piece showed up in their classroom, they were extremely excited. Nek Chand envisioned the piece as some type of bird. But the children knew better: It was a dinosaur.

The children had many conversations about how the sculpture was made, why it was a dinosaur, what it might do. "Would it," they wondered, "ever open its beak so they could see its teeth?" They were familiar with the sharp teeth of Tyrannosaurus Rex. Their dinosaur's beak was made from the elongated necks of two green glass wine bottles, an unknown object, therefore open to interpretation. For these children, it was the site of the dinosaur's teeth. Among all the children, Alonzo had the most passion for the dinosaur.

Drawing to Express Thoughts

One of the MELC's goals was to help children become adept at drawing as a way to express their ideas. Words are slippery. A child can say, "The sun makes the water dry up." But an adult has no idea if the child has any understanding of what evaporation means. If, however, you ask a child to *draw* the relationship between sun and puddle, he must be more precise because drawing requires defining words in pictures.

Drawings give teachers insight into what relationships children have formed. Words are spoken and gone, but a drawing leaves a trace. At the MELC, we used #2 pencils, fine-line black magic markers, or any other mark-makers that enable you to produce detail. Detail reveals how you think. Teachers ask children: "What do these lines mean? And this one? How does it get from here to there?" "Tell me what is happening *here*."

Alonzo had been very resistant to drawing. The teachers thought drawing the dinosaur might, possibly, be an opportunity to overcome his resistance. When Jennifer presented him with a piece of paper the approximate size of the dinosaur and asked him to draw the sculpture, Alonzo could not resist.

The MELC teachers encouraged children to be precise in their drawing, to look carefully at what they were copying, to make their lines closely resemble the lines of the object. Yet, when she proposed the idea, Jennifer would never have guessed that Alonzo would want to draw an *exact* likeness. A great adventure began that lasted 8 days.

Alonzo's Drawing

Alonzo rendered the dinosaur's body with amazing accuracy, but stumbled over the tail, feet, and beak. He could not fit them on the paper or get the proportions correct. Jennifer blamed herself—she had given him *square* paper, thinking only of the body. But with beak, tail, and feet the sculpture was actually *rectangular*. In drawing the body as large as the sculpture, Alonzo had used up the square paper, leaving no room for beak, tail, or feet! Jennifer corrected her mistake by taping additional paper where needed. But with many erasures and taped extensions the product looked messy.

Some children are sensitive to the quality of what they produce. The messiness bothered Alonzo. His solution was to recopy the entire drawing. This time Jennifer gave him paper in the correct proportion. Years later, Jennifer commented, "It was a real lesson for me in how big a challenge a young child will tackle."

Throughout the project, Jennifer documented Alonzo's effort in photos, her own small-scale drawings of his attempts, Alonzo's comments, and her narrative about the project's impetus, process, and outcome. (See also the description of this project from a different perspective in Lewin-Benham, 2006, pp. 125–126.)

The Panel

The final panel was large and comprehensive. It showed:

- Alonzo's huge drawing, almost 5 feet long;
- seven photographs, including Alonzo's hesitation at the project's inception;
- photo captions;
- five small sketches by Jennifer of Alonzo's interim attempts;
- text beside each sketch describing what both Jennifer and Alonzo had done during each attempt.

Jennifer displayed the panel prominently in the Studio. All the children recognized the huge effort. They were so proud of Alonzo's accomplishment. "Come!" they demanded of any visitor, "See Alonzo's dinosaur." Without knowing the phrase *Significant Work*, the children recognized that Alonzo's effort was creative, challenging, an example of competent drawing, and that it had given Alonzo great satisfaction—all hallmarks of Significant Work.

Panel as Window

The dinosaur project is an example of how a wall became a window into a classroom. The panel showed the moment when Jennifer offered Alonzo the challenge. It showed Alonzo's effort to meet the challenge—far beyond what the teachers imagined. And it showed the struggle—something an artist's final product, much less a child's, rarely reveals.

The wall where the documentation hung became a window into:

- the teacher's techniques, including her initial failures;
- the mind of a child, showing how a passionate interest can be the impetus

for extraordinary effort—"Sweaty," in Alonzo's word. (Lewin-Benham, 2006, p. 126);

- the relationship among teacher, child, object, material, problem, and solution;
- the nature of collaboration on a big undertaking: Jennifer and Amelia had helped Alonzo in the final stage—by cutting out the many shapes Alonzo had drawn to represent the glass—so he could glue the pieces onto his final outline.

Without the documentation there for all to see, the process would have been invisible, the effort would have gone unseen, and the project would have faded from memory. But, with the documentation as a constant reminder, the project became part of the class's life:

- a story of trial, error, and triumph;
- an illustration of teaching techniques;
- an example of teacher/child collaboration;
- an instance of bottom-up curriculum development;
- a record of the growth of a teacher;
- a record of the growth of a child.

> **Key Point:**
> When reflection on documentation panels drives curriculum, a significant change occurs in early childhood practice.

Documentation panels can reveal that the structure of an emergent curriculum is, first, belief in children's competence; second, allocation of the time required for something big to happen; third, the range of materials and tools that are available and their role in building skills; fourth, the nature of collaboration. Belief, time, materials, and collaboration. A curriculum emerges when children reflect on documentation of what they have done in collaboration with teachers who believe in children's competence and whose intent is to use time and materials to stimulate thinking.

WALLS THAT ENCOURAGE MINDFUL ACTIVITY

Until recently, with the advent of PET scans and fMRIs, it was not possible to watch someone think. In his sculpture, "The Thinker," Auguste Rodin uses bronze and marble to depict the *posture and attitude* of someone engaged in contemplation. In the section of the novel *Crime and Punishment* that contains Raskolnikov's memoirs, confession, and diary, Fyodor Dostoevsky uses *words* to depict thought. Documentation panels are a new means of watching the mind at work. Most often the work displayed on panels is what I call Significant Work.

Significant Work engages the mind. It elicits complex thought processes; is original and creative; requires collaboration; shows a child's competence; and, above all, is joyful. Hallmarks of Significant Work are wonder, curiosity, concentration, conversation, and laughter—all characteristics of young children who are thinking. A prime example of Significant Work at the MELC occurred when a group of grade school children from Georgetown Day School, a private school in Washington, D.C., adopted the MELC as a community project. By the project's end, the students and MELC children had become fast friends. The MELC children wanted to thank the students in a very big way and discussed the matter with Jennifer. Jennifer gave it some thought and subsequently told the children about artist Marcel Duchamp, who carried miniature models of his work in a display case. The children adapted the idea for their thank you and The Valise Project began. The children made their older friends a case with drawings and models of precious things—of Coco their cat, of the turtle, and other representations of what they loved about the daily life at their school. A photo of students engaged in this project and of their drawing of Coco are shown on the cover. Everything about the project exemplified Significant Work.

The process that yields Significant Work is explained below in relation to Alonzo's Dinosaur.

A Thoughtful Process

Writing about the documentation of a project stultifies what, in reality, is an animated give and take—children's words and actions, teachers' different interpretations, how they disagree, how they reach consensus, their other interactions. The process is dynamic, the outcome unpredictable.

Stage 1: Selecting. Together, teachers sift through their notes to look for specific things: children's passionate interest, a group's train of thought, repeated actions or words, the potential for Significant Work. When teachers read to children bits of their own conversation, it brings them back to the moment when they made the remarks. The experience evokes teachers' ideas of what might lead to Significant Work. *Note:* Teachers' notes do not always yield something with the potential for follow-up!

In the notes that have survived on Alonzo's project, there are no remarks by Alonzo, but there are teachers' comments on his behavior—his resistance to drawing, his love of the "dinosaur." The teachers had a hunch that they might be able to connect the dinosaur, Alonzo, and drawing—they built a relationship.

The selection of a bit of conversation and the connection of that bit to a child's (or children's) behavior is a pivotal moment. It kicks off a new process in the teachers' quest for Significant Work. The bit of conversation and a photo or two might be used to begin a panel.

Stage 2: Brainstorming. During a brainstorm together, teachers hypothesize many possible relationships that could be made between what children said or did and what they might do next. Then teachers consider which relationships can be actualized, which can branch, which are most likely to stimulate children's interest—all important factors in teachers' selection of what to bring to their next meeting with the children. The teachers determine whether there is potential for actions to continue. Had they diagramed Alonzo's potential actions, it might have looked like Figure 10.1.

Stage 3: Vetting the Idea with Children. The teachers bring what they selected back to the group or child who was involved or, possibly, to the entire class. One teacher reads the words the teachers chose as "pregnant." For example, "Yesterday, you said that the shadows on the wall reminded you of the columns at the Arboretum." With Alonzo, the teachers first included him with a group of children to draw the dinosaur, and when they saw that *his* drawing most closely resembled the sculpture, they invited him to make a second drawing.

Figure 10.1. The teachers hypothesized what Alonzo's reactions might be, and for each hypothesis what might happen next.

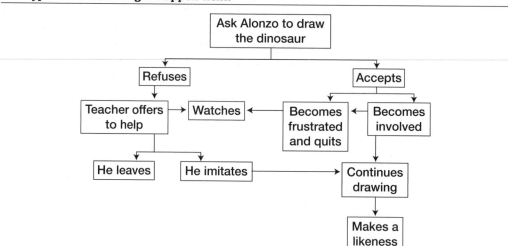

Teachers carefully observe how children react to their own words or how they respond to an invitation. If children's interest is rekindled, "Bingo!" Teachers suspect Significant Work might result. The teachers may, at this stage, add a photo of this conversation and/or a key comment or two to the panel.

Stage 4: Responding to Children's Reactions. Depending on children's re-actions, teachers may continue a conversation with the full class or select a small group, two to five children—the ones most interested—with whom to pursue the topic. During conversations, teachers continue to photograph and take notes. Gradually—over one or several discussions—a project jells. A project may begin simply with the suggestion—from a teacher or a child—of some action the children could take or some product they could make. Again, teachers may add a key photo or comment to the panel, one that is likely to spur more conversation. Sometimes, as with Alonzo, the reaction is quick.

A Way to Listen

Photographing and note taking are threads that run throughout the entire pro-cess of documentation because they are powerful ways to listen. Photographs frame key actions and notes preserve key statements. In a collaborative process, teachers sift through photos and notes looking for ways children's thoughts and actions might branch—those that are most likely to

- hook children's continuing interest;
- engage them in meaningful activity;
- have many potential directions;
- initiate a project;
- result in fruition of a project;
- lead to Significant Work.

Key Point:
Significant Work results when concepts emerge from a thoughtful process.

Throughout the entire process, teachers continue to read back children's remarks to them. Conversations punctuate projects! They contain seeds of what to do next, the meaning of what they have done, and how they will continue.

At any time as a project is emerging, teachers can decide that the moment is ripe to begin a panel. At this initial stage, the panel might contain:

- a simple title–"Alonzo's Dinosaur";
- a single photo or two–Alonzo being offered paper and beginning to draw;
- a short statement–"Alonzo made a strong likeness of the sculpture's body." Statements can include children's words.

> **Key Point:** As panels of children's experiences accumulate on the classroom walls, they become a reflection of children's mental life and developing skills.

As a project continues, teachers add more photos, children's remarks, and perhaps another short statement. In other words, a panel develops along with the project. Panels reveal that children and teachers plumbed their activity for meaning.

DOCUMENTATION AT WORK

Documentation builds curriculum when teachers use one experience as the basis for ensuing experiences.

Natural Objects: The Panel

The MELC children's process of collecting, classifying, and storing natural objects (see Chapter 9) was documented on a panel. It began with a couple of photos of children collecting materials. Once sorting and conversations began, the teachers added more photos captioned with children's words: "Looka this pile of pebbles." "Some big as rocks!" "These leaves crunch!" "They break into little bits!" Comments such as these went on the panel.

When the teachers asked what to do with collections, the children had many ideas: They could

> **Key Point:** *Selecting* what to respond to is the crux of listening.

- crush leaves;
- put pebbles in water and see what would happen;
- paint twigs;
- paint pebbles;
- stick twigs in clay;
- trace leaves.

Their ideas reflected many different techniques they had been learning, techniques that change materials themselves or cause materials to change other things. A photo (maybe two photos) of children using these techniques went on the panel.

Determining what to do with the items once they were sorted was a key step in the project. Therefore, the teachers added a photo to the panel and punctuated it with a few of the children's comments, especially those that revealed the meaning of the activity and were most likely to spur further action.

Teachers' Considerations Spur Action

Among themselves the teachers discussed the children's ideas. For Jennifer, as Studio teacher, the idea of tracing jumped out: If they traced a leaf on acetate, they could put it on the overhead projector and transform something small into something enormous! She suspected that the dramatic change in scale would be very exciting to the children. The teacher/orchestrator ensures that dramatic experiences take place. The Studio teacher brings an artist's perspective to experiences.

Jennifer gathered four older children and asked if each would like to choose a leaf and trace it on tracing paper. Then she explained how to trace over their tracing with a fine-line black magic marker to darken the pencil line. This, she explained, would make the outline visible when projected. Once they had made the tracing darker, Jennifer showed them how to clip their tracing to a sheet of clear acetate (the kind used on overhead projectors), place it on the bed of the projector, and turn on the machine. Thus, she introduced a complex new technique. As she suspected, the children were *very* excited when they saw their small drawing become a huge projection.

Courtney's Work

Courtney chose a frond from a fern, its 30 or so pinnae branching almost symmetrically in pairs opposite one another on each side of the stem, becoming very small as they reached the tip. Courtney spent a long time tracing the leaf and darkening the outline. When she put it on the projector bed and turned on the light, instantly, the drawing became huge! She traced the entire projected image then thoughtfully chose a fine-tipped brush to paint the pinnae different shades of green, mixing the paint herself to match her perception of the varied colors in the natural object. She enhanced her painting by filling in the space around the pinnae with yellow China paint using a sponge, not a brush, to achieve a muted background. Courtney did this with no suggestion from Jennifer. It was a technique Courtney had already learned and thus had in her "resource bank." Jennifer photographed key steps and recorded Courtney's words.

> We got the leaf from off a tree. We picked up leaves with our parents. We took them to school the next day. I traced the leaf with a pencil. Then I got a black pen and traced it on clear paper [acetate]. Then we put it on the projector. It showed on the wall. It was a *big* leaf! We put on the light and then I got a pencil and traced it on big paper. Then I painted it all greens. Then I put yellow China paint around my leaf with a sponge. I dipped it in the container and I smushed it on the paper.

Courtney's description is precise. It contains seven adjectives and eleven different verbs, seven of them reflecting a specific process. Her comments follow one another in a logical sequence. Her statement "It was *big*" responded to projecting the small tracing–about 12 inches–and seeing it fill a 40-inch long sheet of paper.

Courtney's verbal description is as impressive as her painting. She recounts the entire sequence, from collecting with her parents to finishing her painting by filling in the background. She relates the experience in full sentences with proper grammar. Where she doesn't know the word *acetate,* she uses a descriptive substitute–clear

Figure 10.2. The documentation panel of Courtney's fern included the leaf itself, Courtney's tracing of the leaf, and a photograph of Courtney painting a large projection of the tracing. Each item on the panel is explained in Courtney's words.

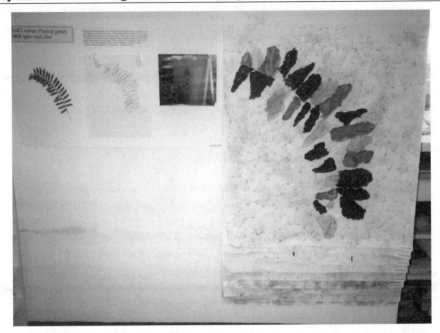

paper. Her logic and sequencing are flawless. The panel reflects both her grammatical and hand skills.

The visually striking result gave other children ideas of what they could do. Nine other children wanted to trace, project, enlarge, and paint a leaf. There were so many paintings, Jennifer mounted them flip-chart style, one over the next, each successive one a bit higher so children's names could be seen. Ten huge paintings took little more wall space than one.

> **Key Point:** Jennifer tossed a ball, Courtney caught it, and the game was on.

Transformation

The documentation showed a transformation in both content (black and white leaf becoming colorful), and process (small leaf becoming large). The documentation reflected content and process. On one panel, direct quotes from Courtney captioned each of ten photos, which showed how the project began:

- children on a walk collecting natural objects; sitting around a table heaped with objects, intently discussing, sorting, and classifying; storing objects on the Studio shelves;
- Courtney selecting the fern frond.

A second panel (Figure 10.2), titled "Fall Leaves: Playing Games with Space and Color," showed the next steps in the process:

- the fern frond;
- Courtney's initial tracing paper clipped to an acetate sheet;
- a photo of Courtney at the easel tracing the projected image of the leaf.

Next to the panel hung the sheaf of enlarged leaves traced and painted by the ten children, Courtney's on top.

The teachers' introduction read: "The children love to collect natural objects when they are outside. We listened to how many things the children said they could do with the objects and decided that they might find it exciting to trace, enlarge, and paint a leaf of their choosing."

USING DOCUMENTATION REFLECTIVELY

As children use panels to reflect on their activities, they watch themselves think. Since the inception of the field of cognitive science (the study of how we think and learn to think), psychologists have attempted to find ways to help students think about their thinking. Panels engage children in thinking about their thinking. Reggio educators call this self-reflective process "revisiting" (see Figure 10.3).

> **Key Point:** The teachers' picking up on a single word mentioned by the children—*trace*—spurred a big project.

When Courtney saw her painting and the documentation of her experience, she commented: "*Here* I was watching the little leaf become a big leaf, but it was the same leaf. The projector made it." She does not yet know that the combination of certain lenses and light can magnify and project. But her comment is an opening for her teacher:

Figure 10.3. Genet and a small group of children revisit two large panels that depict their fall experiences.

- to talk with Courtney about her ideas about the projector;
- to encourage Courtney to notice that a projector's design and a strong light source are essential to its function;
- to experiment with magnifying glasses of different power;
- to examine objects under a microscope.

In such discussions between teacher and child, fanciful and magical thinking ("the projector made it") diminishes, imprecise thinking sharpens, and ideas gradually begin to reflect reality. By studying panels with their teachers, children become mindful about how things work.

> **Key Point:**
> Documentation panels trigger reflective thinking.

Psychologist David Perkins (1992) maintains that intelligence has three components—neural, the biologic functions of the brain and nervous system; experiential; and reflective. Neural intelligence is each person's genetic inheritance. Experiential intelligence accumulates slowly, over a lifetime. These two components of intelligence are difficult to change. But Perkins says reflective intelligence is learnable, that children can be taught to think about how they are thinking. In the examples in this book, we see teachers teaching intelligence and children learning a reflective thought process.

CONCLUSION: WALLS THAT INTRIGUE PARENTS

Loris Malaguzzi spoke of families' "great hunger" for information about their own child's activities in school (Lewin-Benham, 2006, p. 131). Panels satisfy that hunger. They show families photos of their children, children's work products and words, and the complexity of the processes children are engaged in. Thus, families can watch their children learning to think.

Whitney's mother said, "The panels helped me a lot in understanding the projects. What I like is that it was so clear. The words and pictures explain everything. One of the children will explain to you and help you understand the panels, because they know what they have done" (Lewin-Benham, 1998, p. 356).

It is rare for families to be able to see what their children are doing in school. Beyond seeing, families read their children's ideas. Dalisica's grandmother said, "The panels . . . lit up the school. . . . I love it! It . . . helped to understand what was going on" (Lewin-Benham, 1998, p. 355).

Questions to Consider

1. Close your eyes and envision the process of making a panel.
2. Make a rough sketch for a panel of an experience your class has had.
3. Mentally "read" your panel to a small group of children.
4. Can you see yourself making panels in actuality?

CHAPTER 11

Assessing Children's Progress

A mole on your arm,
Will do you no harm.
A mole on the lip,
You're a little too flip.
A mole on your neck,
Money by the peck.
A mole on the back,
Money by the sack.
A mole on the ear,
Money by the year.

—Mother Goose

FOR MILLENNIA people have believed that charms and auguries control their destiny. Whether the omen is good or ill, superstition is a force as strong as any faith. It could be argued that belief in the predictive power of standardized tests is a modern way to put one's faith in destiny. In any event, tests' predictive power is overrated. History shows pointed instances of tests' predictive failure: Einstein failed the entrance exam for a technical college. Edison was considered unfit for elementary school. Winston Churchill, Steven Spielberg, Isaac Newton, and other successful people, some famous, some not, were school failures. School is not effective for some learners and testing raises as many questions as it answers.

The recent chapter in the history of testing began with the *Nation at Risk* report (U.S. National Commission for Excellence in Education, 1983). Since then, children's responses on standardized tests have increasingly been linked to teacher accountability. The first chapter in standardized testing began in the 1800s with political competition between elected school head masters and other politicians. To make themselves appear knowledgeable and important, politicians criticized the head masters who in turn used test results as proof of their success. This left a legacy of political interference in schools that is apparent in the No Child Left Behind (NCLB) legislation. NCLB has tied teaching into knots to meet a one-size-fits-all standard of what children should learn and when they should learn it. NCLB has also driven many fine teachers from the profession.

The cultural divide between Reggio and American schools is most evident in the practice of assessment. The divide stems from beliefs about children. Loris Malaguzzi said that having a joyous early childhood is every individual's birthright. For Reggio educators, early education is not preparation for life; it *is* life.

American school systems, in the main, view early education as preparation for grade school. The word *pre*school implies as much. Our culture is dominated by messages about teaching reading earlier, school readiness, and measuring children's performance against predefined competencies.

In this chapter, I define evaluation and assessment and examine some research about testing and young children. I describe how Reggio educators assess children's progress, and report responses of parents and visitors to the MELC. If you are looking for *proof* that the Reggio Approach produces better results on standardized tests, you will not find it in this book. Standardized tests are not designed to measure the kinds of growth the Reggio Approach fosters.

EVALUATION

Evaluation is a way to show how children perform in comparison to other children. This is done with standardized tests that, through statistical analysis, compare children by negating economic, cultural, or other differences. Test scores are products of evaluation. Some believe that test scores are objective measures of children's progress.

Purpose

Families want to know how their children are doing. Teachers want to demonstrate that their teaching is effective. Administrators want proof that students are performing well enough to keep their schools off "bad" lists. Politicians want to demonstrate that the programs they have funded to boost test scores are working. Yet, there is general consensus that standardized tests should not be used with young children.

The purpose of evaluation is to determine which children have learned material that state standards and preset curricula dictate children should learn. The increase in federal funding for early education and the advent of public school pre-kindergarten programs have resulted in preset curricula and testing for younger and younger children.

> **Key Point:**
> Evaluation is a one-size-fits-all attempt to quantify what children have learned.

Evaluating Young Children

Evaluating children against one another denies individuality. By individuality, I do not mean temperament–shy children versus extroverts–or different "intelligences" (Gardner, 1983). Gardner talks about genetic factors–Mozart, who created a credible musical composition at age 4–or environmental factors–who Mozart might have been had he lived before the pianoforte was invented–or social factors–the influence of others on Mozart (e.g., his father, his audience).

By individuality, I mean the different rates at which systems in the brain develop in different children. I did not walk until I was 18 months old. Had my locomotion been evaluated at 12 months, it might have caused concern. Kurt entered my Montessori class at age 3 and did not speak until 15 months later. Colleagues who taught Kurt's older siblings said his dad was a rigid disciplinarian who demanded perfection. I believed that I should accept whatever Kurt did–or did not do–which meant not asking him to speak. Shortly after he turned 4, Kurt began to speak at every opportunity in fully grammatical sentences with a large vocabulary. He had waited, probably rehearsing silently, until his internal speech matched the patterns he heard around him. Had I pushed him to speak earlier, negative emotional responses might have overwhelmed his brain and blocked the internal rehearsal. Neuroscientists have proven that cortisol, a stress-induced chemical, swamps the brain and causes negative emotions to eclipse cognitive activity (Perry, 1994; Teicher et al., 2003).

Samuel Meisels, president of the Erikson Institute, is a leading authority on early assessment; he is the voice for alternative early assessment. In referring to the Head Start National Reporting System (NRS) first administered in 2003, he states:

> Simplistic approaches to outcome assessment that are uninformed by research, that attempt to compress all a child's experience into a narrow set of achievement items, and that do not take into account the context in which children live and grow will only do harm. The NRS is an example of public policy out of touch with both research and best practice. (2004, pp. 1401–1402)

"Simplistic" tests do not diagnose problems; they merely show that children do not measure up to a standard. Yet, some parents judge their parenting by their child's test scores. I would urge them to look at–and enjoy–their child, not stress about test scores. Children may interpret their parents' stress as a sign that they, the children, are inadequate (Briggs, 1970).

Research makes the case against early evaluation: "The younger the child, the more difficult to obtain reliable assessment data. . . . It is particularly difficult to assess children's cognitive abilities accurately before age six" (Epstein, Schweinhart, DeBruin-Parecki, & Robin, 2004, p. 4).

Tests require answers that are short, fast, and fact-based. Answers on tests are limited to options determined by test designers. The relationships in a test designer's head may be too narrow for the relationships in children's heads or may contain content that a young child has never been exposed to. Tests are never collaborative; they do not reflect the kinds of problems we confront in real life, and rarely allow children to elaborate. Worse, they offer no way to determine the basis for a wrong answer–whether because the child does not know the content or because the child has not acquired the specific thinking skill in which the content is embedded. These constraints are serious impediments to young children's performance and make it impossible to determine the cause of a child's incorrect response.

Teachers know that testing is at odds with young children's capacities. Yet, politics has tied federal funding to test scores, and school systems have tied teachers' salaries or continued employment to test scores. Thus, teachers are pressured to prepare children to do well on tests. It is bad enough to see this pattern in grade school. It is preposterous to ask young children to answer in one right word. Many young children lack motor control to sit for the duration of a test, lack the information to answer fact-based questions, and lack the language skills to express themselves. If young children must be tested, it is better to do so a bit at a time in the natural situation of a familiar classroom with teachers whom they know and trust–and teachers who know them so that teachers can interpret children's responses subjectively, in the context of what they have observed about the children's capacities.

Early education, in the main, consists of classes for 3- and 4-year-olds; kindergarten is the beginning of elementary school. The result has been an emphasis in early education on "readiness." Kindergarten teachers expect that children who have been in preschool will be able to sit still, sometimes for long periods, will know their letters and numbers, and will conform to a program of pre-formulated lessons so that they are "ready" for 1st grade. To meet these expectations, kindergarten has become increasingly academic and is dominated by what is called the "push down" curriculum. And early education teachers have become increasingly prone to "teaching" 3- and 4-year-olds "readiness" skills. I wonder, will the end result of the "push down" curriculum be that babies are expected to pop out of the womb already knowing how to read? In my opinion, "readiness" is being pushed to ridiculous extremes.

Key Points:
- Children, especially when they are young, develop at vastly different rates.
- A well-developed research literature advocates not using standardized tests for young children.

ASSESSMENT

Assessment, as I define it, is a way to show how an individual child performs now in comparison to how she or he performed previously. Assessment is not used to compare children to one another. Assessment is accomplished by accumulating records of a child's performance in many different areas. Assessment is a process, not a product, and it is subjective.

Assessment means that, as children are involved in activities, teachers document initial attempts, reactions, and responses and continue to document as children's content knowledge enlarges, skills increase, memories grow, and expressive abilities expand. Assessment uses systematic ways to accumulate evidence of children's experiences and to ensure that children reflect on their experiences. As children reflect, their responses show teachers how they are thinking; from children's responses teachers determine whether children are learning.

According to the National Childcare Information and Technical Assistance Center, "Multiple measures, conducted at frequent intervals over time, should be used to capture the dynamic nature of young children's learning and should include the families' views on children's learning and development" (Partnerships, Alliances, and Coordination Techniques [PACT], 2010, p. 3). Such techniques are called authentic assessment. Steve Seidel, director of Project Zero, Harvard Graduate School of Education, says that Reggio documentation panels "represent in words and images the working, playing, and learning of groups and individuals" (Seidel, 2001, p. 304).

Key Point: Documentation, as practiced in Reggio schools, combines the kinds of assessment techniques that authorities say are best to use with young children.

AUTHENTIC ASSESSMENT

Authentic assessment is characterized by "systematic observation of children's activities in their day-to-day settings" (Epstein et al., 2004, p. 6). Classrooms, publications, and archives of the Reggio schools provide numerous, detailed case studies of authentic assessment.

Authentic Assessment: The Process

Authentic assessment involves judging children's growth in ways that

- are impartial;
- accurately reflect diverse areas of development;
- show change over time;
- are compatible with how young children behave.

Techniques used in authentic assessment include

- taking regular notes to record what children say;
- taking photos or videos to record what children do;
- maintaining notes and images so they are accessible;
- studying records to see how children are functioning.

> **Key Point:**
> Comparing young children to one another ignores the disparities in different children's paces of development. When parents compare their child's progress to what other children are doing, I answer, "No groom walks down the aisle in diapers," by which I mean that, despite different rates at which children mature, all children develop!

Such techniques enable teachers to compare an individual child's early and later work, thus comparing the child to her- or himself.

Authentic Assessment Techniques: The Evidence

In the MELC, the children new to the school, around age 3, spoke in Black Vernacular English (BVE), a language that differs from Standard English. The children had heard only BVE, had been read to rarely, and had not engaged in much conversation. Moreover, few had the kinds of experiences—trips to a zoo or a museum, stimulating vacations—that are taken for granted in middle-class families. As a consequence, their vocabularies were sparse. Yet, after a year or so, their vocabulary grew, and they spoke Standard English.

We could show changes in the children's language because on panels and in each child's portfolio were the transcripts that provided evidence of initial capacity, change, and progress over time. At the MELC, we used the techniques described below to collect evidence.

Written Notes and Audio Recordings. Each teacher had her own method for taking notes of what children said. Sonya used a large notebook, Wendy a small one, Jennifer a journal. Genet and Deborah used a clipboard that held pages with the heading "What Happened Today" and a dateline.

In many MELC photos, you see the notebook on the floor in front of the teacher as she sits with the full class, on the table where she works with a small group of children, or in her hand as she meets with colleagues to read notes together and debate what they mean.

Figure 11.1. On the end of a shelf unit near the maps, transparent plastic sheet holders contain transcripts of children's conversations about maps.

Transcriptions. Some teachers prefer tape-recordings to handwritten notes. Other teachers use both tape-recorders and notes. Teachers place tape-recorders beside children who are working without a teacher. Transcripts of tapes enable teachers to read conversations they otherwise would miss. Occasionally, transcripts of conversations are hung in clear plastic sleeves alongside the activity that stimulated the conversation (see Figure 11.1).

Photos. Cameras are a primary means of observing children. At the MELC, we took hundreds of slides. They recorded the structures, sculptures, and other constructions children made; children's progress using mark-makers; their social interactions; and their engagement in every other aspect of the school's life. Selecting the slide that best conveyed children's response to an experience involved the teachers in long debates about why a particular image best conveyed an individual child's capacity.

Video. At the MELC, we only used video for occasions such as parent meetings, graduation, conference presentations, or a complex project of short duration, like the "Bridge in Clay," in which two children built a clay bridge to scan the entire 3-foot width of a table (the project is the subject of Chapter 9 in my book *Powerful Children*).

Figure 11.2. Teachers huddle in front of the video screen to debate the meaning of children's actions and words.

Video caught the body language, as no other medium could, of anticipation, frustration, perseverance, and finally, over an hour after the children began, triumph as "De-Marco's hands quickly help Renee press her [clay] slab firmly to his" (Lewin-Benham, 2008, p. 161), completing the bridge, and making the children jubilant. New technologies have greatly advanced how still and video cameras are used in the classroom (see Figure 11.2). Editing, production, and storage are simpler and curricular uses include social negotiations through immediate feedback to children. Children can use certain new cameras themselves. *Note:* Video is most useful when there is an explanation of the context for what is taking place and interpretation of the children's actions. Video is confusing when it reflects teaching behaviors that differ from what a school or teachers state as their beliefs.

Checklists. At the MELC, Jennifer kept a notebook with detailed lists of what children had done. Pages were divided into columns. Down the left-hand side was each child's name and symbol. On the top of each page was the name of a tool, material, or experience. In each column were circles. Whenever a child used something, Jennifer marked the circle. At a glance, she could determine how often any child had been engaged with any tool, material, or experience (see Figure 11.3). Her book became known as the "Magic List" because it enabled teachers to easily see if they had missed engaging some child in using a tool, a material, or in having some other experience. In later years, in addition to marking entries, Jennifer dated them.

Portfolios. The MELC teachers archived children's large works-on-paper in large folders—called portfolios—that Jennifer made from Bristol board, a portfolio for each child.

Figure 11.3. The "Magic List" enables the teachers to see at a glance what experiences each child has had.

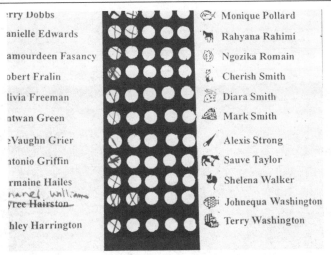

rry Dobbs	Monique Pollard
anielle Edwards	Rahyana Rahimi
amourdeen Fasancy	Ngozika Romain
obert Fralin	Cherish Smith
livia Freeman	Diara Smith
ntwan Green	Mark Smith
eVaughn Grier	Alexis Strong
ntonio Griffin	Sauve Taylor
rmaine Hailes	Shelena Walker
ree Hairston	Johnequa Washington
hley Harrington	Terry Washington

Notebooks. Small works-on-paper were kept in acetate page covers in standard-sized three-ring notebooks, a notebook for each child.

Journals. Computers at the MELC were archaic compared to today's. It is common in many Reggio-inspired schools for teachers to keep a daily journal of their notes and photos and to email them nightly to parents. Teachers explain to parents that every child will not be in every day's journal and are careful to assure parents that over time there is more or less equal coverage of all children.

> **Key Point:**
> Dynamic pictures of children's change over time are collected by means of varied techniques.

Authentic Assessment Techniques: The Products

The products of the techniques described above are used in many ways:

- as assessment;
- as the source of excerpts for panels;
- to show an entire conversation;
- as part of the permanent record of children's growth;
- as the subject matter for parent/teacher conferences or meetings;
- as information about the school's structure and activities.

Here, I describe how to make use of the products of assessment in daily classroom practice.

Assessment. Teachers use records to show parents and the children themselves exactly what they have done. The records, along with teachers' notes, enable teachers to explain what the work product means in terms of what children have learned. Varied records, combined with teachers' interpretations, provide a dynamic assessment

Figure 11.4. Sonya and a small group reread what they have written for a friend's birthday and revise their work until it sounds just right.

that shows not simply what children did but the context—the why, how, when, and where of an experience. Children themselves study their work. In Figure 11.4, the children and Sonya are using a computer to review text they wrote for a friend's birthday and are editing the text collaboratively.

Panels. Children's words, photos of children in action, and occasionally a representative piece of work are carefully selected by teachers to illustrate on a panel what occurred. Panels are *products.* The teachers' selection of materials and their reflection with children about the thoughts and actions shown on the panel are a *process* (see Chapter 10).

Classroom Materials. At the MELC, assessment records became favorite classroom materials. For example:

- Photos were made into albums of individual projects or of an entire year's experiences. Albums were accessible for children and/or parents to peruse.
- Slide shows were shown to children and at parent meetings. (Today, we would use PowerPoint.)
- A slide sorter (the vertical kind, about $20) and magnifying glass were used by children to peruse slides. (Today, children could do this on a computer.)
- Transcripts of children's conversations hung in acetate folders alongside the materials that generated the recording. Teachers read from the transcripts to children to help them remember what they said. Teachers also read transcripts at parent meetings to describe what children were doing.

Through transcripts, children, parents, and others can follow children's train of thought generated by a particular experience.

Permanent Records. Work was rarely sent home but accumulated. When children graduated, teachers gave their family a gift of work showing children's growth over 3 years. When teachers visited homes to meet younger siblings, they saw pieces of the "graduate's" work in the living room, evidence of its importance to families.

> **Key Point:**
> "Documentation . . . ensure[s] that the group and each individual child have the possibility to observe themselves from an external point of view while they are learning" (Rinaldi, 2006, p. 68).

ROADBLOCKS TO AUTHENTIC ASSESSMENT

Apart from the natural resistance to change, a number of factors make it difficult to use authentic assessment.

Unfamiliarity

Lynn Kagan (Professor of Early Childhood and Family Policy at Columbia University) and her colleagues say that, due mainly to lack of training, authentic assessment is "overwhelming" for some teachers who collect "all this stuff" but don't know what to do with it and "don't know what they are seeing when they observe children" (Shepard, Taylor, & Kagan, 1996, p. 10). Reading the documentation on many classroom walls confirms this: Text may be too long, a "lead" thought may be missing, flow may not be logical, or key moments may be overlooked.

There is "serious need for better training of professionals to understand what developmentally appropriate assessment means and how to use new forms of assessment" (Shepard et al., 1996, p. 16). A related problem is that teacher educators themselves may be unfamiliar with documentation techniques. If so, the complex process is open to misinterpretation. Most frequently misunderstood is the role of the teacher in recording, selecting, and reflecting with children.

Some educators, familiar with the word *documentation* but not the techniques, fear that children will "perform" or "pose" for the camera, or act "cute" to make the teacher point her camera at them. I have never seen this happen; just the opposite. Children are oblivious to the picture-taking and recording. Nor have I seen what other educators fear–that photographing and note taking inhibit shy children or solicit extroverts.

> **Key Point:**
> Assessment is authentic *if* it is an integral part of all other aspects of practice; therefore, by nature it is complex and thus daunting to some.

Complexity

The most daunting obstacle to using authentic assessment is its systemic nature. That is, the process of gathering records and using them to reflect with children is inseparable from the curricula that develop when teachers use children's reflections as the basis for what to do tomorrow. Because reflection, assessment, and curriculum are inextricably linked without clear boundaries between the processes, teachers may be at a loss for where to start.

RECONCILING AUTHENTIC ASSESSMENT
AND STANDARDIZED TESTING

Wherever I lecture, the but . . . , but . . . , but . . . of standardized testing comes up. In many teachers' minds, documentation is irreconcilable with the standardized tests they are required to give or the objectives they must prove their children have mastered. I hear statements such as

- But we have to use the (whichever) curriculum to prepare our children for standardized tests.
- But how can we be sure the children are learning enough to be "ready" for kindergarten (or the 4-year-old class, or 1st grade)?
- But there isn't enough time to do these kinds of activities and also cover what we must so our children meet the state objectives.

Examining Core Knowledge Competencies

I studied the 60 competencies, critical and supplemental, that a major urban school system expects 3-year-olds to master. The competencies would be easily mastered in the type of classroom I advocate where self-regulation is established (see Chapter 2), where time and space are structured for Open Flow (see Chapter 4), where there is small-group or one-on-one work (many chapters), where the environment is richly detailed (see Chapter 5), where Meaning-full Conversation is integral to every activity (see Chapter 6), where teachers act with intention (see Chapter 7), and where varied interest-provoking materials are used (see Chapters 5, 8, and 9) to engage children in Significant Work (see Chapters 3, 10, and 12).

The competencies I studied fall into these categories:

- mathematical reasoning and number sense
- children's literature: read-alouds
- oral language
- orientation in time
- scientific reasoning and the physical world

Mastering Core Competencies

I regrouped the competencies according to where children would acquire them in a self-regulated, Open Flow/small-group/well-prepared/conversation-rich classroom. My categories include

- *Vocabulary.* Of the 60 competencies, 14 involve mastering specific vocabulary. So long as the teacher knows what words the standards-gurus consider important, she can include them in conversation or in group activities. Young children's vocabulary expands when words are used and repeated in context, not when children are drilled on word meaning with no context.
- *Pattern recognition.* Twelve of the competencies involve comparing, contrasting, completing, or copying patterns. Teachers must be sure that

among their materials are activities and games that include these skills. Children know how to play many games with no instruction; if children do not, teachers can play a game with a small group to show how it goes. If teachers carefully observe children, encourage them to work independently in small groups, and carefully select children for small groups, children will learn from one another. For children who do not, in an Open Flow day teachers have time to provide one-on-one instruction.

- *Games.* Thirteen competencies, mostly mathematical, can be learned from playing games. As with pattern recognition, teachers must ensure that their classroom has games—commercial, teacher-made, or both—that children know how to play them, and are encouraged to do so.
- *Conversation.* Eight competencies can be mastered by conversing with children. These competencies—typified by children's answering questions about stories—are easily learned by children who regularly engage in Meaning-full Conversation and who are read to regularly and with meaning.
- *Focus.* While everything a child does requires focus, in four of the 60 competencies, focus is the main cognitive process—for example, finding a specific item in an illustration.

As I have stated throughout the book, developing focus is the first order of business for young children. Teachers who want to use authentic assessment techniques must allay their qualms by analyzing how practices in an Open Flow classroom prepare children to meet their school's objectives. I have found some objectives so broad or so numerous and narrow that they are meaningless. I have also found that children in Reggio and Montessori schools possess competencies that far exceed most objectives.

> **Key Point:**
> Reconciling your school's evaluation with authentic assessment techniques is not an insurmountable challenge but does require point-blank attention. It can be accomplished by teachers who are assessment "mavens," that is, those who are naturally inclined to do this kind of analysis and who are willing to take on the task on behalf of their colleagues.

EFFECTIVENESS OF AUTHENTIC ASSESSMENT

I cannot offer statistically significant results from research on authentic assessment to validate the approach as a way to demonstrate what young children learn. What I can offer is a small sample of subjective responses from MELC parents and visitors who observed the school.

Parents' Responses

At the MELC, we periodically asked parents for their responses to the school. Excerpts from comments by a few parents follow (Lewin-Benham, 1998, pp. 354–356).

Ahmed's Mother: "Parent meetings were what helped me the most . . . not based on [making] decisions [about pick-up times or administrative matters], but on what the children were doing. . . . The meetings helped to know what to look at, and what to pay attention to."

Kiesha's Mother: "I relied on the messages for my information–for my understanding of the school and the teachers. I appreciated how you put down the children's dialogues word for word as the children said them."

Daniel's Mother: "I read the journal on the parent board every day. This is the best way for me to know what is going on. The documentation was very helpful, too, in order to know what was happening in the school over a span of time. This summer, we plan to continue using the library."

Georgie's Grandmother: "This is not a place where you just drop your child off. You can see what children are involved in, through the pictures around, and you can see children enjoying themselves in what they are doing."

Cindy's Grandmother: "I thoroughly enjoyed the book sharing program. . . . [It] helped me to become part of the school, and it was valuable for Cindy's learning. . . . I like the panels. . . . It lit up the whole school by putting all the stuff on the wall. I love it! It brightens everything up, and it helped to understand what was going on."

Karen's Mother: "I enjoyed the field trips the most. . . . I feel these experiences opened up the children more, and encouraged them to talk more, and to ask more questions. . . ."

Renee's Mother: "I was new at the motherhood game, but I'm doing it. Whatever I asked, you all took care of it. [The panels and documentation] it's good. It reminds the children of what they've done, and it helps the parents, too."

Alicia's Mother: "Alicia shared a lot with the family, and when there was home researches the whole family participated in the project that she brought home. . . . She made it her business that everyone in the house knew what was going on in the school."

William's Mother: "Parent meetings were the most helpful for me. All of them were helpful. They let me know what is going on. The papers were helpful also. William learned a lot."

> **Key Point:**
> "The school is perceived by families as a precious jewel, almost a redemption" (Amelia Gambetti in Lewin-Benham, 2006, p. 139).

Visitors' Responses

During several national conferences that the MELC hosted, 400 or 500 visitors toured the school. Visitors also came for "MELC Days," formal 1- or 2-day programs with observations, presentations from the staff, and question-and-answer sessions. The following comments are from visitors' written evaluations of a 1-day visit to the MELC. Because we did not ask visitors to sign their name or school, comments cannot be attributed. Here are examples:

I needed to see it at work–the children in the setting, showing that it works by their ease and joy in the environment. I love the music room in use. Slides of Reggio were the least helpful. [They] were more familiar from NAEYC workshops. I was more interested in seeing how it could work in a large U.S. city. It was inspiring. Seeing what I'd read about made the difference in determining ways we could incorporate some principles and more specific projects.

One participant liked best "when we were able to be with teachers and ask questions." She hoped we would expand the program with "more time with teachers to see how they work with the children in the morning."

Another was impressed by "the integration of all the different aspects of learning, and the vision and pedagogy." She appreciated "experienc[ing] both the failures and the things that work including the *important piece* re how ground rules were used to stop the chaos. Very useful to hear the teachers' process. *Every*body is turned on and *passionate* about learning!!" She continues: "I was glad to see keywords–i.e., S. A. Warner, a lot of basic things from Montessori but now added to with all the new learnings, i.e., H. Gardner, Vygotsky, and the R. Emilio [*sic*] work." Her evaluation was signed "Anne [last name illegible] from Phila."

Another found most helpful "being in the classrooms both during and after school," but "needed more coffee to keep going!" She wanted "more framework, structure, and philosophy." The tour with the MELC teachers was her favorite part. She found the teachers' session on "How Does Staff Team Work Impact on Parent Involvement" "most useful in terms of grappling with this issue for our own school."

Another liked best "visiting in school. I especially appreciated teachers expressing their own questions and fears about the program." She would have liked "more time in classroom." She found the tour with the teachers "interesting, but why were [we] not allowed to speak to children?" and said it "would have been interesting to speak to a parent." She evaluated the discussion sessions as "excellent, teachers were honest and articulate."

Another concluded: "Love the school–the organization, the beauty–a child's heaven–the materials were fantastic."

Kathy Porter, a teacher in the Montgomery County [Maryland] Public Schools, wrote, "To wonderful educators: My experience today was something I cannot put into words. You have made me 'revisit' my philosophy of what I know children, *all* children, need to experience. Thank you and keep up the fantastic work. We love you for it."

Accreditors' Responses

In June 1994, the MELC underwent the process for accreditation by the Municipal Preschools of Reggio Emilia. The process took place during the time the MELC was hosting a national conference featuring Reggio educators. Immediately after the conference, the MELC was hosting an "MELC Day" that the Reggio accreditation team observed. Carlina Rinaldi and Vea Vecchi, the accreditors, interviewed participants in the MELC Day about their reactions to the school. Carlina summed up what participants told her: "It is unbelievable what we saw in that school" (Rinaldi, 2006, p. 146).

The Model Early Learning Center received its accreditation in September 1994 (Reggio Children, 1995). The school remains the only school outside their own city that the Reggio Emilia educators have ever accredited.

CONCLUSION: "PROOF" IS NOT ATTAINABLE

Assessment begins when each teacher, school, parent, and community questions their beliefs about children and translates their beliefs into the kinds of practices they want their schools to incorporate. Financing those practices is an ongoing process for parents and school boards. If long-term change in children–growth in skills, empathetic relationships, and analytic capacities–is an important goal, leaders must provide the funds to track children across time using the kinds of techniques described in this chapter.

Most schools lack the funds to follow up on what happens after their students graduate. The information would help improve programs, as feedback from MELC parents on their children's 1st-grade experiences improved the MELC's approach to literacy (Chapter 7). Without such information, we have only the kinds of reactions quoted above. Capturing more information about outcomes is time consuming, expensive, and unlikely to satisfy those who demand "proof" that the Reggio Approach makes a difference.

The greatest difference between standardized tests and authentic assessment is in what each captures. Test questions cover a narrow range of the areas in which young children grow. Authentic assessment records a broad range. Young children grow at such different rates that the narrow range covered by tests cannot provide the comprehensive picture that authentic assessment strives to capture. Were standardized testing to be mandated for early education and were teachers of young children to teach to a test, schools would be forced to curtail the very experiences that build thinking skills, encourage collaboration, instill self-regulation, and develop empathy.

Questions to Consider

1. List what information you would require about children's progress to satisfy you that they are learning.
2. What would you use to show parents that their children are progressing?
3. What would you use to demonstrate to administrators and funders that your school is up to par?
4. How would you make the case that something other than standardized testing should be used to show children's progress?

CHAPTER 12

Significant Project Work

Flying-man, Flying-man up in the sky,
Where are you going to, flying so high?
Over the mountains and over the sea—!
Flying-man, Flying-man,
Can't you take me?

—Mother Goose

C HILDREN'S IMAGINATION is boundless, and they are willing to tackle anything, as shown in the nursery rhyme and the scenarios in this chapter. It was mid-October, a new school year. As you entered the MELC, you saw a display with photographs of all the children under the title, in large letters, "Who We Are." It was called the Photo Board. The photos were black and white, portraits that captured each child's uniqueness. Under each photo was the child's full name.

The display was striking, spacing exact, no extraneous details. The emphasis was on each child's expression. It was the first thing the children showed visitors, who always exclaimed with pleasure. Since its installation, children had not tired of studying the display, sometimes a single child, sometimes a small group, other times a child and admiring adult. However, it was clearly adult work. Because the display had no work by children, the children's presence was missing.

In this chapter, I describe a project from the MELC, a project from Reggio, and contrast a beginning American process with a mature Reggio process.

AN MELC STORY

The problem was how to add children's presence, in the form of their work product, to the Photo Board. Neither teachers nor children had confronted such a problem. The teachers decided to clarify the problem for themselves before presenting it to the children. Looking back 17 years later, Jennifer said, "There is so much we didn't know!" Had they been experienced, the teachers might have involved the children more in the process or encouraged children to make more use of one another's ideas.

Starting the Project

In 1994, we understood the problem as giving children a presence. Today, we would add: *how teachers improve their own ability* to see individual differences among children and *how to help teachers learn about children's problem solving abilities*. More specifically:

- Do children *focus*?
- How long will children *sustain attention*?
- Will children *collaborate*? Who will be leaders? Who will be imitators? What other roles will they play? Will roles change?
- What *meaning* will children find in the work?
- What *relationships* will they make between this project and other experiences?

Because the MELC teachers placed great emphasis on activities that helped children understand the meaning of friendship, for this project the teachers tried to develop questions with social implications:

- What can you learn about your friends by looking at the Photo Board?
- How could you learn more?

Good questions focus teachers' observation and hook children's interest.

> **Key Point:**
> As a project is launched, teachers must analyze what their intentions are.

Possible Interpretations

If the MELC teachers' intent was to see if children would learn about their friends from the Photo Board, they would observe the children with questions such as these in mind:

- Does discussion of a favorite panel cause children to talk about one another?
- Do children respond to visual impressions? "Gerald's nose is flat. Courtney's braid stands straight up. Arminta has a big smile."
- Do children respond to auditory patterns? "Donald's name got a 'D' just like Derrick's. Terrell's picture is next to Tom's because their last names are both Brown."
- Do children respond to social or emotional feelings? "I want to work with Courtney 'cause we friends."

The teachers also wondered if children would understand the nature of the materials they were using because there were potential problems in altering the Photo Board: What if children wanted to *color* the photographs? Would they know you cannot color a high-gloss black and white photo? What if they wanted to add pictures like they had drawn for their friends' birthday gifts? Would they have the spatial sense to see that there was no room for pictures on the Photo Board? Materials have constraints—too stiff, shapeless, opaque, too slick, too dark, too light. Could children match a material's property to the requirements of a project?

Reggio educators call this process of thinking about what might happen "making hypotheses." Before a project begins and during complex projects, teachers have to push hypotheses to logical conclusions.

One Hypothesis. In the MELC, the teachers engaged the children in many discussions about friendship, what it means to be kind, to help someone, to say things that make someone feel good. Teachers and children had discussed how Miss Wendy's welcoming hugs made them feel. They had discussed the friendship between their cat, Coco, and the goldfish. The children feared Coco would hurt the fish, but discovered that Coco just wanted to look at it. Brandi noticed: "Coco don't even put out his paw." The children were very familiar with panels about Coco's relationships. Because they had studied them many times, they recalled every detail of the exchanges between cat and goldfish, cat and turtle, cat and them.

Frequently, children had pored over the Birthday Book, full of portraits they had made and what they had written about their friends. The teachers had read them the comments such as: "Derrick always play with the trains." Or, "Brandi like Tesha best." Would the children understand that you learn something about a friend from such comments? From reading children's comments about one another, would viewers feel children's presence on the Photo Board?

A Different Hypothesis. The teachers could suggest that the children model what they did on the Photo Board after a project in the Studio called "A Hundred Tiny Doors." Covering the huge bottom panes of two windows, "Doors" was a favorite project—miniature collages using "sequins, bugle beads, scraps of theater gel, mini-paper clips, assorted beads and buttons" (Lewin-Benham, 2006, p. 117). During the project, every child had participated, some filling one "door" with the tiny items, others filling several. Would the children want to make miniature assemblages? They would be small enough to fit on the Photo Board. Would mini-collages tell children anything about one another?

The teachers had a practical concern about the "Doors" idea: Because the original "doors" were mounted on windows, light shone through their transparent backing. Light couldn't shine through the Photo Board. Would that deter the children? Would they consider sparkly, shiny materials beautiful enough?

A "Doors"-type project was significantly different from the first hypothesis. If the children decided to do "Doors," could the teachers back off the idea of describing friends? Teachers' ideas don't always resonate with children's. "Doors" were certainly beautiful and, as the poet Ralph Waldo Emerson (1912) said, "beauty is its own excuse for being."

Third Hypothesis. If the project were "Doors," the children would have to solve a number of problems—size, material selection, production. These problems raised pros and cons.

Pros:

- The children loved the "Doors."
- They had worked industriously.
- The children enjoyed using myriad tiny objects to fill small spaces.
- There had been a huge amount of collaboration.
- "Doors" had been an early catalyst to draw parents, the shimmering bits beckoning them to look closely, children pulling their parents to "Come! See!"
- Teachers and children had hoped there might be another similar project.
- Another "Doors" project would probably evoke the same long, concentrated span of work and yield something equally beautiful.

Cons:

- Exactly where on the Photo Board would the "Doors" go?
- How big should each be?
- From what would the backing be made?
- What objects would they use on the backing?
- Would the colors be limited or whatever any child wanted to use?
- Would the project be worth the time? In other words, would it develop new skills, help children acquire new content, or expand the meaning they assigned to things?

> **Key Point:**
> Because projects can take many possible directions, teachers weigh the pros and cons of how different projects might develop before embarking on a project *and* at key junctures in an ongoing project.

In undertaking a project, teachers consider what their intention is and what they and the children might learn. Forming hypotheses can reveal whether a project has the potential to develop in rich ways. A central issue is how interesting the project will be to the children; that is, will it cause them to focus? Encourage them to work collaboratively? Stimulate conversation? Engage them in making meaning?

Deliberating

The teachers continued their deliberations. A project often flies in wide circles before homing in. The teachers considered what differences there would be among older and younger children. Some were in their 3rd year together and had made many different things. Some were brand-new.

- Would new children require more structure? For example: Would they gather materials from the shelves, or choose from a selection the teachers made?
- Who would decide what material to use for the backing, teachers or children?
- What would new children think of the "Doors" on the window panes?
- How much would the older children help the younger ones?
- Could the older children reason through the constraints in the project?
  - material for the backing should neither overwhelm the materials nor clash with the Photo Board;
  - items would need to attract attention;
  - size: There was little space, only 1½ by 2½ inches for each child.

> **Key Point:**
> There are times for teachers to give answers directly, times to collaborate with children as they search for their own answers, and times merely to listen and observe.

"Thinking about what is possible is in itself an act of inventing, discovering, and planning" (Reggio Children, 1995, p. 10).

Challenge: The Backing. Jennifer would have to have many conversations with children about choosing a backing. The children would have to consider the qualities of various materials:

- Were cardboard and corrugated paper pretty enough?
- Were wallpaper samples too patterned?
- Was fadeless art paper too bright?
- From the large collection of cardstock—chrome coat, shiny, slick, matt finish, white, quiet beige, pale pastels—which would work best?
- Would she, Jennifer, strike the right balance between suggesting and listening?

Complication: Measurement. There was another complication: How would children figure out how large to make the background pieces? Malaguzzi said that the answer to such problems "involves neither a simulation nor a laboratory experiment, but originates from a problem the children have made their own" (Malaguzzi et al., 1995, p. 16).

> **Key Point:**
> Serious
> questioning
> before the start
> of a project
> is a hallmark
> of a reflective
> practice.

Five-year-olds do not know how to use rulers. Some are just learning one-to-one correspondence; others are learning qualitative relations—more than, less than, and equal. If the children themselves made the backings, they would have to deal with problems in both number and measurement. Malaguzzi (1997) said,

The school should start from concrete problems and situations so as to ensure more immediate and lasting interest and motivation. . . . We are convinced that measurement is the best and most useful channel through which five-year-olds can approach the world of numerical and mathematical languages. (p. 16)

A REGGIO STORY

Reggio teachers begin projects by clarifying their intentions. They wonder how individual children explore and observe children with questions such as these in mind:

- How aware are children of what tools and materials they will need?
- Can they choose materials that suit a particular task?
- Can children use materials skillfully to achieve their goal?
- Are children competent tool users?
- To what extent would children help one another, imitate one another, seek help from another child or an adult?

To launch a project, teachers carefully form questions that will provoke children's interest without putting teachers' ideas in their heads (see Chapter 6). How to suggest without directing is not always clear.

The Reggio publication *Shoe and Meter* (Malaguzzi, 1997) tells the story of children who have asked a carpenter to build a specific table for their classroom. He has agreed to do so but needs measurements.

The carpenter immediately puts the children on guard: "Do you know how to make measurements?"

Their reply is swift: ". . . Do you really know how to make a table exactly like this one?"

And so the adventure is launched.

Some of the children say it's hard, some say that you just have to start, that the table has too many measurements, that you need numbers. The general apprehension, however, only thinly conceals their strong desire to set off on the adventure. (pp. 18–19)

First Steps

First, the children try counting and measuring with their fingers. Aware that something is amiss, two children bring paper: "We have to draw the table so we can understand it" (p. 21). On their drawings of tables they also draw computers, pencil holders, and more items that represent the *functions* of a table. The drawings are charming but confusing. The teachers step in and take a table outside the classroom, where it is isolated from its functions.

The children measure the table with every part of their body, soon realizing that using a leg requires less work than using fingers. They get nowhere using their bodies and begin to bring objects—a ladle from the kitchen, a book. The children have mastered one certainty: A measuring object can be either too short or too long! But they are far from using consistent measurement, and they seem to be stuck.

First Teacher Intervention

Watching thoughtfully, the teachers concur that a more concrete example of using their whole body might help the children see the need for a consistent measure. The children have had some experience measuring long jumps so the teachers suggest they make long jumps and measure them. But, the children discover that the first jump, which measures four of Tommaso's feet, measures only three of the teacher's feet! As the children make more jumps, discrepancies increase! Jumps measure five of one child's feet, six of another's.

A big breakthrough: The children measure their feet against the teacher's and realize that her foot is bigger because it occupies more space. As the teachers suspected, this new understanding gives the children a new idea. Pier Luigi: "Why don't we get a string and measure the whole thing at one time and then cut it when we get to the end of the table?" (p. 33).

And they're off in a direction that results in two strings that measure the table—one for the length, the other for the width, which the children call "shortness" (p. 35). But they are not satisfied. They realize they have no numbers. The children don't say this in so many words, but show it in their actions. Daniela measures the string with her fingers, counting out loud as she does so. Her expression shows something is still not right!

Daniela and Tommaso leave and return with strips of paper, put a strip next to the string, and Daniela writes 1, 2, 3. . . . For the first time in the project, the children have added numbers to measurement and are using numeric symbols! Daniela, with some impatience: "Numbers go on forever! We can't write them all!" (p. 38).

Tommaso observes that there must be lines between the numbers. His comment spurs Daniela to make what she calls a "measuring stick" (p. 39), combining numbers and lines. The other children think this is such a good idea that they *all* make measuring sticks! "So 'meters' of subjective and arbitrary lengths are created" (p. 41). Despite discrepancies, each meter has numbers with marks to indicate progression. Several are quite precise, but . . . "Here, in fact, the scandal explodes. The various sticks measure the table as 78, 41, 20, 23, 44" (p. 43). Each child's stick shows a different measure for numerical value. Meter is still subjective.

Second Teacher Intervention

Hoping children will see the problem, the teacher suggests they line up the sticks. One stick has marks over each number to represent that number's value. Another has the same number of marks *between* each number to try to make equal distances. It is a creative but varied collection. As the children study the sticks they have lined up, they concur: They must pick the meter "with the right numbers!" (p. 45).

It seems they are getting close, but then . . . Tommaso says, "Let's measure the table with my shoe!" (p. 51). After working with an abstraction, numbers, they revert to a concrete object, a shoe! The children put a long strip of paper on the table and count how many shoes it measures: The paper is six and a half shoes long (see Figure 12.1). No matter which end of the table they start counting from, the length remains six and a half shoes. They are on to something. They measure the width and, voila! They have their measurements: The table is six and a half shoes by three shoes.

Third Teacher Intervention

Again, the teacher intervenes suggesting that the children *draw* their results.

The teacher's suggestion lends clarity to the situation. This type of loan should always be made based on a guarantee of results in terms of the advancement of the children's knowledge; otherwise it becomes more of a transmission of adult knowledge that is not in tune with the children's research and the procedures they are working out for themselves. (p. 54)

Figure 12.1. With great care Tommaso aligns a shoe with the table's edge, uses his hand to mark the place where the toe lands, then moves the shoe forward, placing the heel exactly where the toe was.

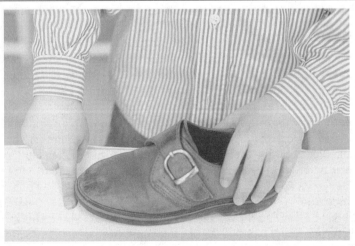

© Preschools and Infant-toddler Centers–Istituzione of the Municipality of Reggio Emilia (Italy), from the book *Shoe and Meter* published by Reggio Children.

Tommaso Has a Breakthrough. Tommaso suggests that they look for a "real meter stick" (p. 54), goes himself, and returns immediately with a folding ruler. He measures his shoe. It is 20 centimeters long.

A piece of good luck: The fold in the ruler falls on 20, the exact size of Tommaso's shoe! Amazingly, the shoe and the ruler coincide. The children find it funny that the ruler's folds go 20, 20, 20. They conclude that they simply have to add up the 20s! They easily add three 20s with a calculator, then add 5 for the leftover "little piece" (p. 58). They do the same for the "shortness [width]," which measures three shoes, or 60. So, they have numbers–125 x 60.

The table is now covered with:

- the children's number lines;
- four drawings, one on each side of the table, of meticulously outlined shoes;
- the number 125 on each long side and the number 60 on each short side.

The children are taking no chances that the carpenter might misread their instructions. They are using all the measurement systems they have devised.

When Breakthroughs Occur. The breakthrough from the concrete shoe to the symbolic ruler seems to have occurred out of the blue. The brain sometimes works like that, especially when the mind is prepared. These children's minds were prepared by:

- the concrete, firsthand experience of needing to give accurate measurements to a carpenter;
- their teachers' listening, which is as much about when to be silent as when to intervene;
- the classroom, equipped with measurement tools that the children had undoubtedly seen used;
- the availability of the calculator, which the children knew how to work, including the plus key.

Conceptual breakthroughs result from brain processes that we cannot observe. Something calls the brain to action, to recollect past experiences, to rapidly retrieve memories from where they are stored. Something kicks in analytic processes to elaborate, synthesize, and in the process build relationships. Neuroscientists say that the potential number of connections among brain cells is, essentially, infinite. When children are engaged in Significant Work they are building brain networks.

Another Conundrum! But one breakthrough does not a solution make, especially in complex work. And, when concepts–such as how numbers and measurement work together to form a useful system–are being formed, they tend to be unstable. In other words, it requires repetition for the brain to consolidate tentative understanding so that it can be applied in future situations.

Marco now notices that the number on the bottom of Tommaso's shoe is not 20, but 29! Such a conflict throws the brain into a state of disequilibrium. The children begin to argue about whether 20 or 29 is right; but Daniela says emphatically: "The meter [meaning the ruler] doesn't make mistakes" (p. 60).

Emphatic as she is, Daniela does not prevent the huge eruption that follows. Children begin taking off their shoes. Many shoes have different numbers. The confusion could derail the project!

Fourth Teacher Intervention

The teacher brings the children back on track, reminds them that the carpenter is waiting, and suggests that they *draw* the table with its measurements. To do so, the children will have to blend the language of number and the language of picture. Combining an abstract representation (number) and a drawing is another huge conceptual challenge.

The children's drawings are combinations of meters, numbers, shoes, and schematics of the table. Each child's interpretation is different. One shows a top view of the table, another the table top with legs extending from opposite corners, another a disaggregated collection of top, legs, and thickness. Daniela's has a small square with two circles in it. She calls it a "secret drawing" (p. 65), but later explains that the square is an imaginary hole through which you can see both the table leg and the foot, represented by two circles, one inside the other.

As an aggregate, the children's drawings represent every different part of the table, each with measurements for the carpenter. Some children took great pains to count the exact number of centimeters. Others decided it was important to *see* measurements, so encircled the table legs with paper on which to write the numbers. Others turned the table upside down to make measuring easier. One found a measuring tape to take the circumference of a leg and in the process realized that all the legs would be the same. In all drawings, the shoe remained the preferred measure.

Tommaso made another remarkable breakthrough. With his foot alongside the table leg, he said: "It's half of half of half of the shoe" (p. 71), realizing that a unit can be broken into smaller units. The remark shows Tommaso's intuitive understanding of division and, by deduction, multiplication, the inverse mathematical function. Young children's minds can grasp these concepts.

A Big Debate

A heavy debate ensues among the children. The teachers keep out. Finally, Alan, the children's emissary to the teachers, explains their dilemma: Which would the carpenter better understand, the measurement with shoes or with numbers?

The teacher responds that the children must make that decision. There is a clamor of voices, with numbers seeming to be favored. But when the teacher suggests a show of hands, all vote for the shoe! Realizing their own inconsistency, the children break into hearty laughter and ask to vote again. The vote is taken: four to two, meter over shoe. Clearly, there is some reluctance to part with the shoe, a cherished object in this complicated project.

Fifth Teacher Intervention: A "Reconnaissance"

The teachers convene a meeting of the children, a "reconnaissance," what in Reggio parlance is a time to talk about everything they have done so far. The children want to examine their drawings. After much discussion, they concur that numbers

Figure 12.2. Any good carpenter would be able to build a table using the detailed specifications that resulted from the children's efforts and their collaboration.

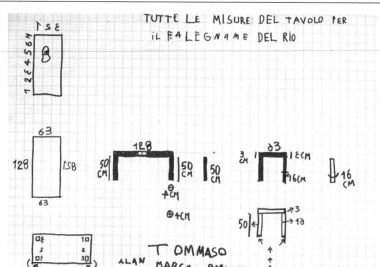

must be on the drawings. They also decide that each child should make a new drawing. Then, the group will choose the best features and combine them into one drawing to give to the carpenter. Selecting best features to combine into a final product is a common procedure in many Reggio projects.

The children reach agreement: Three children will make the drawing, but all will sign it. It is remarkably sophisticated, drawn on graph paper (the children's choice) with top and side views of the table, arrows pointing from table part to number, and one small rectangle with a drawing of the shoe. The numbers 1, 2, and 3 are on the width, and the numbers 1 through 6 are on the length. Overall, the drawing is neat and entirely intelligible.

The children present the drawing to the carpenter (Figure 12.2) along with a letter specifying that they want oak wood with a yellow top. Toward the end of the letter, they add cautionary notes: "Be careful because if you work in a hurry you might make a mistake . . . [and] put your glasses on so you can see better" (p. 86). In closing, they tell the carpenter to have fun and they give him their phone number in case he does not understand something.

The story *Shoe and Meter* reveals the structure of Reggio projects:

- Children's interest is the starting point.
- The challenge is novel and complex.
- The teachers provide time for children to try out their ideas, watching closely and making comprehensive records of what the children do.

- If the children get stuck, the teachers intervene to help the children move toward the goal; if interventions instead lead the children on a tangent, the teachers allow time for the children to try out their ideas.
- At propitious moments, the teachers bring the group of children together to pool ideas.
- The teachers allow whatever amount of time it takes to meet the challenge.

> **Key Point:**
> When children are deeply engaged, Reggio teachers neither rush them nor lead them to a solution.

THE CONTRAST

In the end, the MELC teachers followed neither of the more complicated hypotheses. As Jennifer said, there was so much they did not know in 1993! Jennifer provided materials for all children to personalize their own photo. She selected pieces of shiny paper, some transparent, others embossed, all in complementary colors. Each child chose the pieces he or she liked and glued them in place, no backing boards, no measurement required. The mini-collages added a sparkle that pleased everyone. The consensus was that the Photo Board now indeed showed the presence of children (Figure 12.3).

Figure 12.3. As you entered the MELC, you faced a floor-to-ceiling photo mural of the children; across the top is a collage made collaboratively, and under each child's photo is a mini-collage that was made by that child alone.

Figure 12.4. An integrated collection of best practices, such as the Reggio Approach, represents a paradigm shift in early education.

THE PARADIGM	SHIFT
Preplanned Lessons	**Thoughtful Intentions**
Whole Class	**Small Group**
Preset Curriculum	**Emergent Curriculum**
Lesson Planning	**Process Planning**
Teacher/Aide	**Teacher/Teacher**
Schedule Driven	**Interest Driven**
Ho-Hum Spaces	**Provocative Places**
Time Bound	**Space Provoked**
Bulleting Boards	**Documentation**
Teacher-Lecturer	**Teacher-Collaborator**
Loud Colors	**Gentle Hues**
Cluttered Spaces	**Intentional Spaces**

The differences between the two projects–Photo Board and *Shoe and Meter*–are as wide as the ocean separating Washington, DC, and Reggio. Yet both projects represent a paradigm shift: a change in the structure of early childhood practices (Figure 12.4).

The MELC Context

The MELC teachers, as Jennifer knew, had not yet acquired much understanding of their role. But they worked for whatever amount of time was necessary–even until late in the evening–to clarify their ideas, study notes of the children's words and actions, and consider possible next steps. At the time, Reggio-inspired work had barely begun in the United States. Our relations with educators in Reggio Emilia, and especially Amelia Gambetti, were our touchstone. The MELC experiences have since become a touchstone for what American children can achieve using the Reggio Approach.

In summer 2010, at an international gathering in Reggio Emilia, Amelia Gambetti was a presenter. During her lecture, she called her time at the MELC "one of the most moving experiences of her life," her voice breaking as she described the school's environment, providing "the best for children who had nothing" (Lecture, Reggio Emilia, Summer 2010).

The Reggio Context

The MELC children had no experiences that were remotely comparable to the Reggio children, who were highly primed by past experience to tackle projects with many complexities. The Reggio teachers were seasoned and highly skilled in the arts of observing, listening, stepping back, knowing when to intervene, making suggestions, and forming questions that direct children's attention in ways that lend clarity to their confusion or point their investigation along fruitful paths.

Reggio teachers understand that seemingly fruitful paths may, in fact, be dead ends. They are comfortable with uncertainties, false starts, and explorations that proceed at children's pace. They realize that the mind forms new concepts gradually, and if given time, children eventually become more skilled at using concepts as the basis for analytic thinking and at expressing themselves in different modes or languages. Any best practice allows the time for children to learn something, to seem to forget it, to learn it again, and with repeated experience to make the word, idea, or action their own. These processes, like the movement of glaciers, are largely hidden from sight. Reggio educators are, above all, masterful at reading clues about children's understanding from the children's most nuanced actions or comments.

Were anyone to question whether the *Shoe and Meter* project was "worth the time," I would respond: When you have created a process yourself–as the Reggio children created a standardized measurement system–you may forget the outcome, but are likely to remember how you got there. Therefore, you can do it again. Equally important, what is likely to transfer from this experience to others is your confidence in your ability to solve tough problems and the sweet taste of succeeding at a big effort.

CONCLUSION: BUCKING CULTURAL IMPERATIVES

Reggio educators are decades removed from their beginnings. My hope is that in the United States' hurry-up culture, we will not conclude that Reggio practices "don't work." Our tendency is to allow only a few years to try something before we move on to a newer trend. My hope is that the culture surrounding Reggio-inspired schools in the United States will allow them time–the most precious gift to a teacher or a child– to find their way. My hope is that we will have many touchstones where the belief in children's competence flourishes and where teachers become masters in the arts of intention, intervention, and listening.

The *Shoe and Meter* project is a metaphor–an example of how, when given the time, children resolve complex undertakings, in this case creating a system with abstract symbols by using the languages of words, drawings, numbers, letters, gesture, movement, and more. The project is an illustration of how children translate among all these languages, drawing on them creatively to express ideas that are in formation. The project provides glimpses of how children's brains analyze new challenges–how children's sensory experiences and movements inform, misinform, or fail to inform their analytic processes. The project highlights the nature of collaboration among children and between teachers and children and it provides a clear picture of the teacher's role in a project–her intention, when she intervenes, how she does so, and the result. *Shoe and Meter* is a rare window into how children's minds form concepts: in this project a sense of the meaning of standardized measurement.

As for the Photo Board project, it lived on in the MELC's entryway. It more than satisfied the teachers' goal of bringing the children's presence to the display. The Photo Board lured visitors and made each family proud of its son or daughter. It drew parents into friendships as they called one another's attention to their child's work, praised every child's effort, and shared the pleasure of the sparkling outcome. The project offered children in next year's class a model for their own personalization of the Photo Board, a model they could either copy or vary—the choice presently undecided, but pregnant with possibilities.

And in fact, that is where we are with Reggio-inspired schools in America— pregnant with possibilities.

Questions to Consider

1. Consider a project you might undertake and write hypotheses for the different ways it could develop.
2. Explain what hypothesis you might have developed for changing the Photo Board.
3. Analyze the teachers' actions in the *Shoe and Meter* project according to the roles of the teacher described in Chapter 7.

CHAPTER 13

EXCEL

See saw, sacaradown,
Which is the way to Boston Town?
One foot up the other Foot down,
That is the Way to Boston Town.

—Mother Goose

THINK OF THIS CHAPTER as a series of lenses to look at where you are going in your practices. The analogy is an eye checkup. As the optometrist slips lens after lens into the holder in front of your eyes, the letters on the chart continually become clearer. The chapter title EXCEL is an acronym. Each letter stands for a cluster of best practices. No cluster is more important than another. Like the lenses the eye doctor uses, each is important in the process of the exam. I explain the acronym in the first part of this chapter.

The questions in the second part of the chapter help you focus on your practices more clearly. EXCEL is a self-test to help you see what you consider important. Seeing what we consider important is a way to confront our beliefs.

The third part of the chapter has ideas for how to use EXCEL, either on your own or with a group, to help you change your practices. I suggest reading the full chapter before beginning to answer the questions in part two.

UNDERSTANDING THE ACRONYM EXCEL

The acronym EXCEL stands for

E–Environment
X–eXchanges
C–Conversation
E–Evidence
L–Language

The cluster of practices together indicates the quality of children's experiences. The selection reflects my beliefs about what constitutes excellent early education. Others might select differently. Here, I describe the meaning of the acronym EXCEL.

E—Environment

In early education, from birth to about age 8, the environment *is* the curriculum. Jean Piaget (1950), father of constructivist theory, believed that each child's intelligence develops from experiences with objects in the environment. Lev Vygotsky (1934/1986), father of socio-cultural theory, believed that the interaction of adults in children's experiences determines how an experience will affect children's thinking. Reuven Feuerstein, father of the theory of mediated learning, believes adults' interactions—if they are intentional, convey meaning, and transcend from the immediate to the past or future—are *the* determining factor that makes us human (Feuerstein et al., 2006). Reggio practices integrate constructivist, socio-cultural, and mediated-learning theories. A challenge in early education is to integrate the beliefs of Piaget, Vygotsky, Feuerstein, the Reggio educators, and other best practices.

Reggio educators believe the environment is so important that they call it a "third teacher." This means they trust that what children learn from each other and from using items in the classroom is equally important to what they learn from working with a teacher.

As you read the questions on the environment, consider: Every question suggests conditions that either restrict children's access to ideas or, if changed, could make ideas more accessible. By "idea," I mean a child's ability to construct new meaning through his or her actions with or without an adult's interaction.

> **Key Point:**
> The environment either constricts what children can experience or puts a world of relationships within children's reach.

X—eXchanges

The central idea in Vygotsky's (1934/1986) socio-cultural theory is that we learn as a result of our interactions—or exchanges—with the environment but especially with one another—child/child, child/adult, or adult/group. Reggio educators believe that teachers' primary role is to listen, to know when to intervene, and to do so in a way that enables children to clarify their own thinking. Feuerstein's theory would put it this way: Adult intervention in children's activities has three essential characteristics: (1) intention, (2) meaning, and (3) transcendence (Feuerstein et al., 2006). Intention means that adults give serious thought to why they are intervening, select a particular meaning that they intend to convey, make children aware of their intent, do whatever is necessary to convey that meaning, and then encourage children to connect the meaning to something that happened in the past or could happen in the future.

Looking at an episode in the *Shoe and Meter* project, described in Chapter 12, the teachers' *intent* in suggesting that children make a long jump is to remind children how they once used standard measurement. The teachers make the suggestion because they see a parallel between how children measured their jumps and what they need to do to measure the table. The *meaning* is the children's dawning realization that measurement must be consistent and must use numbers. The *transcendent* ideas are that there are ways to measure other than with one's body and they can be applied to tables, long jumps, or universally. The teachers understand that children's desire to give instructions to the carpenter is the motivation for their actions. Thus, to maintain the motivation, the teachers thoughtfully consider precisely when and how to intervene as the project evolves. The proof that the teachers are completely cognizant of every minute in the project's life is that they have documented it with exceptional detail in words and photos.

eXchanges are based on adults'

- selecting something of importance to communicate;
- knowing how to arrest children's attention;
- sensitively listening or watching children's responses as keys to children's emotional and cognitive states;
- using their intention to change children's state–stimulate a desire to participate, excite children about new cognitive skills, engage empathetic feelings, and the like–and to keep motivation high.

C—Conversation

I determine whether children are self-regulated by how they behave when you engage them in conversation. Conversation is a way to observe whether children can:

- focus their attention;
- maintain focus;
- think logically, that is, stay on topic and make responses that relate to what others are saying;
- restrain impulsive behavior;
- monitor what they are doing as they do it;
- retrieve relevant content and concepts from their memory;
- express their ideas fluently.

To me, conversation is important because it helps develop the brain's attention systems. Attention is the basis for all learning. A child who cannot focus cannot learn. Helping children become self-regulated means "training" the attention systems so that in time children are able to regulate by themselves. Some children need to be taught these skills. Smiley faces, gold stars, threats, and punishments such as time outs are external rewards or incentives for children who do not have internal controls. External incentives motivate children to work for the reward. They do not help children work for the joy of the work, nor do external rewards help build internal control. Conversation is also important because it helps in developing the brain's linguistic systems.

E—Evidence

By evidence, I mean both the work children themselves have produced and the documents teachers make or collect:

- notes or recordings of what children say;
- photos of children's significant actions that
  - capture the moment of discovery;
  - seize a perplexed face;

- arrest the expression that says, "Aha!"
- reveal a group's attempt to solve a problem, like using body parts to measure (Malaguzzi, *Shoe and Meter,* 1997);
- freeze hands as they skillfully manipulate;
- snag a series of images that show a skill as it evolves;
- catch an emotion when children empathize, show friendship, feel sorrow;
- watch a misadventure and perhaps its righting.

    Note: Having a camera always ready, knowing what to shoot, having adequate light, a favorable angle on the children, and the object of children's attention in view–all at the same instant–is often a matter of luck. But when caught, such photos are invaluable in showing children's growth. Photos also show teachers' increasing understanding of what the work means and of their own growth.

- video, a more difficult medium than photos because video requires interpretation to explain what the teacher's intention is, the meaning of the clip, its transcendent value, and the context that surrounds or gave rise to the content;
- lists of what children have been engaged in along with other records that teachers keep on a regular basis.

> **Key Point:**
> Evidence is the basis for assessment and therefore for reflective teaching.

L—Language

    By language, I mean the diverse modes of expression in which humans communicate their ideas. There are hundreds. I focus on:

- spoken or written words in which ideas relate logically to one another;
- symbols, such as numbers, pictograms, or letters;
- gesture, facial expression, body language, and other movements;
- visualization and spatial representation;
- marks on paper that reveal how children move their hands and how they manipulate any kind of mark-maker;
- musical expression;
- using the hands to wield tools and shape objects in clay and other natural or man-made materials;
- responses to natural paradoxes such as light, shadow, holes, rainbows, air, water, temperature, and other phenomena;
- responses that reflect understanding of oneself and others.

> **Key Point:**
> Language is both the means through which individuals exchange ideas and the means through which the mind receives, stores, manipulates, accesses, and expresses ideas.

    I use the phrases *Meaning-full Conversation* and *language-full experiences* to emphasize the importance of using language fully. By fully I mean using extensive vocabulary, standard grammar, fluent expression, as well as using language in its verbal (speaking or reading aloud), graphic (writing), and silent (reading to yourself) modes.

PUTTING EXCEL TO WORK

In this section, are the five topics in the acronym EXCEL. I pose nine or ten questions for each topic. Under each topic is a list of considerations; all describe conditions that are *undesirable*. Note your reaction to each condition and respond to the questions. Your responses can help you analyze your own practices and determine what you do in each area of practice addressed in this assessment. In the third section of this chapter I provide additional guidance on how to use EXCEL to change your practice, either by yourself or with the support of a group of colleagues.

E—Environment

In the early years, the environment *is* the curriculum. Examine your environment to assess what possibilities your environment provides for children's minds to grow.

1.   Is the room cluttered or orderly? For signs of clutter, consider whether you see these things in your classroom:
     *   cardboard boxes of surplus supplies such as tissues, sponges, paper towel, toilet paper, cleanser, and the like;
     *   materials piled on shelves so that individual puzzles, games, or manipulatives cannot be seen without lifting off other items;
     *   walls covered with commercially produced posters or decorations;
     *   mismatched containers that hold materials;
     *   containers so large that you cannot see the contents inside;
     *   sets with many pieces–blocks, LEGO, trains–without a storage system that makes pieces visible, orderly, and easy to take out and put away;
     *   small objects–beads, animals and people, grocery items, housekeeping items–stored without being sorted by category, color, size, or some other classification system;
     *   pencils, crayons, or markers not stored by color;
     *   crowded shelves.

2.   Are the materials that are available to children mainly colored plastic, or are there wood and other natural materials? Consider whether
     *   textures to arouse the tactile sense are mainly limited to wooden shelves, Formica tables, and plastic toys;
     *   colors to arouse the visual sense are mainly limited to a narrow range or to intense hues. (Remember: The human visual system can distinguish about 2 million colors.);
     *   objects that children can handle are mainly limited to circles, squares, triangles, rectangles, spheres, and cubes with no ovoids, ovals, cones, pyramids, or other shapes, especially those reflecting the complexity of the natural world such as spirals, fractals, and irregular or compound shapes;
     *   there is little or nothing to arouse the senses of smell, sound, and taste.

3.   Are there commercial products or children's work on the walls? Consider whether

- wall displays are mainly commercially produced;
- memos, procedures, and other written materials that have little direct relation to children are in evidence.

4. Is there a large collection of art materials—open-ended, multi-purpose, diverse, and enabling children to be precise—that is visually accessible and within reach? Consider whether

- art materials are mainly limited to tempera paint, crayons, thick markers, play dough, wiggly eyes, glue sticks, blunt scissors, school paste, construction and painting paper, and not much else;
- materials are too high for children to reach;
- materials are in a cupboard or otherwise out of children's sight;
- art materials are located in different parts of the room;
- there is no central place that clearly acts as a studio.

5. Are there thin-line black and colored markers and a mark-making area? Consider whether

- markers have only thick tips;
- markers are in only 12 or 16 colors;
- markers are uncapped or dried out;
- markers are isolated from paper.

6. Are manipulative materials in good condition, plentiful, varied, and orderly? Consider whether

- parts are missing—for example, no strings with the beads, no board for pegs, not enough pegs to fill boards, no cylinders, cones, pyramids, ovoids, or other non-rectilinear shapes or solids;
- items with working pieces are broken—for example, the door on the stove, the drawers in the cash register, the body parts of dolls;
- objects are scratched, chipped, or dented;
- quantities of blocks, LEGO, or other sets are insufficient to create large or complex constructions;
- there are no imaginative "found" objects to mix with blocks, train sets, or to use in play areas;
- overall there is little choice of materials.

7. Are the imaginative play areas detailed, attractive, and complex? Consider:

- dress-up clothes
  - there are none;
  - dress-up clothes are dirty, ragged, or torn;
  - storage is inadequate so clothes are piled on shelves, stored in chests or boxes, or lying on the floor.
- housekeeping area
  - sparsely appointed—not enough dishes to set a table for four, not enough pans, pots, or baking dishes to stimulate varied pretend play;
  - no real cans or cartons among food items;
  - nothing of beauty to give the area character or aesthetic quality.
- grocery
  - sparse collection of food items;

          – no "real" item such as cash register or shopping cart;
          – food is all make-believe with no real cans or boxes (empty, of course);
          – all major food groups–protein (dairy and meat); fruits and vegetables; carbohydrates; fats, oils, sweets (in limited amounts)–are not represented.

8. Are there awe-inspiring collections of natural materials? Consider whether

   • there are no natural materials or too few natural materials to attract children's attention;
   • natural materials lack variety;
   • natural materials are broken–shells chipped or fragments, leaves crumbled, bird's nest scraggly, insects missing parts;
   • there are no ways to protect natural materials such as compartmented boxes, lined trays, pieces of felt, or special cases;
   • there is no magnifying glass or loop;
   • there are no books in which to research shells, rocks, leaves, bark, or other natural materials;
   • plants are not groomed or are wilting;
   • aquariums or cages are poorly equipped with nothing for animals to hide or play in;
   • animals' facilities are dirty;
   • manufactured "natural" objects substitute for the real object from nature.

9. Are there mirrors, light tables, and climbing/crawling structures? Consider

   • mirror
     – only one mirror;
     – mirror(s) is plastic and distorts images;
     – no mirror in which children can see their full body;
     – mirror is hung too high for children to see themselves.
   • climbing/crawling apparatus
     – there is none;
     – designed for children under age 3, not 4 or older.
   • light table is poorly designed–for example, the bulbs can be seen through the Plexiglas, the surface is not evenly lit, is too bright, or the frame extends too far onto the top;
   • there are few materials that are colored, transparent, or shiny;
   • there are no materials that reflect or transmit light;
   • there is no object such as the pyramid, kaleidoscope, periscope, or other large Reggio-type structure.

X—eXchanges

    The kinds of eXchanges that take place among children, children and teachers, and children and the environment reveal what the role of the teacher is.

1. Do you tell the children what to do, or do children choose? Consider whether

   • you name the children and direct what they do;
   • you alone, not collaboratively with the children, make lists of class helpers.

2. Is use of time determined by a schedule or by children's span of interest? Consider whether
   - a posted schedule lists activities at regular intervals of 15, 20, 30, or some other increment of minutes;
   - the schedule lists "pull-out" sessions for individuals or groups of children;
   - the schedule lists such classes as music or language that the full class attends on a regular basis;
   - children who are concentrating are interrupted to change activities;
   - children who are concentrating are told to stop so others can have a turn;
   - children who are concentrating are told to stop so they can work with the teacher.

3. Do children use "indoor voices"? Consider whether
   - the tone of the classroom is loud;
   - children call across the room;
   - you call across the room.

4. Do children hit, punch, push, and so on?
5. Do children run around the classroom?
6. Do children cooperate readily when asked to do something? Consider whether
   - children resist your suggestions, refuse to work with you, or ignore what you ask;
   - children are rude to peers and adults;
   - transitions are disorderly.

7. Do children work collaboratively in small groups? Consider whether
   - children play alone or do not play together with open-ended toys like blocks;
   - children do not use imaginative play areas with their friends;
   - most work is with the full class.

8. Are children disciplined by internal or external controls? Consider whether
   - there is a time-out chair;
   - a behavior chart lists children with stars or other marks by their name under categories such as "is quiet," "sits still," "listens quietly," "walks";
   - you call children's attention to the chart;
   - you reprimand children by yelling;
   - you reprimand children in noticeable ways–dragging, pinching an arm;
   - you insist that children apologize to one another in words that you provide;
   - you frequently take children who misbehave out of the classroom.

9. Do children guide one another pleasantly? Consider whether
   - children are bossy with one another;
   - children imitate your words to discipline their peers;
   - children do not share roles of leader and follower.

C—Conversation

When and how conversation takes place reveal whether children are self-regulated, whether the day is organized by a schedule or is an Open Flow day, and whether the teacher listens to the children with intention.

1. Is there a full-class meeting every day? Consider whether

    -   full-class conversations happen
        -   occasionally;
        -   rarely;
        -   almost never;
    -   days have no structure because whether there is a full-class meeting or when it takes place is generally unpredictable.

2. Do full-class conversations flow from children's remarks, follow something children are interested in, or only flow from a topic you suggest? Consider whether

    -   most topics of conversation are teacher-generated;
    -   your questions and comments do not generate problem solving or critical thinking;
    -   you usually have an answer you expect the children to give;
    -   children mainly respond in unison or use scripted or formulaic words;
    -   children seldom make spontaneous remarks;
    -   aside from show-and-tell, children rarely speak about what interests them;
    -   teacher-talk dominates;
    -   your questions lead children toward what *you* have decided to do;
    -   talk is teacher-initiated and in a teacher/child/teacher pattern rather than initiated by anyone to someone specific or to everyone.

3. Is full-class conversation multiway with children addressing one another, or do children mainly answer you and rarely one another?

4. Do children listen respectfully to one another, or do they pay little attention when other children talk?

5. Do children pay attention during a full-class conversation? Consider whether

    -   *Most* wiggle, squirm, crawl away, or chatter among themselves:
        -   usually;
        -   sometimes;
    -   *Some* wiggle, squirm, crawl away, or chatter among themselves:
        -   usually;
        -   sometimes.

6. Are conversation topics free-flowing, or are they formulaic—the calendar, attendance, show-and-tell?

7. Can children sustain conversation and stay on topic for an extended time such as 20–30 minutes? Consider whether

    -   children rapidly lose interest in a free-flow conversation:
        -   usually;
        -   sometimes;
    -   few children respond on topic:
        -   usually;
        -   sometimes.

8. Do topics of conversation reflect what children will do or have done during the day? Consider whether

- there is little conversation about activities children have been or will be engaged in;
- you do most of the talking and provide most of the information.

9. Are all adults in the classroom engaged in the conversation? Consider whether

- the second teacher does not join the conversation;
- the aide does not join the conversation;
- interns do not join the conversation;
- parents or other visitors do not join the conversation.

10. Is there much conversation between you and children one-on-one or in small groups? Consider whether small-group and one-on-one conversations are mainly

- greetings;
- about behavior;
- instructions;
- lessons from a Teacher's Guide;
- preplanned, formulaic lessons;
- unrelated to what children are engaged in.

E—Evidence

Evidence consists of children's work products that provide a window into each child's thought processes and development. The quality of evidence is a window into teachers' beliefs, expectations, planning, and implementation.

1. Is children's work creative? Consider whether work does not vary from child to child; it all looks pretty much alike.
2. Is children's work complex? Consider whether

- work requires
  – few steps;
  – little tool use;
  – few hand skills;
- work involves little or no problem solving;
- work is not challenging or novel;
- work does not provide new content or concepts.

3. Is children's work original? Consider whether

- work is derivative;
- work copies a pre-made plan.

4. Is children's work stored individually? Consider whether

- there are no individual folders for each child's small work on paper;
- there are no individual portfolios for each child's large work on paper;
- there are not other individual containers for other kinds of each child's work.

5. Is selected work displayed? Consider whether

- work by all children is usually displayed together;
- work by an individual child or small group of children is rarely displayed.

6. Are there documentation panels on the walls? Consider whether

   - there are no documentation panels;
   - there are a limited number of documentation panels;
   - you are not sure how to make documentation panels;
   - you don't have time to make documentation panels.

7. Do children spontaneously examine or discuss work on display? Consider whether

   - children never or seldom spontaneously examine or discuss work on display;
   - children take little or no notice of what is on display.

8. Do children take parents or visitors to look at their work?

9. Does work product show evidence of collaboration? Consider whether

   - children's work, for the most part, is done by an individual child;
   - children are not allowed to collaborate;
   - children are not encouraged to collaborate;
   - work is cooperative in that different children participate but there is little or no discussion, debate, suggestions, or negotiation;
   - work is cooperative in that different children add a piece but the outcome is predictable and therefore children's contributions have no impact on the direction the work takes.

L—Language

Languages, broadly defined, are powerful tools that the brain uses to receive and process information and to express itself.

1. Do children speak in full sentences, elaborate their statements, and use standard grammar? Consider whether

   - some children
     - are weak in all these areas;
     - could be stronger than they are;
   - children use lots of expressions that they learn from television;
   - children use lots of noises that they learn from television.

2. Do children express themselves in varied ways? Consider whether children demonstrate

   - little creative gesture and facial expression;
   - few meaningful body movements;
   - little or no symbolic representation;
   - disregard toward other living things and people;
   - un-empathetic interactions;
   - illogically stated thoughts.

3. Do children use a variety of tools facilely? Consider whether the following are absent:

   - scissors that cut;
   - wire cutters (for clay);
   - wire cutters and strippers (for wire);

- needle and thread;
- vegetable peeler;
- stapler;
- tape;
- ruler;
- glue;
- mark-makers.

4. Do children use mark-makers on their own initiative as readily as they use words? Consider whether
   - some children have weak hand skills;
   - some children strongly resist drawing;
   - only a few children draw all the time.

5. Is children's vocabulary above average? Consider whether
   - children use fewer words than is typical of their age;
   - some children's vocabulary is sparse.

6. Do children love to listen to books? Consider whether
   - children are restless during stories:
     - many;
     - some;
     - few;
   - children name favorite books:
     - many books;
     - some books;
     - few books;
   - children ask to be read to:
     - most children;
     - some children;
     - few children.

7. Is the in-classroom library generously stocked? Consider whether the library is stocked:
   - well;
   - fairly well;
   - poorly.

8. Is there nonfiction as well as fiction?
9. Are there magazines?
10. Is the stock enlarged or are reading materials replenished regularly?
11. Is there an in-classroom listening area for music and books?
12. Do children sing, play instruments, or listen to music daily?
13. Is there access to a great variety of materials that encourage or support children's urge to express language in written or other graphic form? Consider whether the following are absent:
    - papers in many colors, thicknesses, finishes, and degrees of transparency, from cardstock and cellophane to rag, tinsel, and tissue;
    - all manner of mark-makers;

- clip boards so children can carry writing paper where there are no tables or outside the school on excursions;
- envelopes, especially small ones, to hold messages.

14. Are varied materials absent that would encourage children to express their thoughts symbolically?
    - wire from single strands to rolls of chicken wire, in different metals and thicknesses;
    - organized collections of buttons, bells, shells and other varied items to string;
    - different thicknesses and textures of cardboard;
    - beads, bangles, baubles, feathers, and sequins;
    - miscellaneous hardware;
    - looms;
    - rope, string, raffia, streamers, and fabric strips to weave or use in other ways;
    - clips, brads, tacks, staples, rubber bands, and other fasteners;
    - used postage stamps;
    - natural materials from the animal, vegetable, and mineral kingdoms.

USING EXCEL TO RATE YOURSELF

I have written EXCEL for anyone interested in changing their practices. EXCEL can be used either individually or with a group. Here, I describe possibilities for two different uses.

You, Yourself, and EXCEL

If you use EXCEL as a personal tool, privately, the questions can help you have a dialogue with yourself about various aspects of your teaching. If you are in the process of rethinking your practices, I suggest using EXCEL as you begin the change process. Then, put your answers away. At the end of the school year or 8 or 9 months after you first use EXCEL, answer the questions again without looking at your earlier answers. After you have completed answering the questions a second time, compare the two sets of answers. The comparison will show you what has changed.

If none of your answers has changed, consider talking with a trusted colleague about your beliefs and goals. If a few answers have changed, consider whether the changes occurred mainly in one area of practice. Recall what you did to change and particularly consider whether it was a conscious effort. If so, recall your state of mind, put yourself in the same frame of mind, and tackle a second area of practice. I suggest initiating your first changes in an area that is most comfortable or compelling for you.

EXCEL as a Group Exercise

If you have embarked on a change process with your co-teacher or with a group of teachers and are using EXCEL together, begin with each person answering the questions privately and putting the answers away.

As a group, agree on which area of practice addressed in EXCEL is the area you want to discuss first. Schedule a regular time for meetings, and at each meeting choose one of the questions in the area you have selected to discuss. Ask someone to take notes and to circulate the notes after the discussion. (A different person can take notes at each session.)

At a next session, use the notes to develop an action plan—things you will tackle as your first steps toward change. Each person's change agenda can be different from the others. If a question stymies you, let me know via my website: annlewin-benham. com. I'll be glad to clarify.

EXCEL addresses wide-ranging practices, far more than a group may want to tackle in a year or two. If some members of the group are reluctant to change, draw on the group for help in exactly what to do to begin; perhaps one person can act as coach for another. As a tool to foster discussion about change, EXCEL should be "eaten" in small bits, but thoroughly chewed and given digestion time! EXCEL is designed to be used in a reflective manner, not as a punishment/reward exercise. Therefore, encourage a group spirit that is supportive, where neither bragging nor blame is allowed.

Tips for Using EXCEL

The objective of EXCEL is to provide you with a tool for self-analysis that, through your answers, can help you keep track of and demonstrate growth in your understanding of reflective teaching.

Remember: As you consider the items in the assessment, notice that the examples are all undesirable. It is better *not* to do the things, to have the conditions, or to see the children's behaviors that are listed!

- If several of your answers are "no" or "sometimes," consider developing a plan and timeline for change.
- If you cannot answer a question easily, come back to it at a later time; or, choose a different area because the place you chose to begin may be the least compatible with your nature.
- Begin with the area that is most comfortable for you.
- Take a single question into the classroom and for a week jot down answers based on what you see yourself doing, on how your classroom looks, or on what the children do or say. In other words, ground your answers in the reality of what you observe.
- Because change is tough, tackle one of your teaching behaviors at a time, or change one small facet of your practice at a time. Move thoughtfully!

CONCLUSION: BEST PRACTICES AND SIGNIFICANT WORK

As we read in the epigram for Chapter 1, Alice and the Cheshire Cat agree that if you don't know where you're going, any road will get you there. A welter of voices confounds teaching practices—the morning drive time expert whose advice is contradicted by the lunch time speaker's message, who in turn is trumped by the expert on the evening news. Each expert has a different idea of what is "best." In this tumultuous sea, teachers need a life raft. Beliefs, as emphasized in Chapter 1, are that raft. Beliefs anchor all we do.

I believe that testing, as commonly used, is competitive, pressures teachers who in turn pressure children, and provides a distorted picture of achievement. Testing fails to capture the growth–or lack of growth–that is observed by classroom teachers who know far more about their children than any test can reveal. Testing can undermine attempts to use best practices. In Chapters 11 and 13, I have suggested ways to gather and use evidence to support what you know as a teacher. In all other chapters, I have shown what I believe are effective ways–best practices–to support and encourage young children to grow.

Embedded in the best practices I describe are detailed examples of what I call Significant Work. Significant Work is creative, original, complex, competent, language-full, and joyful. Reread the scenarios throughout the book, but especially in Chapters 6, 8, 9, and 12. Significant Work is the opposite of work that is banal, ordinary, simplistic, slip-shod, and dull. Use the scenarios as another lens with which to consider whether the work in your classroom reflects best practices.

Significant Work sparks children's engagement so that they develop skills that will help them throughout their lives. These skills include focus, self-reflection, empathy for others, linguistic prowess, and analytic abilities. And, especially in Chapters 2 through 5, 7, and 10, I have described teaching that exemplifies what are generally called best practices. They are powerful practices. The teaching I have portrayed seeds children's minds with significant content that is full of big ideas, the kinds that resonate throughout one's life.

Glossary

Atelierista. The name used in Reggio schools for the studio teacher, an experienced arts or crafts person who brings the perspective of someone skilled in the use of materials and tools to a school's faculty.

Authentic assessment. Using evidence that accumulates over time of what children say and do. The evidence is the basis for determining how children are developing and for comparing each individual child's work to his or her own earlier work.

Big experience. An out-of-the-ordinary outing, excursion, or happening in the classroom that varies from the typical day.

Collaborate. A process in which teachers and children discuss, negotiate, disagree, and reach consensus about what to do or how an activity will change as it unfolds.

Co-regulate. The responsive back-and-forth communication between two people in which they exchange gestures, expressions, words, or actions that are influenced by their partner's actions.

Conversation. Dialogue focused on a topic in which a pair or a group exchanges ideas, opinions, and information based on what the members of the pair or group say.

Conversation Tool Kit. A cluster of techniques that teachers use to engage children in conversation that is meaning-full, that evokes responses from all involved, and that enables children to develop both self-regulation and increasingly large vocabulary, correct grammar, and expression that is on-topic, fluent, and succinct.

Design. A plan in which form, function, and aesthetics are equally important; design can refer to the literal layout, the look, or the items in the physical space, to a master plan for the structure of all an organization's functions, or to an individual's thoughtful consideration of his or her actions.

Document (verb). The process whereby teachers systematically collect evidence of what children do and say, archive the evidence for over 2 or 3 years, display carefully selected pieces, and use it to engage children in reflecting on their thoughts and actions.

Emergent Curriculum. Content that grows from teachers' thoughtful observation of children's interests and teachers' collaboration with children in shaping activities that build on those interests. (See also Collaborate.)

Evaluation. A system to measure children's development against widely used benchmarks for what children's capacities should be at a particular time, age, or grade level.

EXCEL. An acronym for a process of self-assessment that teachers can use to examine their classroom environment, their interactions with children, their use of conversation, how they gather and use evidence to assess children's progress, and how they encourage language development.

Flow. Mihaly Csikszentmihalyi's term for anyone engaged in a task to an extent that they lose track of time and awareness of anything but the task itself. Significant Work is produced by people in flow.

100 Languages. A metaphor with which Reggio educators refer to children's capacity to learn how to use any of the virtually unlimited means of human expression and to learn the attributes and functions of numerous ones.

Hypothesize. To consider the possibilities for what might happen in light of what has happened and what you know in general.

Individualized Instruction. Teachers' lessons to a child one-on-one; that is, when a teacher teaches something to one single child at a time.

Intention. Teachers' determination that they will convey the meaning in a stimulus to a child or children and the authority with which they make it clear that they expect the child or children to focus on the matter at hand.

Items. The equipment, materials, and tools that are available for children's use.

Lessons. Content or skill presented by a teacher to an individual child or to a small group of two to six children.

Materials. The wealth of natural and man-made objects that children can explore to learn the attributes and functions of each one. Materials include everything from alphabets to zoo animals and from beetle wings to yellow markers.

Meaning. Content related to anything in time or space. Meaning is represented in a trace (footprint, outline), a symbol (flag, map), or an abstraction (speech, words in a phonetic alphabet, numerals that form a system with which to calculate). Meaning is communicated in speech, writing, gestures, graphics, or any other way in which humans convey something to one another.

Meaning-full. Content that can branch in different directions and has the potential to help people build many different relationships.

Mediate. Intervention by an adult in children's activities. Mediation is characterized by intention (I, the teacher, want you to know this), meaning (I have selected this stimulus for a particular reason), and transcendence (I will encourage you to make a connection between this stimulus and something you have experienced in the past or can imagine for the future).

Negotiated Curriculum. Classroom work that grows out of teachers' observation of children's interests; it is a lively process–that can span quite a number of days–in which teachers and children hypothesize and debate how their interests might develop. (See also Collaborate, Emergent Curriculum, Hypothesize.)

"Normalized." Maria Montessori's term for children who are self-regulated and capable of concentrating for long periods.

Open Flow. A day in which there is a usual time for full-class meeting(s), lunch, and nap, but in which long blocks of time are unscheduled so that children can pursue their interests without interruption.

Orchestrate. A technique in which, by thoughtfully watching children and listening to them, a teacher ensures that a class is self-regulated, that the children stay focused, that projects move forward, and that parent involvement, documentation, or other activities move along.

Panel. A board, as large as 3 by 4 feet, on which teachers lay out the evidence they have selected of children's activities. Panels hang on classroom walls and are the basis for teachers and children to reflect and converse on what they did and what they might do next.

Pedagogista. The name used in Reggio schools for a master teacher, who may be a psychologist, who works with several schools and takes part in dialogue on subjects that range from projects to design, parent issues, teacher education, budget, children with special needs, and more.

Research. Reggio teachers' process of observing, note taking, reflecting, and hypothesizing; when educators follow a scientific-type process through which they collaborate with peers and with children on projects and other activities.

Self-Regulation. Children's ability to focus, sustain attention, keep on track, suppress behavior that might disrupt others, and respond with increasingly empathetic and/or analytic thought processes.

Significant Work. Activities that engage children, cause them to concentrate intently for long periods, are joyful, and produce work that is original, creative, complex, language-full, and shows evidence of children's competence.

"Third Teacher." How Reggio educators refer to the classroom and school environment. They design with great attention to every item and therefore trust that a child engaged in an activity on his own or with other children learns as much as if he were working with a teacher.

Transcendence. Thinking of how something you are currently doing or contemplating relates to something you did in the past or might do in the future. Teachers who "mediate" encourage children to make such relationships. (See also Mediate.)

Appendix: Answer to the Question at the End of Chapter 7

- The *orchestrator* is seen in the assembly of a small group of children and the fact that the group is working outdoors.
- The *researcher* is seen in the observation of the children's activity and in the teacher's not intervening when the children's trials fail to cover the shadow. It is the research mind that encourages experimentation even when the adult knows it will be a dead end.
- The *designer* is seen in the fact that the children know that in their school they can find a sheet and tape.
- The *documenter* is seen in the fact that the children's dialogue has been recorded and their activity has been photographed.
- You cannot see the *collaborator* or *mediator* in the vignette. But this does not mean that these roles were not played before the short conversation in the example or that they will not be played as the vignette continues to unfold.

References

Baumrind, D. (1967). Child care practices anteceding three patterns of preschool behavior. *Genetic Psychology Monographs, 75(1)*, 43–88. Retrieved September 19, 2010, from http://www.devpsy.org/teaching/parent/baumrind_styles.html

Bellis, M. (2009). The history of adhesives and glue. Retrieved January 10, 2010, from http://inventors.about.com/od/gstartinventions/a/glue.htm

Berk, L., & Winsler, A. (1995). *Scaffolding children's learning: Vygotsky and early childhood education.* Washington, DC: NAEYC.

Bondavalli, M., Mori, M., & Vecchi, V. (1990). *Diana hop!: Advisories for three year old children.* Reggio Emilia, Italy: Diana Pre-School.

Briggs, D. C. (1970). *Your child's self-esteem.* New York: Random House.

Bruner, J. (1996). *The culture of education.* Cambridge, MA: Harvard University Press.

Carroll, L. (1941). *Alice's adventures in wonderland.* New York: The Heritage Press. (Original work published 1871)

Cartwright, A., & Curthoys, I. (1996). A neural network simulation of the vestibular system. Retrieved February 15, 2009, from http://resources.metapress.com/pdf-preview.axd?code=ex0taw18f4fj6lrr&size=largest

Cavallini, J., Filippini, T., Transcossi, L., & Vecchi, V. (2008). *We write shapes that look like a book.* Reggio Emilia, Italy: Municipality of Reggio Emilia and Reggio Children.

Central Conference of American Rabbis. (2007). *Mishkan T'Filah: The reform siddur.* New York: Author.

Csikszentmihalyi, M. (1990). *Flow: The psychology of optimal experience.* New York: HarperCollins.

Diamond, J. (2005). *Collapse: How societies choose to fail or succeed.* New York: Viking.

Dickinson, D. K., & Tabors, P. O. (2002, March). Fostering language and literacy in classrooms and homes. *Young Children, 57(2)*, 10–18.

Emerson, R. W. (1912). The rhodora. In T. R. Lounsbury (Ed.), *Yale book of American verse.* New Haven, CT: Yale University Press. Retrieved June 3, 2009, from http://www.bartleby.com/102/38.html

Epstein, A. S., Schweinhart, L. J., DeBruin-Parecki, A., & Robin, K. B. (2004). Preschool assessment: A guide to developing a balanced approach. *Preschool Policy Matters, 7*, 1–12. New Brunswick, NJ: National Institute for Early Education Research. Retrieved February 5, 2009, from http://nieer.org/resources/policybriefs/7.pdf

Fernald, J. C. (1947). *Funk & Wagnalls standard handbook of synonyms, antonyms, and prepositions.* New York: Funk & Wagnalls Company.

Feuerstein, R., Feuerstein, R. S., Falik, L., & Rand, Y. (2002). *The dynamic assessment of cognitive modifiability.* Jerusalem: International Center for the Enhancement of Learning Potential.

Feuerstein, R. S., Feuerstein, R., & Falik, L. (2004). *User's guide to the theory and practices of the Feuerstein instrumental enrichment–BASIC program.* Jerusalem: International Center for the Enhancement of Learning Potential.

Feuerstein, R., Feuerstein, R. S., Falik, L., & Rand, Y. (2006). *The Feuerstein instrumental enrichment program: Part I and Part II.* Jerusalem: International Center for the Enhancement of Learning Potential.

First direct recording made of mirror neurons in human brain. (2010, April 13). *Science Daily.* Retrieved August 24, 2010, from http://www.sciencedaily.com/releases/2010/04/100412162112.htm

Gardner, H. (1980). *Artful scribbles: The significance of children's drawings.* New York: Basic Books.

Gardner, H. (1983). *Frames of mind: The theory of multiple intelligences.* New York: Basic Books.

Greenspan, S. I., & Shanker, S. G. (2004). *The first idea: How symbols, language, and intelligence evolved from our primate ancestors to modern humans.* Cambridge, MA: Da Capo Press.

Hughes, L. (1994). Harlem. *The collected poems of Langston Hughes.* New York: Knopf. (Original work published 1951)

Kandel, E. (2006). *In search of memory: The emergence of a new science of mind.* New York: Norton.

Kantrowitz, B., & Wingert, P. (1991, December 2). The best schools in the world. *Newsweek,* pp. 50–52.

Lamb, C. (1913). Mrs. Battle's opining on whist. In E. Rhys (Ed.), *The essays of Elia* (p. 40). London: J. M. Dent. (Original work published 1823)

Lewin, A. (1998). Bridge to another culture. In C. Edwards, L. Gandini, & G. Forman (Eds.), *The hundred languages of children* (2nd ed., pp. 335–357). Greenwich, CT: Ablex.

Lewin-Benham, A. (2006). *Possible schools: The Reggio approach to urban education.* New York: Teachers College Press.

Lewin-Benham, A. (2008). *Powerful children: Understanding how to teach and learn using the Reggio Approach.* New York: Teachers College Press.

Lewin-Benham, A. (2010). *Infants and toddlers at work: Using Reggio-inspired materials to support brain development.* New York: Teachers College Press.

Malaguzzi, L. (1985). *Brick by brick: The history of the "XXV Aprile" People's Nursery School of Villa Cella.* Reggio Emilia, Italy: Reggio Children.

Malaguzzi, L. (1991). *The very little ones of silent pictures.* Reggio Emilia, Italy: Coi Bambini.

Malaguzzi, L. (1997). *Shoe and meter: First approaches to the discovery, function, and use of measurement.* Reggio Emilia, Italy: Reggio Children.

Malaguzzi, L., Castagnetti, M., Rubizzi, L., & Vecchi, V. (1995). *A journey into the rights of children: As seen by children themselves.* Reggio Emilia, Italy: Reggio Children.

Mann, C. C. (2005). Unraveling khipu's secrets. *Science, 309*(5737), 1008–1009. Retrieved February 15, 2009, from http://www.sciencemag.org/cgi/content/short/30957371006

Margueron, J-C. (2003). Emar 2003 overview: Research in the country of Ashtata Emar I and II Syria. *The Shelby-White Leon Levy Program for archaeological publications.* Retrieved February 15, 2009, from http://www.fas.harvard.edu/~semitic/wl/digsites/Mesopotamia/Emar_03/

Meisels, S. (2004, May). Should we test 4-year-olds? *Pediatrics, 113*(5), 1401–1402.

Ornstein, R., & Thompson, R. (1984). *The amazing brain.* Boston: Houghton Mifflin.

Partnerships, Alliances, and Coordination Techniques (PACT). (2010). *Assessment and evaluation: Becoming an educated consumer. Part I: Child assessment.* Fairfax, VA: National Child Care Information and Technical Assistance Center.

Perkins, D. (1992). *Smart schools.* New York: Free Press.

Perkins, D. (1995). *Outsmarting IQ: The emerging science of learnable intelligence.* New York: Free Press.

Perry, B. C. (1994). Neurobiological sequelae of childhood trauma: Post traumatic stress disorders in children. In M. Murburg (Ed.), *Catecholamine function in PTSD: Emerging concepts* (pp. 253–276). Washington, DC: American Psychiatric Press. Retrieved September 10, 2010, from http://www.healing-rts.org/tir/perry_neurobiological_sequelae_of_childhood_trauma.pdf

Piaget, J. (1950). *The psychology of intelligence.* New York: International Universities Press.

Pinker, S. (1994). *The language instinct: How the mind creates language.* New York: HarperCollins.

Posner, M., Rothbart, K. K., Sheese, B. E., & Kieras, J. (2008). How arts training influences cognition. In M. Gazzaniga (Ed.), *Learning, arts, and the brain* (pp. 1–10). New York: Dana Press.

Ratey, J. (2002). *A user's guide to the brain: Perception, attention, and the four theaters of the brain.* New York: Vintage.

Reggio Children. (1995). Reggio accreditation! *Innovations, 2*(4), 6. Detroit, MI: The Merrill-Palmer Institute.

Reggio Children. (1998). *Children, spaces, relations: Metaproject for an environment for young children* (G. Ceppi & M. Zini, Eds.). Reggio Emilia, Italy: Author.

Reggio Children. (2004). *Children, art, artists: The expressive languages of children, the artistic language of Alberto Burri.* Reggio Emilia, Italy: Municipal Preschools.

Rinaldi, C. (2006). *In dialogue with Reggio Emilia: Listening, researching and learning.* London: Routledge.

Sacks, O. (2002). *Oaxaca journal.* Washington, DC: National Geographic Society.

Seidel, S. (2001). Understanding documentation starts at home. In C. Giudici, C. Rinaldi, & M. Krechevsky (Eds.), *Making learning visible: Children as individual and group learners* (pp. 304–311). Cambridge, MA: Harvard Graduate School of Education and Reggio Emilia: Reggio Children.

Shepard, L. A., Taylor, G. A., & Kagan, S. I. (1996). *Trends in early childhood assessment policies & practices.* Los Angeles: National Center for Research on Evaluation, Standards, and Student Testing, University of California.

Shin, E., & Spodek, B. (1991). *The relationship between children's play patterns and types of teacher intervention.* East Lansing, MI: National Center for Research on Teacher Learning. (ERIC Document Reproduction Service No. ED332803)

Spaggiari, S. (2000). To be amazed by children. In S. Sturloni & V. Vecchi (Eds.), *Everything has a shadow except ants* (pp. 8–9). Reggio Emilia, Italy: Reggio Children.

Stevenson, R. L. (1985). Happy thought. *A child's garden of verses* (p. 34). Avenel, NJ: Children's Classics. (Original work published 1913)

Sturloni, S., & Vecchi, V. (2000). *Everything has a shadow except ants.* Reggio Emilia, Italy: Reggio Children.

Teicher, M. H., Andersen, S. L., Polcari, A., Anderson, C. M., Navalta, C. P., & Kim, D. M. (2003). The neurobiological consequences of early stress and childhood maltreatment. *Neuroscience Biobehavioral Reviews, 27(1/2),* 33–44.

This to That. (2010). Retrieved February 15, 2010, from http://inventors.about.com/gi/dynamic/offsite.htm?zi=1/XJ&sdn=inventors&cdn=money&tm=73&gps=37_817_869_567&f=00&tt=2&bt=1&bts=1&st=17&zu=http%3A//www.thistothat.com

Thurber, J. (1943). *Many moons.* New York: Harcourt, Brace and Company.

The U.S. Market for Infant, Toddler, and Preschool Products. (2003). (Vols. 1–3, 2nd ed.). Retrieved April 3, 2008, from http://www.packagedfacts.com/Infant-Toddler-Preschool-834131/

U.S. National Commission for Excellence in Education. (1983). *A nation at risk: The imperative for educational reform.* Washington, DC: U.S. Department of Education.

Vygotsky, L. (1986). *Thought and language.* (A. Kozulin, Trans. & Ed.). Cambridge, MA: The MIT Press. (Original work published 1934)

Wayne's Word. (1996). Orchids (Orchidaceae): The world's smallest seeds. Retrieved August 7, 2010, from http://waynesword.palomar.edu/plfeb96.htm

Wilson, F. (1998). *The hand: How its use shapes the brain, language, and human culture.* New York: Pantheon.

Wolf, M. (2007). *Proust and the squid: The story and science of the reading brain.* New York: Harper.

World Resources Institute. (2001). No end to paper. Retrieved August 11, 2010, from http://earthtrends.wri.org/features/view_feature.php?theme=6&fid=19

Index

Adams, Ansel, 75
Aesthetics, 3, 9, 14–15, 16
  developing aesthetic sense, 74–76
  impact on children, 74–75
  and materials, 56–57
  and Reggio design, 71
Assessment, 1, 5, 15, 154–168. *See also* EXCEL
  authentic assessment
    process, 157–158
    roadblocks to, 163
    and standardized testing, 164–165
    and teacher self-assessment, 185–186, 192–193
    techniques, 158–161
    uses for records, 161–163
  brief history of testing, 154
  defined, 157
  effectiveness of authentic assessment, 165–167
    parents' responses, 165–166
    visitors' responses, 166–167
  evaluation and young children, 155–157
    defined, 155
    purposes, 155
    reasons against, 156–157, 168, 197
Astatke, Genet, 105, 152, 158
Attention, 5, 14, 16, 31, 38, 91, 92, 170, 185, 201. *See also* Brain, Focus
  and the brain, 53, 84, 85, 116, 119, 140, 185
  in infants/toddlers, 118–119, 121
  and materials, 25, 52, 53, 54, 57, 69, 72, 120, 172, 189
  not paying attention, 20, 31, 32, 191
  teachers' capturing, 30, 34, 93, 95, 99, 109, 143, 181, 185
Azzariti, Jennifer, 46, 88, 104, 105, 106, 121, 122, 123, 144, 145, 146, 147, 150–151, 158, 160, 169, 172, 173, 179, 180

Baldwin, Wendy, 40, 43, 45, 46, 105, 106, 158, 170
Barley, Deborah, 105, 158
Beliefs about children, 1, 5, 6, 7–18, 196
Best practices, 1, 3, 12, 180, 181, 197
Blocks, 53, 68
Brain. *See also* Focus, Movement, Relationships, *Training* the brain
  and aesthetics, 79
  attention systems, 118–119
  classification, 138
  and comparison, 88
  and conversation, 84–85
  and environment, 66, 67
  evidence of thinking, 146
  and focus, 84, 88, 116, 118, 119, 165
  forming judgment, 139
  and hand, 114, 115–116
  and imitation, 93
  and listening, 111
  and materials, 111, 113
  memory, 10, 16, 43, 56, 119, 143, 146, 185. *See also* Conversation
  and precise words, 114–115
  prepared minds, 176
  procedures, 63–64
  processes at work, 181
  and relationships, 83, 84, 85, 136, 137, 143, 176
  repetition, 118, 119, 176
  same/different, 87
  senses, 56, 62, 75
  transcendence, 137–138. *See also* Transcendence
  vestibular system, 119
Brain research, 5
  mirror neurons, 11
Bruner, Jerome, 96
Burri, Alberto, 121

Chand, Nek, 144

Changing practices, 4, 5, 6, 183–197

Classroom environment, 3
  and commercial interests, 69–70
  as curriculum, 66–79
  design failures, 67–69
  and furniture, 67, 68, 69
  and materials, 67, 68, 69, 70
  and teacher self-assessment, 183–184, 187–189

Classroom manager, 34, 60

Collaboration, 6, 9, 43, 44, 58, 59, 60, 66, 67, 71,
    100, 122, 128, 133, 134, 138, 143, 146, 162,
    168, 170, 171, 178, 179, 180, 181, 189, 190, 193,
    199, 200, 201
  and classroom design, 66
  with families, 127
  in Reggio, 3, 8, 10, 11, 12, 23, 26
  among teachers, 99, 104, 106, 108, 109, 148, 172

Competence, 1, 2, 3, 4, 9, 117–118, 181
  and bottom-up practices, 14, 146
  discouraging, 117, 154
  encouraging, 102, 113
  and intentional teaching, 100
  in Montessori children, 31
  Reggio belief in, 6, 9, 12, 26, 79, 173
  results of growth in, 96, 113, 118, 145, 165, 197,
    201
  teachers' belief in, 23, 109

Complexity, 33, 49, 53–54, 67, 73, 101, 125, 153,
    163, 187

Concentration, 1, 3, 4, 16, 53, 171
  and challenge, 54, 117–118
  and interruptions, 62, 108, 190
  in Montessori, 29, 31, 35, 200
  in Reggio, 23
  and self-regulation, 60, 104
  and Significant Work, 146, 201
  in teachers, 98

Content, 83, 84
  as basis for concepts, 80, 85
  conversation and, 80, 82, 86, 93
  enlarging, 130, 131, 157, 197, 199, 200
  examples, 80, 85
  and literacy, 80
  meaningful, 11, 200
  in pre-packaged curricula, 62
  relation to context, 84, 186
  and tests, 156

Conversation, 4, 11, 12, 80–96
  and brain function, 84–85

designing conversations, 100–101
  examples, 144
  and EXCEL, 185, 190–192
  and focus, 11, 80, 81–83, 90, 91, 94, 95, 96, 101,
    105–107, 185, 199
  impact of, 95–96
  is and is not, 81–82
  and literacy, 84
  and meaning, 83
  and memory, 82, 83, 84
  in projects, 82–83, 86–88
  and self-regulation, 20
  and slowing down, 44, 88
  and teacher self-assessment, 185, 190–192
  why use, 90

Conversation Tool Kit, 1, 82
  maintaining focus, 94
  managing conversation, 91–92
  selecting topics, 93–94
  techniques, 90–91
  times for conversation, 92–93
  zero cost of, 96

Csikszentmihalyi, Mihaly, 16, 19, 200

Cultural mediator, 21–22

Curriculum
  align curriculum and assessment, 96, 163,
    164–165
  bottom up, emergent, negotiated, 14, 57, 137,
    146, 180, 199, 200
  environment as curriculum, 66–79, 67, 100,
    183, 187
  and open flow, 62
  and panels, 49, 51, 142–143, 146, 149, 163
  standardized, 15, 19, 31, 32, 59, 62, 155, 157,
    164, 180

Design, 1, 199
  and aesthetics, 74–76
  of class program, 22
  of classrooms, 5, 57, 76–79, 109, 189
  commercial design, 69–70
  detail in, 69
  failures, 67–68
  impact of, 66, 67
  and intentional teachers, 99–101
  of lessons, 29, 102–103
  of Montessori materials, 3, 25
  principles of, 72–74
  process, 76–78, 79
  in Reggio, 9, 10, 70–71, 79

Design *(continued)*
  of teaching roles, 103–104
  teacher as designer, 66, 74, 201
Dewey, John, 1
Diamond, Jared, 76
Documentation, 5, 10, 36–51, 141–153. *See also*
    Panel
  and cognition, 143
  effective, 49–50
  to generate curriculum, 49, 51
  how children use, 142–143
  is and is not, 36–38
  learning to document, 50
  role in a project, 41–43
  and teacher self-assessment, 185–186, 192–193
  use of, 38–39
  vs. commercial material, 141
  way to involve parents, 39–41, 141–142
Drawing, 46, 47, 55, 79, 93, 105, 115, 131, 132,
    135, 138, 186, 194
  Alonzo's dinosaur, 144–146, 147, 148
  and brain, 139
  and change of scale, 150
  compared to words, 144
  in Reggio, 8, 9, 15, 125, 126
  resistance to, 144
  in Shoe and Meter project, 174, 176, 177, 178,
    181

EXCEL, 5, 183–197
  Conversation, 185. *See also* Conversation
  defined, 183
  Environment, 183–184. *See also* Classroom
    environment
  Evidence, 185–186. *See also* Assessment
  eXchanges, 184–185. *See also* Self-regulation
  how to use
    by yourself, 195
    with a group, 195–196
  Language, 186. *See also* Literacy
  questions to assess your
    Conversation, 190–192
    Environment, 187–189
    Evidence, 192–193
    eXchanges, 189–190
    Language, 193–195
  tips for using, 196

Family involvement, 1, 3, 4, 5, 10, 18, 36–51
  gathering materials, 135–136

  meetings and events, 48
  messages to home, 47–48
    examples of, 45, 136
    process for writing, 134–135
  reading panels, 153
Feuerstein, Reuven, 10, 86, 88, 109, 137, 184
Focus, 4, 5, 10, 14, 21, 34, 43, 52, 54, 62, 66, 71,
    86. *See also* Brain, Conversation
  and classroom design, 66
  cannot maintain focus, 29, 32, 62, 67, 91
  and materials, 116, 120
  on relationships, 106, 140, 170
  and self-regulation, 201
  and Significant Work, 197
  as a teaching technique, 92, 107, 170, 172, 200
Fried, Itzhak, 11
Froebel, Friedrich, 1

Gambetti, Amelia, 10, 47, 180
Gardner, Howard, 10, 118, 139, 155, 167
Glue
  ancient uses, 122
  in the classroom, 123
  modern uses, 122–123
Goldsworthy, Andy, 75
Greenspan, Stanley, 98, 118, 126

Hand, 30, 59, 64, 68, 126, 128, 136, 139, 157, 160,
    186, 192, 194
  and brain development, 114, 115, 116, 117, 118,
    120, 133
  and infants/toddlers, 116, 123, 126
  and use of scissors, 123–124
Hughes, Langston, 55
Hundred languages, 9, 111, 112, 126
  defined, 127, 200

Independence in children, 52, 63–64
  fostering, 6, 29, 55, 56, 61, 64, 65, 68, 165
  thwarting, 56, 62, 104
Intentional teaching, 1, 3, 5, 6, 17, 29, 40, 97–110,
    181, 200
  and affect, 98
  and choosing, 100
  and conversation, 82, 86, 90, 91, 92, 95, 101,
    185, 190
  defined, 97–98
  during an experience, 109–110
  impact of, 184
  intention and emotion, 98

to involve families, 10
and projects, 170, 172
in Reggio, 35, 36, 173
in toddlers, 137

Joy, 1, 2, 6, 9, 30, 48, 55, 63, 74, 76, 85, 96, 118, 119, 133, 143, 146, 154, 166, 171, 185, 197, 201

Kagan, Lynn, 163

Labels, 50–51
Listening, 1, 6, 10, 21, 51, 62, 71, 100–101, 102, 148–149, 181. *See also* Brain
    barriers to, 100
    environment that supports, 5, 69, 194
    process of, 43, 51, 83, 90, 91, 100–101, 102, 104
    in Reggio, 12, 142, 181
    results of, 71, 111
    and teaching techniques, 97, 105, 106, 108, 109, 149, 173, 176, 185, 200
Literacy, 34, 96, 186
    Black Vernacular English, 158
    books, 23, 31, 33, 37, 38, 55, 57, 58, 60, 62, 75, 77, 87, 126, 189, 194
        extending children's interests with, 92, 93, 130
        involving families with, 166
        making books, 26, 171
        making children book lovers, 68, 69
    content/context, 84
    content/concept, 85
    and conversation, 80–96, 84, 91
    designing to foster, 102–103
    and families, 44, 103, 168
    and labels, 50–51
    pressure to achieve, 17
    scripted curricula, 31
    and teacher self-assessment, 186, 193–195

Malaguzzi, Loris, 1, 3, 8–9, 13, 26, 47, 71, 153, 154, 173
Many Moons (Thurber), 43–44
Materials, 1, 111–124. *See also* Glue, Paper, Scissors
    accessibility, 54
    aesthetics of, 56–57
    availability of, 55, 67–69
    and the brain, 119
    and building competence, 117
    children's drive to explore, 113
    and culture, 111–112, 116, 117

defined, 113
in an established class, 58–59
and focus, 118–119
khipu, 120
manageability of, 55–56
markers, 115
with new children, 58
and record keeping, 120
ribbon, 115
and slowing down, 116
and their stories, 120–124
two lives, 113
utility of, 56
Materials and relationships, 125–140
    and children's products/stories, 133
    finding materials, 127–130
    forming judgments, 139
    gathering materials, 134–135
        with families, 135–136
    man-made materials, 127–129
    natural materials, 129–131
    natural materials in use, 131–133, 149–152
    stories of natural materials, 130–131
Meaning-full conversation, 1, 5, 11, 186
Measurement, 105–106, 173–177, 179, 181, 184, 186. *See also* Projects
Meisels, Samuel, 156
Memory, 56, 57
Meyer, T, 71–72, 79
Model Early Learning Center, 2
    developing self-regulation, 34–35
Montessori, Maria, 1
Montessori materials
    binomial cube, 54
    trinomial cube, 54
Montessori method
    differences from Reggio Approach, 3
    "grace and courtesy," 30
    group lessons, 29–30
    materials, 3
    new children, 28 -29
    "normalized" children, 28
    and Open Flow, 65
    and practical life, 2
    walking on the line, 30
Movement, 9, 12, 15, 22, 23, 24–25, 56, 100, 107, 126. *See also* Hand
    and brain, 25, 30, 75, 83, 117, 119
    and imitation, 93
    and infants, 119, 126

Movement *(continued)*
and language, 186, 193
and Montessori method, 28–30
and precision, 29, 109, 126
in projects, 24, 181

National Association for the Education of Young
Children (NAEYC), 3

Open Flow, 1, 4, 5, 16, 52–65
beginning, 62–65
curricula, 62
eliminating schedules, 63–65
essential features, 52–60
classroom items, 52–54, 58–59
with new children, 60
organization, 54–57
with settled children, 60
space/time structure, 57–60
how it looks, 60–62
barriers, 62
time blocks, 61
and teacher as orchestrator, 107

Paint
and conversation, 94
displaying, 151
examples, 89, 151
and independence, 56, 68
and infants, 126
ready-mixed, 68
in Reggio, 38, 71, 78
uses of, 130, 131, 149, 150, 151
in well-prepared environment, 55, 74, 108,
125
Panel. *See also* Documentation
as assessment device, 158
contents of, 145, 150
examples, 85, 89, 151, 153
families' reactions, 153
as product for reflection, 162
revisiting panels, 152–153
what panels reveal, 145–146
Paper, 114–115
ancient uses, 120–121
games with, 114
and infants, 121
kinds of, 114
properties, 114
with toddlers, 114

transforming paper shapes, 121
Papert, Seymour, 83
Parents. *See* Family involvement
Perkins, David, 113, 153
Piaget, Jean, 3, 184
Porter, Elliot, 75
Posner, Michael, 5, 14
Projects, 1, 5, 49
barriers, 55, 100, 116, 135
challenges in, 172–173
and collaboration, 58, 59, 201
and conversation, 10, 14, 80, 86, 136, 149
and families, 36–51, 153, 166
hypotheses about, 170–172
and materials, 125, 128–129, 139
in panels, 38, 143–146
stories of. *See also* Reggio Approach
Alonzo's Dinosaur, 144–146
Courtney's Leaf, 150–152
Here We Are, 169–173, 179, 182
A Hundred Tiny Doors, 171
Our Families and Us, 4, 44–47
Pollution, 94–95
Representing Different Selves, 86–88, 89
Valise Project, 146–147
starting a project, 169–170, 173–174
techniques, 41, 43, 46, 51, 61, 83, 91, 102, 107,
108, 135, 142–143, 147–148, 149, 184, 200

Reflection, 10, 12
Reggio Approach, 1, 2, 3, 5
and aesthetics, 79
American interest in, 4
and best practices, 12
cultural context, 8–9
difference from American practice, 7, 18
and intentional teaching, 97
and materials, 3, 5, 56
and open flow, 65
projects, stories of
Amusement Park for Birds, 126
Blacks and Whites, 121
Natural Materials, 131, 133
Shoe and Meter, 173–179, 181
reconnaissance, 177–178
relationships, 70–71
and self-regulation, 21–22, 23
structure, 16–17
structure of projects, 178–179
teachers' expertise, 181

teachers' roles, 99
theory, 11
Relationships, 14, 17, 25, 66, 71, 116, 137, 140, 146, 147, 170, 200, 201. *See also* Brain
  and classroom design, 66, 67, 71, 72, 79, 184
  and concept formation, 71, 105, 109, 131, 136, 138
  and conversation, 96
  and documentation, 36, 38, 40, 142
  and drawing, 144
  failing to build, 67, 68
  and families, 38, 40
  how to establish, 140
  with infants, 119
  and materials, 111, 113, 125–140, 125–126, 127, 130, 133
  pleasure in, 119
  in Reggio practice, 70, 71
  and small groups, 23
  and socio-cultural theory, 11, 70, 82
  spurred by documentation, 143
  in testing, 156

Sacks, Oliver, 112, 138
Scenarios, 4
  conversation and meaning, 82–83
  disruptive children, 19, 23
  filmy gauze material, 125
  intention and intervention, 99
  intentional teaching roles, 109–110
  intervention, 7
  late speaker, 155–156
  measuring height, 105–107
  natural materials in use, 131–133
  path of a falling leaf, 113
  peeling/coring an apple, 117
  simple materials/complex relationship, 125–126
  sorting and classifying, 149
  teaching with intention, 99
  unsettled children, 53–54
Scheduled day, 32–33
Scissors
  ancient uses, 123
  with children, 123–124
  modern uses, 123
Scripted kindergarten, 31–32
Self-regulation, 1, 3, 4, 5, 16, 19–36
  and conversation, 20
  and movement, 24–25, 107

and rights/responsibilities, 26–27
and teacher intervention, 25–26
and teacher self-assessment, 184–185, 189–190
typical approaches to, 20
Senses. *See also* Brain
  aesthetic sense, 66, 74, 76
  appeal to senses, 12, 16, 56
  and brain, 15, 68, 79, 181
  limiting sensory awareness, 187
  and meaning, 56
  and nature, 62
  sensory awareness, 9, 138
Shoptaugh, Sonya, 27, 41, 44, 46, 55, 86, 105, 106, 158, 162
Significant work, 1, 146–147, 169–182, 196, 197
Small-group work, 9, 11
Socio-cultural theory, 11, 70, 82, 184
Space/time use, 9, 14, 100
Spaggiari, Sergio, 107
Studio teacher, 9

Teacher development, 10
Teacher's role, 3
  being flexible, 104
  as classroom manager, 60
  as collaborator, 108
  as designer, 74–76, 99–104
  as documenter, 108, 147–148
  dual role, 17
  holding conversation, 80–96. *See also* Conversation
  as mediator, 109
  and open flow, 57–60
  as orchestrator, 11, 99, 107–108, 109
    of conversation, 101, 109
    of experiences, 150
    of flow, 109
    invisibility of, 107
  redesigning roles, 103–104
  as researcher, 10, 104–107
    hypothesizing, 105–107, 148
  teacher intervention, 174–178
Training the brain, 14, 16, 52, 53, 56, 63, 75, 114, 185. *See also* Brain
Transcendence, 63, 86, 91, 137–138, 184, 200, 201. *See also* Brain

Vygotsky, Lev, 3, 11, 184

Water table, 53

Photo credit: Tanya Clark, Academy Leader, CAPCS Amos 2 Early Childhood Campus, Washington, DC

About the Author

Ann Lewin-Benham is an author who uses stories from the classroom, findings from neuroscience, and theories from psychology to build bridges between research and the classroom. Her first two books, *Possible Schools* and *Powerful Children*, show the complex practices of the Reggio Approach in a school she founded and directed in Washington, DC, for Head Start–eligible families. Her third book, *Infants and Toddlers at Work*, shows how materials can support the development of brain structures in children from zero to 3 years old.

In her early years, Ann was a teacher and teacher educator, founding schools as alternatives to lock-step education. In frustration at schools' seeming inflexibility, she worked in informal education, founding and, for the next 20 years, directing a children's museum, a pioneering effort in the new field of education in hands-on museums. When Ann again founded schools, she established two that were harbingers of the soon-to-be charter school movement—one, a school for teenage dropouts, became the safety net for an urban public school system; the other, the Model Early Learning Center, is the subject of her first two books.

Currently, in addition to writing, Ann lectures frequently and works side-by-side with teachers in their classrooms, where she demonstrates the techniques about which she writes.